WOMEN'S SPORTS

WHAT EVERYONE NEEDS TO KNOW®

WOMEN'S SPORTS
WHAT EVERYONE NEEDS TO KNOW®

JAIME SCHULTZ

OXFORD
UNIVERSITY PRESS

OXFORD
UNIVERSITY PRESS

Oxford University Press is a department of the University of Oxford. It furthers
the University's objective of excellence in research, scholarship, and education
by publishing worldwide. Oxford is a registered trade mark of Oxford University
Press in the UK and certain other countries.

Published in the United States of America by Oxford University Press
198 Madison Avenue, New York, NY 10016, United States of America.

"What Everyone Needs to Know" is a registered trademark of
Oxford University Press.

© Oxford University Press 2018

Library of Congress Cataloging-in-Publication Data
Names: Schultz, Jaime, author.
Title: Women's sports : what everyone needs to know® /
Jaime Schultz.
Description: New York, NY : Oxford University Press, 2018. |
Includes bibliographical references and index. |
Identifiers: LCCN 2017054908 (print) | LCCN 2018000951 (ebook) |
ISBN 9780190657727 (updf) | ISBN 9780190657734 (epub) |
ISBN 9780190657703 (pbk. : alk. paper) | ISBN 9780190657710 (cloth : alk. paper)
Subjects: LCSH: Sports for women. | Sports—Sex differences. |
Sex discrimination in sports. | Women athletes—Health and hygiene.
Classification: LCC GV709 (ebook) | LCC GV709 .S38 2018 (print) |
DDC 796.082—dc23
LC record available at https://lccn.loc.gov/2017054908

1 3 5 7 9 8 6 4 2

Paperback printed by LSC Communications, United States of America
Hardback printed by Bridgeport National Bindery, Inc., United States of America

For Nella and Sylvie, or Sylvie and Nella—whichever they prefer.

CONTENTS

FIGURE AND TABLES xiii
ACKNOWLEDGMENTS xv
ABBREVIATIONS xvii

1 Why Women's Sport Matters 1

Why does sport matter? 1
Why does girls' and women's sport matter? 2
What counts as a sport? 5
Case study: Is cheerleading a sport? 6

2 A Brief History of Women's Sport 10

How long have women played sport? 10
What marked the beginning of the modern age of sport and what did it mean for women? 13
What were the medical rationales for keeping women out of sport? 17
What were the aesthetic rationales for keeping women out of sport? 19
What were the social rationales for keeping women out of sport? 20
Were the 1920s the "golden age of sport"? 21
What were industrial leagues? 21

*How did the history of racial and ethnic segregation and oppression
affect sport for American girls and women?*   23

*When and how did physical educators change their collective
philosophy about competitive sport for girls and women?*   27

3 The Influence of Title IX   29

What is Title IX?   29

How has Title IX influenced girls' and women's participation in sport?   30

How do athletic programs comply with Title IX?   33

*If athletic departments do not directly receive federal funding, are
they exempt from Title IX?*   34

Is Title IX to blame when athletic departments cut men's programs?   35

What is gender equity?   36

Do we still need Title IX, as it applies to athletics?   37

*How does Title IX apply to cases of sexual harassment and
sexual violence?*   37

4 Gender and Sport   41

Do the terms "sex" and "gender" mean the same thing?   41

How does gender affect girls' and women's participation in sport?   42

What are some examples of gendered differences in sport?   44

*How do uniforms express gender differences in men's and
women's sport?*   46

What is the feminine apologetic?   48

Is muscularity a gendered characteristic?   49

5 Sexualities and Sport   53

What were the historical concerns about women's sexuality in sport?   53

Does "sex sell" women's sport?   54

What is the Lingerie Football League?   57

What is homophobia? 58

What are some of the ways that homophobia affects women's sport? 60

Are there sports opportunities organized specifically for LGBTQ athletes? 63

Are things getting better for gay, lesbian, bisexual, and queer athletes? 64

6 Sex Segregation — 66

Why do we segregate sport on the basis of sex? 66

Should we segregate sport according to sex? 68

Are women closing the "muscle gap" in sport? 70

What are some examples of sex-integrated sport? 71

Why do girls and women play softball while boys and men play baseball? 73

Is there really any such thing as "throwing like a girl"? 75

Does Title IX permit girls and women to play on boys' and men's teams? 76

Does Title IX permit boys and men to play on girls' and women's teams? 77

What are "sex tests" in women's sport? 78

What is hyperandrogenism? 81

What policies do organizations follow with regard to transgender athletes? 83

7 The Olympic and Paralympic Games — 87

How is the Olympic Movement organized and what role do women play in its organization? 87

How long have women been competing in the Olympic Games? 90

What Olympic sports have been the most difficult for women to gain access? 91

Do women compete in the same Olympic sports as men? 96

Are there any negative consequences to adding new sports and events to the Olympic program? 98

Do all National Olympic Committees send female athletes to the Games? 99

What are the Paralympic Games? 101

How is the Paralympic Movement organized and what role do women play in the organization?   103

Do men and women compete equally at the Paralympic Games?   104

Do all National Paralympic Committees send female athletes to the Games?   106

Do the Paralympic Games receive the same amount of media coverage as the Olympic Games?   106

8 Women, Sport, and the Media   109

Do male and female athletes receive the same amount of coverage in sport media?   109

Isn't this difference in coverage based on consumer interest?   110

How does the coverage of women's sport differ from the coverage of men's sport?   111

Are sportswomen of color treated differently in sport media?   114

Are Muslim women treated differently in sport media?   118

Are there any significant themes that emerge in the media coverage of parasport or female athletes with impairments?   119

Has new and electronic media changed the coverage of women's sport?   121

What is the status of women in sport journalism?   122

What types of challenges do women sport journalists face?   123

Are women journalists allowed in men's locker rooms?   126

9 Professional Opportunities   129

What is the status of women in coaching positions?   129

What is the status of women in other positions of authority in sport?   132

Are there any professional sports in which women earn the same amount of money as men?   135

In what sports are pay disparities between men and women athletes the widest?   137

How do the WNBA and other professional women's leagues survive?   141

Why aren't women's professional sports more successful?   144

10 The Sport–Health Connection   146

Is sport healthy?   146

Do female athletes have health concerns that are different from those of male athletes?   148

Does menstruation influence women's sport participation?   150

What is the female athlete triad?   151

In what sports are female athletes most susceptible to disordered eating patterns?   152

Is it OK to compete in sport while pregnant?   153

What performance-enhancing drugs do women use and what are the effects?   155

Does sport put girls and women at risk for sexual violence?   160

There is a lot in the news concerning sexual abuse scandals in sport: Is this a new phenomenon?   163

What is being done to address and prevent sexual abuse in sport?   166

11 Moving On   169

If sport provides so many benefits, why don't all girls and women participate?   169

Are there any places where it is illegal for women to play sport?   171

Is sport a human right?   173

What is Sport for Development and Peace?   175

Are things getting better for girls and women in sport?   177

NOTES   181
BIBLIOGRAPHY   211
INDEX   239

FIGURE AND TABLES

Figure

3.1 Net Outcome of NCAA Added and
     Dropped Teams   35

Tables

7.1   Women's Participation in Olympic
      Summer Games   92
7.2   Women's Participation in Olympic Winter Games   93
7.3   Introduction of Olympic Women's Sports   94
7.4   Evolution of the Paralympic Summer Games   105
11.1 Sport and the Millennium Development Goals   176
11.2 Brighton Declaration on Women and Sport:
      The Principles   179

ACKNOWLEDGMENTS

I owe my gratitude to a number of people who have helped with this book. I deeply appreciate Lucy Randall's editorial guidance. It was a pleasure to work with her and the staff at Oxford University Press, including Gina Chung and Hannah Doyle, as well as with project manager Rajesh Kathamuthu and copy editor Daniel Hays. The Press secured two excellent reviewers, and I am grateful to Rebecca Alpert and the anonymous scholar who helped me strengthen the manuscript. Several friends and colleagues generously offered their expertise throughout the writing process. Thank you to Shireen Ahmed, Mianne Bagger, Jonna Belanger, Paulina Rodriguez Burciaga, Erin Buzuvis, Megan Chawansky, Brenda Elsey, Sarah Field, Kristine Newhall, Maureen M. Smith, Nancy Williams, and Amy Wilson. Finally, and as always, I offer my eternal love and gratitude to Team Schef: Paul, Nella, and Sylvie.

ABBREVIATIONS

AAGPBL	All-American Girls Professional Baseball League
AAS	Anabolic-androgenic steroids
AAU	Amateur Athletic Union's
ACL	Anterior cruciate ligament
AIAW	Association of Intercollegiate Athletics for Women
CTE	Chronic Traumatic Encephalopathy
FBS	Football Bowl Subdivision
FIBA	Fédération Internationale de Basket-ball/ International Basketball Federation
FIVB	International Volleyball Federation
FIFA	Fédération Internationale de Football Association/ International Federation of Association Football
FSFI	Fédération Sportive Féminine Internationale
hGH	Human growth hormones
IAAF	International Association of Athletics Federations
IF	International Sports Federation
IFBB	International Federation of Bodybuilding and Fitness
IOC	International Olympic Committee
IPC	International Paralympic Committee
LLB	Little League Baseball
LPGA	Ladies Professional Golf Association
MLB	Major League Baseball
NBA	National Basketball Association

NCAA	National Collegiate Athletic Association
NFL	National Football League
NHL	National Hockey League
NOC	National Olympic Committee
NPC	National Paralympic Committee
OCR	Office for Civil Rights
PED	Performance-enhancing drug
SDP	Sport for Development and Peace
UFC	Ultimate Fighting Championship
UN	United Nations
USAG	USA Gymnastics
USLTA	United States Lawn Tennis Association
USOC	United States Olympic Committee
WADA	World Anti-Doping Agency
WNBA	Women's National Basketball Association
WTA	Women's Tennis Association
YWCA	Young Women's Christian Association

WOMEN'S SPORTS

WHAT EVERYONE NEEDS TO KNOW®

1

WHY WOMEN'S SPORT MATTERS

Why does sport matter?

For better or for worse, sport matters. It brings together friends, families, communities, and stadia full of strangers. It rallies nations and stokes rivalries. Sport gives us a sense of history, a sense of tradition, and a sense of identity. It instills civic pride, affords temporary escape during difficult times, transcends social boundaries, and acts as an agent of social change. Sport has sparked riots, incited wars, and paved the way for diplomacy and reconciliation. Sport is dramatic, it is uncertain; it stirs our passions and tests the boundaries of what it means to be human.

There is, of course, a dark side to sport, one riddled with problems that include corruption, cheating, violence, injury, greed, discrimination, and exploitation. Even so, we remain sports crazed. The rates of consumption are telling. A 2014 global survey found that in France, 65 percent of adults followed sport. This was the low end of the scale. India provided counterbalance: 93 percent of the population identified as sport fans. The United States fell somewhere in the middle, where 70 percent of Americans follow sport, a diversion to which they each devote an average of 7.7 hours per week.[1] In 2016, sport in the United States was a $500 billion industry, while the global sport industry amounted to $1.3 trillion.[2]

Individuals who choose to follow sport can consult a variety of media outlets. At least 20 percent of urban US newspapers are devoted to the coverage of sport, but television, for now, reigns supreme. Of the more than 7 billion people in the world, an estimated 3.6 billion television viewers saw at least one minute of the 2012 Olympic Games. The 2014 Fédération Internationale de Football Association (FIFA) Men's World Cup reached a global in-home audience of 3.2 billion people, and 750 million tuned in for the 2015 FIFA Women's World Cup. Advertisers paid $5 million for each thirty-second commercial that aired during the National Football League (NFL) Super Bowl 50 (2016) as 111.9 million viewers made the game the third most watched broadcast in US television history, just behind the 2014 and 2015 Super Bowls.

Electronic communication and personal devices are quickly catching up to television as the favorite ways to consume sport. Television viewership for the 2016 Rio Olympics was down from the Games four years earlier, but there was a 29 percent increase in online streaming as 100 million users streamed 3.3 billion minutes of Olympic coverage.[3] One study found that 70 percent of sport fans who use social media check their devices during a meal, 58 percent do it in the bathroom, 33 percent do it in meetings, and 9 percent do it in church.[4] In other words, sport profoundly affects our daily lives.

Why does girls' and women's sport matter?

Sport is more than a cultural product. Organizers have long promoted the advantages of athletic participation for boys and men, arguing that it provides opportunities for physical activity and teaches important values, including a strong work ethic, teamwork, commitment, determination, leadership, goal setting, how to recover from setbacks and failure, how to perform under pressure, and the pursuit of excellence. We now accept that those same attributes are vital for girls and women.

Research shows that sport is also a matter of health and well-being. Girls who play sport, in comparison to their non-sporting peers, show lower risks for obesity, certain cancers, diabetes, and osteoporosis. Those same female athletes are less likely to engage in risk-taking behavior, including smoking, illicit drug use, and risky or unprotected sex, and they are are less likely to become unintentionally pregnant. Through sport, girls and women learn new skills, how to take control of their bodies, and how to push the limits of their physical potential.[5]

Sport also offers psychological, social, academic, and professional benefits. On average, high school girls get better grades, graduate at higher rates, and more often go on to college if they play sports. Athletic involvement correlates with higher levels of confidence and self-esteem, positive body image, motivation to achieve long-term goals, lower incidence of depression, and decreased suicidal thoughts and tendencies. Very few women will play sport professionally, but lessons learned at any level of play can translate into career success. A 2014 global survey ascertained that 94 percent of high-level senior businesswomen played sport; 52 percent of them played at the collegiate level.[6] EY Women Athletes Business Network and espnW surveyed 400 women executives on four continents for their 2017 report, "Why Female Athletes Make Winning Entrepreneurs": 74 percent of respondents believed that a background in sport can accelerate a woman's career, 66 percent believed that athletes make exceptional candidates for jobs, and 75 percent stated that competitiveness is an asset to their leadership style.[7]

Sport provides opportunities for girls and women to engage in positive relationships, build social networks, and gather in safe spaces. Sport is fun, but it also facilitates social inclusion, integration, and gender equity. Athletic engagement can be a source of empowerment and provide a means to challenge discrimination by giving girls and women an active presence in public spaces, greater mobility, leadership opportunities, powerful role models, and by breaking down gender stereotypes. As women's sport becomes a global phenomenon, the emergence of athletic opportunities in developing countries, one journalist remarked, "represents a mold-breaking departure from traditional definitions of femininity."[8]

Playing sport has the power to transform the way girls and women think about themselves and, in turn, how others regard them. Anecdotal evidence from India, for instance, suggests that entire communities benefit from inclusivity. The introduction of compulsory athletics for all schoolchildren in the northern state of Harayana, along with the prominence of several female sports heroes, coincides with decreased rates of female feticide, girls' mortality, and "honor killings." Ritu Jagnal, a Haryana-based activist, found that citizens' "attitude to women is changing and that is reflected in the rise of its women athletes. . . . It will still take time—social shifts cannot happen overnight—but it is happening."[9]

For these and other reasons, the United Nations Educational, Scientific and Cultural Organization insists that "the practice of physical education and sport is a fundamental right for all." In accordance, a number of organizations have launched programs designed to advance sport for girls and women. These include the International Working Group for Women in Sport, European Women and Sport, the US State Department's Empowering Women and Girls Through Sports Initiative, the International Olympic Committee's (IOC) Commission on Women and Sport, and the IOC's partnership with the United Nations to "promote women's empowerment through sports." There are also myriad groups that operate on local, state, regional, and national levels that continually remind us why sport matters to girls, women, and their communities.[10]

Sportswomen provide powerful and visible role models by exhibiting their physical capabilities, mental tenacity, and tactical awareness. Would "running like a girl" or "throwing like a girl" remain effective insults if more spectators saw the way girls *actually* run and throw? Watching girls' and women's sport reminds us of the participants' humanity. Even today, stereotypes about female frailty, weakness, and passivity persist. The popular media is riddled with images that dehumanize women as sexual objects. Sport shows women as active subjects. Consider all the physical, mental, and social benefits that can come from playing sport. Who wouldn't want that for girls and women? Why deny half the population the right to develop in the same ways we agree are important for boys and men? Women's rights are not just about women—they are about maximizing the potential of an entire community.

What counts as a sport?

Sports are human inventions. They develop at particular times and places for a variety of reasons. In the past, societies considered shin kicking (pretty much what it sounds like) and eye gouging (also fairly explanatory) as sport forms. At one time or another, Olympic competitors engaged in croquet, tug of war, and live pigeon shooting at the Olympic Games. Relatively recent additions to the Olympic program include karate, skateboarding, and surfing. The International e-Sports Federation is lobbying for the inclusion of competitive video gaming at future Games. Our ideas about sport are constantly evolving.

Organizations such as the IOC have tremendous power when it comes to determining what counts as a sport. For the IOC to consider adding a sport to the Olympic program, that sport must have an official international governing body, a requisite number of national governing bodies, a history of international championships, and, for women, must be played in at least forty countries on three continents. (For men, it must be played in at least seventy-five countries on four continents—a discrepancy that indicates women lag behind on a global scale.) Olympic sports tend to favor former colonial powers and wealthy nations with the means to export and popularize their pastimes throughout the world. As a result, we are not likely to see the national games of Afghanistan (buzkashi), Bangladesh (kabaddi), or Columbia (tejo) represented at the Games.

What counts as a sport also tends to favor those activities invented by and for men and in accordance with what we think of as "masculine" attributes, such as strength, power, and aggression. Coupled with the historic exclusion of girls and women, sport constitutes a "male domain," as scholars have characterized it—a "masculine preserve."[11] Historians argue that a more complete understanding of our sporting past requires reconsidering definitions of sport to account for varieties of female physicality. For example, Nancy Struna identifies spinning competitions in Colonial America as a "feminine-defined sport form." Divided into teams, women and girls "transformed a significant domestic activity into a contest" by racing to spin skeins and knots of yarn from raw linen and cotton.[12] Other scholars propose more attentiveness to "physical culture," which includes activities such as dance, calisthenics, purposive exercise, and active leisure.

With these qualifications in mind, *sport*, as it I discuss in this book, refers to physical, institutionalized, nonutilitarian contests. This unfortunately ignores a range of human activities, but it makes the subject manageable. I also approach girls' and women's sport primarily from a US perspective, resulting in a regrettably partial view of the subject.

Case study: Is cheerleading a sport?

If we continue the discussion on Olympic recognition, the answer to this question is "maybe." But a better answer depends on who you ask, why you're asking, the particular function and role of the cheerleader, and a variety of other considerations. A brief look at the history of cheerleading, its connection to gender, and its "sportization" process demonstrates that asking whether cheerleading is a sport is much more complicated than a yes-or-no answer allows.

The role of "cheer leader," as it originated in late nineteenth-century intercollegiate sport, was reserved for men, and there was a great deal of prestige associated with the position. "As a title to promotion in professional or public life," reported *The Nation* in 1911, "it ranks hardly second to that of having been a quarter-back."[13] During the next few decades, girls and women appeared periodically on the sidelines, but it remained a male-dominated enterprise.

In the wake of World War II, more girls and women began to cheer, and by the mid-1970s approximately 95 percent of all participants were female. It was during this time, and specifically with the passage of Title IX (discussed in Chapter 3), that the question of whether cheerleading is a sport became important. School administrators hoped they could count female cheerleaders as athletes to bolster their numbers and show compliance with the law that forbids sexual discrimination in any educational program that receives federal funds. However, the Office of Civil Rights ruled that cheerleading was an "extracurricular activity," not a sport, and that athletic departments could therefore not count cheerleaders as athletes under Title IX.[14]

As girls took to new athletic opportunities, they began to turn away from cheerleading. Looking to revive the activity, cheer organizers developed competitive or all-star cheerleading, which they differentiated from sideline or supportive cheerleading, although both versions became increasingly athletic. By the twenty-first century, as the National Center for Catastrophic Sports Injury Research's Frederick O. Mueller described it, cheerleading had transformed into a "contact sport that involves all types of gymnastic stunts, pyramids, and partner stunts as well as throwing flyers high in the air and catching them (we hope)." In fact, Mueller's data for the center's annual report determined that high school and collegiate cheerleading accounted for 64.8 and 70.6 percent, respectively, of all catastrophic injuries reported for girls and women in sport.[15]

Accordingly, members of the American Medical Association made it a matter of policy to recognize cheerleading as a sport. The organization, along with a host of others, contends that the designation will make the activity safer by giving the athletes access to athletic trainers, equipment, and practice facilities, and by requiring proper certifications for coaches. Indeed, a growing number of states have reclassified cheerleading as an official high school sport. However, there has been an interesting response from the leaders of major cheer organizations, many of who are reluctant to subject what they call an "athletic activity" to the same rules that govern scholastic sports. This reclassification would require putting limits on eligibility, training periods, and the duration of a competitive season. The sports designation would also cut into the profits of the lucrative cheer industry, which operates independently from schools.

At the collegiate level, too, various factions debate whether cheerleading is a sport. In 2010, a federal district judge in Connecticut ruled it was not a sport and that Quinnipiac University violated Title IX by dropping its women's volleyball team to promote competitive cheer to varsity status. In response, a number of schools banded together to form the National Collegiate Stunts and Tumbling Association (now the National Collegiate Acrobatics and Tumbling Association [NCATA]) and changed the name of their sport from competitive cheer to acrobatics and tumbling. All member schools consider acrobatics and tumbling a varsity sport and, backed by USA Gymnastics, the NCATA is pushing for National Collegiate Athletic Association (NCAA) recognition. A rival organization, USA Cheerleading, has proposed a similar sport for NCAA consideration.

In light of this circuitous evolution of cheerleading, it was somewhat surprising that in 2016 the IOC voted to provisionally recognize it as an Olympic sport. The decision meant that the IOC will provide the International Cheer Union with at least $25,000 annually for three years to promote the sport. During that period, the union can apply for full Olympic recognition in the Summer Olympic Games.[16] In the meantime, sports such as squash, which dates back to the 1830s and boasts more than 20 million players worldwide, continue to languish without Olympic representation.

So why cheerleading, and why now? These questions, as with many of the questions raised throughout this book, do not have simple answers. Instead, they are connected to issues of power, privilege, and politics. In thinking about the progress and pitfalls that characterize women's sport, it is important to remember that the subject cannot be isolated from larger historical, cultural, and social issues but, rather, is deeply implicated in the ways we think about women's rights, bodies, gender, sexuality, race, ethnicity, social class, religion, and (dis)ability. Women's sport matters.

2

A BRIEF HISTORY
OF WOMEN'S SPORT

How long have women played sport?

Women have always engaged in various sport forms. Much of our knowledge about these activities is pieced together from archeological evidence, artistic renderings, and literary traces, all of which are subject to the fickle nature of interpretation. In addition, a Western bias shapes much of the sport history scholarship, such that it ignores myriad civilizations and their athletic practices. "Historians have tended to assume that civilization began with the ancient Greeks," write June Kennard and John Marshall Carter, "but grand civilizations existed twenty-five centuries before the Greeks; and, further, the Greeks borrowed much from these civilizations."[1] This historical blind spot leaves undocumented the athletic experiences of an uncalcuable number of past societies—"the people without sport history"—as anthropologist Susan Brownell describes them.[2] There is evidence that women participated in ball games in ancient China and Mesoamerica, as two examples. Just the same, most sport history begins in Greek antiquity, and ideas about ancient Greece undeniably influenced the development of modern sport.

With these qualifications in mind, we do know that women in ancient Greece and Rome had limited sporting activities. Their mythologies includes tales of athletic women and goddesses, such as Artemis (the Roman Diana), goddess of the hunt and an expert archer. The Amazons, a legendary tribe of warrior women in Greek mythology, were skilled at riding horses, fighting, and archery (DC Comics' Wonder Woman is an Amazonian descendent). In his epic poem *The Odyssey*, Homer describes a ball game played by Nausisca and her maidens. And Atalanta was a formidable, if mythological athlete who regularly bested men in hunting and wrestling. Hoping to avoid marriage and confident in her abilities, she declared that she would only wed the man who could beat her in a footrace. With that, Aphrodite, goddess of love, gifted three golden apples to a desperate Melanion, who tossed them at Atalanta's feet during the race, thus distracting her enough to win the race and her hand in marriage.

The ancient Olympic Games (776 BCE–393 CE), held at the shrine for Zeus, king of the gods, in Olympia, were part of the cycle of Panhellenic Games that included the Pythian Games in Delphi, the Isthmian Games in Corinth, and the Nemean Games in Nemea. Greek women did not compete at or attend these events, and the ideology of separate spheres—which assigned men to public life and confined women to matters of the home—precluded most Greek women's athletic engagement. There were a few noteworthy exceptions, however. Pausanias, writing in 175 CE, described maidens running short footraces in the Herean Games, staged in honor of the goddess Hera. In the Greek city-state of Sparta, girls and women exercised to prepare them for motherhood and to bear and care for healthy offspring. Spartan girls raced, wrestled, and threw the discus and javelin. The colony of Cyrene on the northern coast of Africa also boasted accomplished women athletes.

Sport in ancient Rome became increasingly spectacular— something that Roman citizens watched rather than something in which they participated. Men and women flocked to gladiator contests and chariot racing during this time. There is evidence that a few women fought as gladiators, but the combatants were primarily men.

Following the fall of the Roman Empire, sport in medieval Europe (fifth to fifteenth century CE) was divided strictly along class lines. The aristocracy delighted in medieval tournaments, in which women played auxiliary roles. Outside these tournaments, aristocratic women joined in field sports, such as hunting, horseback riding, hawking, and falconry. Middle-class women, it seems, were restricted to the role of spectator as men competed in archery, running, jumping, and wrestling contests. For the peasantry, sport happened during fairs and seasonal festivals. Women ran smock races (footraces that awarded smocks to the winners) and took part in folk football—a wild, no-holds-barred precursor to soccer, rugby, and American football. And at least as early as the fifteenth century, English milkmaids incorporated their milking stools into a stick and ball game. "Stoolball" is an antecedent of both cricket and baseball, though men in both sports denied these "feminine" roots.

The Renaissance originated in Italy and spread throughout Europe in the sixteenth and seventeenth centuries. According to scholar Allen Guttmann, women of this era ice skated; played stoolball and other ball games; boxed; and raced by foot, horse, and boat (in Venice). Noble women enjoyed sport as well. Mary Queen of Scotland hunted, Katherine of Aragon golfed, and Anne Boleyn was an archer.[3]

In Colonial America of the seventeenth and eighteenth centuries, sporting practices were tied to geography, religion, ruling ideology, and social hierarchy. The Puritans of New England, for example, censured blood sports and gambling, but these and other pastimes prospered elsewhere in the colonies. The necessities and adverse conditions associated with settlement, homesteading, and frontier life often precluded sport as we think of it today. Still, women and men raced horses and boats, played games, and gambled on blood sports and other pastimes.

Colonial America was not just about the colonists but also about the colonized, enslaved, indentured, and dispossessed. Well before European settlers arrived in the "New World," Native American women participated in physical contests, footraces, and ball games. Later, enslaved women recalled African traditions and forged new recreational activities on those rare occasions they found themselves with respite from toil. Combative activities, such as boxing and wrestling, held multiple meanings during the era of slavery. Such pursuits were a way to assert status, played out in courtship rituals, and provided occasions for personal expression and entertainment. Importantly, combat sports were also a means through which individuals could resist violence and oppression. As historian T. J. Desch Obi argues, "Female slaves would practice wrestling as part of the ritual performance and contest, and those techniques were put to good use when faced with rape or brutality."[4] More than mere amusement, sport has held a variety of meanings throughout history.

What marked the beginning of the modern age of sport and what did it mean for women?

Emerging around the middle of the nineteenth century in Europe and, later, North America, modern sport was significantly different from primitive, ancient, and medieval forms. Guttmann characterizes these differences in terms of secularism, equality of opportunity to compete, and in the conditions of competitions, specialization of roles, rationalization, bureaucratic organization, quantification, and the quest for records.[5] A number of milestones developed with the transition to modern sport, including the first boat race between Oxford and Cambridge (1829); Alexander Cartwright's rules of the Knickerbocker Base Ball Club (1845); golf's first Open Championship (1860); the first men's track meet between Oxford and Cambridge (1864); the establishment of England's Football (soccer) Association (1863); the first intercollegiate

American football game between Princeton and Rutgers University (1869); the formation of the Rugby Football Union (1871) and Baseball's National League (1876); the first official lawn tennis tournament at the All England Croquet and Lawn Tennis Club in Wimbledon (1877); the inventions of judo (Kanō Jigorō, 1882), basketball (James Naismith, 1891), and volleyball (William Morgan, 1894); and the first modern Olympic Games (1896). The engineers of modern sport primarily designed it to be for and about (white) boys and men—as a way to develop a particular version of masculinity against the supposedly "emasculating" forces of industrialization, urbanization, and immigration. Still, ambitious women have always dared to compete.

During the Victorian era (named for England's Queen Victoria, 1837–1901), white middle- and upper-class women found themselves bound by dictates of gentility. This did not entirely preclude sport, however. Croquet began as a pastime of the elite class and later flourished with middle-class Americans in the 1860s and 1870s. By the 1880s, lawn tennis began to eclipse the popularity of croquet, and women first joined the Wimbledon Championships in 1884, though they played a decidedly less vigorous game than they do today. Confined by restrictive clothing, rules, and social mores, women's tennis at the turn of the twentieth century was more social activity than physical activity. On the well-manicured grass of stately manors or within the confines of exclusive country clubs, tennis, as well as golf, were indicative of conspicuous leisure and consumption.

American women's colleges, established after the Civil War (1861–1865), provided students with programs of gymnastic and callisthenic exercises, and administrators soon added sports such as baseball and field hockey to the curriculum. In 1892, one year after Naismith invented basketball, Senda Berenson introduced the sport at Smith College. Basketball quickly became popular and spread throughout the country's colleges, high schools, Young Women's Christian Associations

(YWCAs), and settlement homes. At the first official women's intercollegiate basketball game in 1896 (University of California vs. Stanford University), physical educators worried about "rough and vicious" play.[6] Consequently, leaders adapted the game for girls and women, confining players' movement to designated zones and limiting, if not eliminating, physical contact between competitors (see Chapter 4).

In truth, decorum and propriety were luxuries accorded to the upper classes. The daily lives of working-class women required active physicality, and they often lacked the discretionary income, time, and energy to devote to sport. In some instances, sport provided moneymaking opportunities (a prospect the elite found "vulgar"), and women boxed, played baseball, wrestled, and performed feats of strength, often to the delight, if not the curiosity, of the ticket-buying crowd. From the mid-1870s to the late 1880s, pedestrianism, or competitive walking, was a popular pastime in which men and women raced for time and distance. "Pedestriennes" such as Bertha Von Hillern and Mary Marshall drew onlookers by the thousands.[7] In 1878, England's Ada Anderson, who peppered her stunts with songs, speeches, and comical pranks, performed at Brooklyn's Mozart Garden, where management constructed an oval track for the occasion. Anderson completed a quarter mile every fifteen minutes for 1,000 consecutive quarter hours, which amounted to more than twenty-eight days of walking. The *New York Times* reported that bystanders were "so fascinated by the spectacle of a woman on the track performing a feat of which the majority of men would be incapable, that they watch her for hours at a time, day after day, with unflagging interest."[8] Soon, six-day pedestrian races captured public attention. The first American women's contest took place at New York City's Madison Square Garden. As the *Times* reported with a ring of pity, the event involved "18 unfortunate women whose poverty has compelled them to undertake the six-day's walk."[9]

The invention of the safety bicycle (so named for its safety features, including front and rear wheels of equal size) led to the cycling boom of the 1880s. Six-day bicycle races replaced pedestrian events while, outside of competitions, women found new physical, political, and sartorial freedoms astride a bike. Feminists, particularly those working to get the vote, exhorted the real and symbolic values of "the wheel." Susan B. Anthony called it a "freedom machine," and Elizabeth Cady Stanton declared that "many a woman is riding to suffrage on a bicycle."

Wherever women rode, they found that the long cumbersome skirts of the Victorian era were incompatible with cycling, and they adapted their clothing to suit the two-wheeled fad. Of particular public interest was women's adoption of "bloomers" (named for women's rights activist Amelia Bloomer), or baggy pantaloons that allowed safer and freer movement. Although bloomers never really caught on in the world of fashion, girls and women wore them in physical education classes, and "Bloomer Girl" baseball teams barnstormed across the United States.

Because of the freedoms associated with the bicycle, civic, religious, and medical leaders denounced "wheelwomen." Detractors claimed the bicycle caused women to lose their composure, to push their bodies in harmful and unseemly ways, and that cycling would lead to unchaperoned escapades with morally suspect suitors. Critics issued warnings about potential spinal deformities, uterine displacement, damage to women's reproductive organs, and the masturbatory effects of riding astride. Among the most preposterous arguments was that women would develop "bicycle face," a supposedly permanent condition marked by bulging eyes and clenched jaw.

In these urgings against women's cycling, there are three primary rationales used against women's participation in sport in the early twentieth century, as identified by scholars Tess Kay and Ruth Jeanes: the medical rationale, the aesthetic rationale, and the social rationale (discussed, in turn, next). As a result, Kay and Jeanes argue, the history of women in sport has been "one of substantial exclusion."[10] Even into the twenty-first century, the residual effects of these rationales continue to exert powerful influences.

What were the medical rationales for keeping women out of sport?

Many of the arguments against a woman's participation in sport had to do with her presumed delicate constitution, combined with her obligation to devote her energies toward her ultimate purpose: bearing and raising healthy children and preparing herself for the "cult of domesticity." Most notably, there were grave concerns about what sport might do to women's reproductive functions. In 1898, the German *Journal of Physical Education* noted that

> violent movements of the body can cause a shift in the position and a loosening of the uterus as well as prolapse and bleeding, with resulting sterility, thus defeating a woman's true purpose in life, i.e. the bringing forth of strong children.[11]

This attitude spread far and wide. In England, women's soccer was popular with both participants and spectators around the time of World War I. Yet, from 1921 to 1971, the English Football Association banned women's teams from club grounds, arguing the game was "quite unsuitable for females." Cynics expressed similar concerns in Brazil. As one man wrote to Brazilian president Getúlio Vargas, "a woman cannot practice this violent sport without seriously affecting the physiological equilibrium of her organic functions, due to the nature that disposes her to be a mother." Vargas apparently agreed. In 1941, the National Sports Council decreed that girls and women "will not be allowed to practice sports incompatible with the conditions of their nature," and Brazilian women could not legally play soccer again until 1979.[12]

For much of the nineteenth and twentieth centuries, middle- and upper-class women were bound by the myth of female frailty. As author Collette Dowling defines it, "The theory behind the frailty myth was this: Women could not be allowed to follow their own pursuits—physical or mental— because every ounce of energy they could generate was needed for maintaining the reproductive process." There were, of course, exceptions to this rule. Dowling argues that communities draw on women's strength "only when the economy needs it—during wars, while men are away, or when helping to pioneer new lands."[13] Even more, enslaved women, agricultural laborers, factory workers, ranch hands, and domestic servants could not afford to abide by the logic of the frailty myth. Their everyday existence required strength, strain, and stamina.

Connected to the myth of female frailty was the theory of vital energy. Perhaps a 1921 *New York Times* author described the theory best:

> Every girl, it seems, has a large store of vital and nervous energy upon which to draw in the great crisis of motherhood. If the foolish virgin uses up this deposit in daily expenditures on the hockey field or tennis court, as a boy can afford to, then she is left bankrupt in her great crisis and her children have to pay the bill.[14]

With only a finite quantity of vigor on which to draw, girls and women must not waste it on sport (or higher education, politics, or countless other pursuits).

Menstruation—that "eternal wound" in a woman's body— also drained a women's vital energy account and was paramount among the worries of physicians and health reformers, especially with regard to sport.[15] Even as late as 1939,

Dr. Stephen Westmann characterized menstruation as an injury "in the most sensitive part of a woman's body," declaring that "no sportsman would ever dream of competing with a wound in his vital organs!" As such, he continued emphatically, "*complete abstinence from activity in sport is absolutely imperative in the menstruating woman.*"[16] Over time, physicians came to the general understanding that moderate or light exercise served a variety of health purposes, but violent and competitive sports would certainly lead to ruin (see Chapter 10).

What were the aesthetic rationales for keeping women out of sport?

There were several aesthetic concerns about women in sport. First, critics charged that it was not something at which attractive girls and women excelled. In his 1939 book, *Farewell to Sport*, for instance, acclaimed sportswriter Paul Gallico wrote that "unattractive girls are comparatively good sports. Pretty girls are not. The ugly ducklings, have taken to sport as an escape and to compensate for whatever it is they lack, sex appeal, charm, ready-made beauty."[17]

The second concern was that sport participation *made* a girl or woman unattractive. Sport would cause "bicycle face" or other disfiguring afflictions, shrink a woman's chest, and build hideous, bunchy, butch-y muscles. In "masculine" sports, such as track and field, women's "charms shrink to something less than zero," assessed one journalist in 1936.[18]

The third concern was that women competing made an ungainly and unsightly spectacle. Baron Pierre de Coubertin, a primary architect of the modern Olympic Games, consistently disapproved of women's participation (see Chapter 7). On women in the winter sport of bobsleigh, Coubertin wrote in 1908,

Seeing a lady with her skirts lifted sliding in this position, usually scratching up the runway with two small pointed sticks which she holds in her hands and which help her steer the sleight, that sight represents a true offense to the eyes. Nothing uglier could be imagined.[19]

It was a position de Coubertin, and others, expressed often.

What were the social rationales for keeping women out of sport?

The social rationale, in this context, refers to the mentality that sport is really about masculinity and therefore contrary to idealized femininity. Sport would "masculinize" female athletes, confuse gender roles, and undoubtedly lead to social ruin. In 1912, Dr. Sargent, writing for *Ladies' Home Journal*, posed the question, "Are athletics making girls masculine?" His answer was affirmative. Sports, he wrote, "tend to broaden the shoulders, deepen the chest, narrow the hips, and develop the muscles of the arms, back and legs, which are all masculine characteristics."[20] Social rationales against women in sport were not just about women—they were about preserving sport as a place for boys and men and guarding masculine qualities as their own. The apprehension was twofold: Sport ruins women and women ruin sport.

Like so many other rationales against women's athletic participation, anxieties about femininity persist today. As just one of countless examples, Helen Grant, the United Kingdom's minister of sports, equalities and tourism, remarked in 2014 that athletic women

don't have to feel unfeminine. . . . There are some wonderful sports which you can do and perform to a very high level and I think those participating look absolutely radiant and very feminine such as ballet, gymnastics, cheerleading and even roller skating.[21]

To be clear, there is nothing wrong with ballet, gymnastics, cheerleading, and roller skating, but this type of comment reasserts the idea of "gender-appropriate sport" (see Chapter 4) instead of redefining femininity to include a range of athletic pursuits.

Were the 1920s the "golden age of sport"?

Sportswriters, including Gallico, looked back fondly on the 1920s as sport's "golden decade."[22] While it is true that many sporting heroes made their mark during this era, it was also a time of racial segregation, ethnic prejudice, and rank sexism. A few sportswomen made headlines in the twenties, including swimmers Sybil Bauer and Gertrude Ederle, who in 1926 became the first woman and the fastest person to swim the English Channel. The American public greatly admired tennis players such as Helen Wills and Suzanne Lenglen. Between 1919 and 1927, the French Lenglen ruled the courts. Playing a balletic style of tennis in her short sleeveless dresses and without a corset, Lenglen's daring fit well in the flapper era.

At the same time, women physical educators began to worry about "excessive" competition and "violent" athletics. They were increasingly dismayed by the exploitation and sexualization of girls and women in male-governed, commercial sport. In addition, this type of sport favored the highly skilled few at the expense of the masses. By the 1920s, "moderation" became the primary curricular focus as educators attempted to suppress competitive and intercollegiate contests. Eventually, most women physical educators argued vehemently against highly competitive sports, including women's Olympic involvement, well into the 1950s. As an alternative, they promoted "play days" that emphasized cooperation under the banners of "play for play's sake" and "a sport for every girl and a girl in every sport."

What were industrial leagues?

This was the kind of sport against which women physical educators railed. Historian Lynne Emery defines industrial sport as athletics sponsored by an industry (e.g., insurance companies, banks, textile companies, and bottling plants), designed to benefit both employees and the business. The theory behind providing athletic opportunities was that they made for healthy, happy, and loyal workers, and helped advertise the company. Industrial sports for women began to take off in the 1920s and continued through the 1960s as teams and individuals competed in tennis, bowling, volleyball, baseball, softball, track and field, swimming, golf, and field hockey. Basketball was especially popular, and without industrial teams, Emery argues, the Amateur Athletic Union's (AAU) national women's basketball championship, first held in 1926, could not have survived.[23] The US Olympic team prospered too. In 1929, sportswriter John Tunis remarked that it was "mainly the girls" who worked for "the big industrial concerns, the big banks, the big insurance companies, and large corporations," that represented the nation on the Olympic stage.[24]

The most famous woman to emerge from American industrial leagues was Mildred "Babe" Didrikson (later Zaharias), who excelled in nearly every sport she tried. In 1930, as a junior in high school, Didrikson took a stenographer's position with the Employers Casualty Company of Dallas; but her real job was to play for the business's basketball team, the Golden Cyclones. During the next three years, she earned All-American honors and, in 1931, led the Cyclones to the national AAU championship. Employers Casualty also sponsored a women's track and field team. At the 1930 national AAU meet, Didrikson won the javelin and baseball throw. At the same competition the following year, she was the leading scorer, with wins in the long jump, a world-record performance in the baseball throw, and a national record in the 80-meter hurdles.

The subsequent 1932 championships also served as the Olympic trials. Didrikson, the only member on the Employers Casualty team, won the shot-put, javelin, 80-meter hurdles, and baseball throw and tied for first place in the high jump to earn 30 points and the national team title—solely on her own. The second-place team, the Illinois Women's Athletic Club, included twenty-two athletes who, all together, scored 22 points. American Olympic officials limited Didrikson to three events at the 1932 Games in Los Angeles, where she won gold medals and broke world records in both the javelin and the 80-meter hurdles. She also tied for first in the high jump, but officials demoted her to silver-medal status, arguing she "dived" over the bar, which amounted to a breach of protocol but was not, apparently, a disqualifying offense.

After trying to make a living off sport during the height of the Great Depression, Didrikson turned to golf in the late 1930s. She won eighty-two tournaments, including a streak of fourteen in a row, and became one of the founding members of the Ladies Professional Golf Association. In 1950, three years after her untimely death from cancer at the age of forty-five, the Associated Press named Didrikson the greatest female athlete of the half-century. That may have been an understatement.

How did the history of racial and ethnic segregation and oppression affect sport for American girls and women?

In the pre-civil rights era, American sport was subject to the same de facto and de jure forms of racial, ethnic, and religious segregation that affected every facet of social life. Swimming pools, perhaps more than any other site of sport, reflected the ugly racism of the Jim Crow era. Gold-medal-winning Filipina American diver, Victoria Manalo (later Draves; discussed in Chapter 8), could only swim in public pools on "International Days." At mid-century, she, along with other Asian, black, and Latina/o swimmers, were allowed just one day of the week to swim, after which officials drained and cleaned the pool.

Women of color faced multiple and intersecting forms of discrimination based on sex, gender, race, ethnicity, and often social class. Some created their own sporting spaces, motivated by what sociologist Nicole Willms calls "a push–pull phenomenon: the pull of shared culture—language, food, customs—and the push of being ostracized by the mainstream culture."[25] Other women joined multiethnic or segregated organizations, teams, industrial leagues, schools and colleges, the Police Athletic League, and religious institutions that promoted girls' and women's sports.

Settlement homes also offered educational, social, and recreational prospects to local communities. The Dennison Settlement House in Boston, for example, sponsored Chinese American women's basketball teams in the late 1920s and 1930s. A Jewish team backed by the Chicago Hebrew Institute won the 1921 Central AAU Girls' Basketball Championship, and Young Women's Hebrew Associations and similar religion-based organizations provided athletic outlets.[26] In 1920s and 1930s California, Buddhist temples and Young Women's Buddhist Associations established basketball leagues and teams for Japanese American girls and women. Enthusiasm for the sport developed into "J-Leagues"—Japanese American community basketball leagues and tournaments that continue to thrive today.[27]

Segregated organizations were a matter of necessity, especially when it came to exclusive sports such as tennis, in which Lenglen, Wills, and other white champions refused to take on challengers of color. Athletic and country clubs, as well as clubs established for specific sports and competitions (such as figure skating and bicycle racing) regularly denied membership to African Americans, Jews, Asians, Latina/os, and those they considered of lower social standing. Many public facilities maintained the color line as well. Consequently, in 1916, a collective of African American professionals formed the American Tennis Association (ATA). Lucy Slowe was the first ATA female champion and, throughout the 1920s, women such as Lula Ballard, Isadore Channels, and Ora Washington jockeyed for ascendancy. Washington won the ATA's national singles title eight times in nine years, and between 1929 and 1927, she won twelve consecutive doubles championships.

She also excelled in basketball, playing for the Germantown Hornets, a team sponsored by a "colored" Philadelphia YWCA. Later, Washington captained a team backed by the *Philadelphia Tribune*, which regularly publicized the accomplishments of black sportswomen.[28]

"Although athletics carried the stigma of being 'not truly feminine' for black women," argues historian Amira Rose Davis, sport "also provided an opportunity to demonstrate the strength and health of the race."[29] Like Ora Washington before them, Margaret and Roumaina Peters were shining examples of "race pride." The sisters ruled the ATA courts from the late 1930s to the early 1950s, and they attended Alabama's segregated Tuskegee Institute (now Tuskegee University) on athletic scholarships. At a time when women physical educators of all races and ethnicities shunned highly competitive sports programs, Tuskegee was a rarity. It was also a great success. Between 1937 and 1951, Tuskegee's Tigerettes track program dominated AAU competition, winning fourteen of fifteen outdoor titles and five of six indoor titles. In 1948, Tuskegee graduate and high jumper Alice Coachman became the first black woman to win an Olympic gold medal.

Tennessee Agricultural and Industrial State College (now Tennessee State University) borrowed liberally from Tuskegee's program to develop the next preeminent track program in the nation. In 1955, with a team of just six athletes, Tennessee State won its first national AAU championship. The Tigerbelles would go on to defend that title every year from 1956 to 1968, losing the 1969 championship by just 1 point. Between 1948 and 1968, Tigerbelles accounted for twenty-five of the forty medals that US women won in track and field. Among them was the incomparable Wilma Rudolph, who won a bronze medal at the Melbourne Games of 1956 and three gold medals at the 1960 Olympic Games in Rome.

Althea Gibson was another beneficiary of women's athletics at historically black institutions, having attended Florida Agricultural and Mechanical College for Negroes (now

Florida Agricultural and Mechanical University) on an athletic scholarship. Gibson deserves special mention in this history for desegregating not one but two "country club" sports in the mid-1900s. Gibson got her start playing paddle tennis in New York's Police Athletic League. Black philanthropists, impressed with her talents, financed her participation in the ATA. Taking the mantle from the Peters sisters, Gibson won ten straight ATA championships between 1947 and 1956. All the while, ATA officials, black journalists, and white supporters, including former champion Alice Marble, lobbied the United States Lawn Tennis Association (USLTA) to desegregate the game. Unable to withstand the pressure, USLTA relented in 1950. Gibson entered the US National Championship at Forest Hills, becoming the first black athlete, male or female, to break tennis's color line. Six years later, she won the French singles event, the Wimbledon doubles title, and the US Nationals and repeated the same honors in 1958. In tennis's amateur era, however, Gibson was unable to support herself in the now lucrative sport. She turned her attention to professional golf, becoming the first African American woman on the tour.

Sporting practices provided ways for people to assert their humanity under even the worst circumstances. In the late nineteenth and early twentieth centuries, the US and Canadian governments established schools for aboriginal children, the curriculum of which was designed to strip them of their "Indian-ness" and assimilate them—"civilize" them—according to Anglo-Saxon values. In the US, tens of thousands of Native American boys and girls attended on-reservation schools and off-reservation boarding schools, where they endured unfathomable horrors and abuse. Yet, even in the harshest conditions, sport provided an opportunity for pride, escape, and joy. Basketball was particularly popular for girls. At the 1904 World's Fair in St. Louis (held in conjunction with the Third Olympiad), the girls' team from Fort Shaw Indian Boarding School in Montana won the title of "World Basketball Champions."

Women of Japanese descent also became casualties of US governmental policies. Following the December 7, 1941, Japanese attack on Pearl Harbor that brought the United States into World War II, President Franklin D. Roosevelt issued Executive Order 9066, setting in motion the incarceration of 120,000 people of Japanese ancestry, including American citizens, most of who lived on the West Coast. Between 1942 and 1946, government agents forced these individuals to leave their homes and businesses and confined them behind barbed wire in internment centers that were located in some of the most desolate areas in the country. Despite the dehumanizing circumstances, prisoners organized sports teams and leagues, the results of which appeared regularly in camp newspapers. Interned girls and women played table tennis, basketball, and volleyball, but softball emerged as the most popular pastime, providing "an important component to the morale needed to endure their imprisonment," writes historian Samuel O. Regalado.[30]

When and how did physical educators change their collective philosophy about competitive sport for girls and women?

In the 1940s and 1950s, a new generation of physical educators and students began to push for more competitive athletics. After studying the issue, physical educators conceded to the prevailing attitudes of the time, and a number of schools started offering varsity women's sports. In the Cold War era that followed World War II, the US Olympic Committee also began to reconsider its apathy toward women's sports, as American teams found themselves at a disadvantage in international competitions against Soviet and other Eastern Bloc countries that developed and promoted female athletics.

In 1967, the American Association for Health, Physical Education, and Recreation's (now the American Alliance for Health, Physical Education, Recreation and Dance) Division for Girls and Women's Sports established the Commission on

Intercollegiate Athletics for Women that, in 1971, became the Association for Intercollegiate Athletics for Women (AIAW), designed to govern, structure, and provide championships in women's college sport. The AIAW differed significantly from the NCAA, which, at the time, had no interest in governing women's athletics. The AIAW opposed the NCAA's commercial stance and instead adopted an explicitly educational philosophy that included minimizing travel during the week so that student-athletes could focus on their studies, allowing athletes to transfer schools without penalty, and, initially, prohibiting off-campus recruiting and athletic scholarships.

Combined with the burgeoning women's movement and the enactment of Title IX (see Chapter 3), the 1970s was a revolutionary period in the history of women's sport. By 1980, the AIAW had nearly 1,000 institutional members, provided participation opportunities for approximately 125,000 college women, and offered 35 national championships in 17 sports. During this time, the NCAA, which repeatedly opposed Title IX throughout the 1970s, made motions to take over the governance of women's intercollegiate athletics. In 1981 and 1982, the NCAA offered championships in women's sports and many AIAW-member institutions switched their allegiance, finding that the NCAA provided better funding and resources. As a result, the AIAW lost a lucrative television contract with NBC and in 1982 suspended operations. A judge subsequently dismissed the AIAW's antitrust lawsuit against the NCAA, and the women's organization that provided so much for so many officially folded in 1983. Although the decision marked the end of a revolutionary era, the efforts of pioneering sportswomen and organizers through the 1970s set the stage for what we might call the modern era of *women's* sport.

3

THE INFLUENCE OF TITLE IX

What is Title IX?

Title IX of the Education Amendments of 1972 is an amendment to the Civil Rights Act of 1964. It states, "No person in the United States shall, on the basis of sex, be excluded from participation in, be denied the benefits of, or be subjected to discrimination under any education program or activity receiving Federal financial assistance." Title IX applies to all public and private educational institutions that receive federal funds and addresses ten areas, including access to higher education, career education, education for pregnant and parenting students, employment, learning environment, math and science, sexual harassment, standardized testing, and technology. But it has become most widely known for its influence on sport.

There are three general aspects of Title IX as it applies to athletics:

1. Participation: There must be equal opportunities for male and female students to participate in sports. This does not mean identical sports but, rather, equal participation spots. Football, with approximately 100 participation opportunities, tends to skew the numbers because there are no female equivalent sports that require that many team members.

2. Scholarships: At scholarship-granting colleges and universities, male and female student athletes must receive scholarship dollars proportional to their participation.

3. Other benefits: Sometimes called a "laundry list," these benefits include equitable (not necessarily equal) treatment in the provision of equipment and supplies; scheduling of games and practice times; travel and daily allowances or per diems; access to tutoring; coaching; locker rooms and practice and competitive facilities; medical and training facilities and services; housing and dining facilities and services; publicity and promotions; support services; and recruitment of student athletes.

In 2002, Title IX was renamed the Patsy T. Mink Equal Opportunity in Education Act, in honor of one of its principal authors and the first Asian American woman and woman of color to serve in the US Congress.

How has Title IX influenced girls' and women's participation in sport?

It was not until 1975 that Congress approved Title IX language specific to sport. At that time, elementary schools had one year to comply with the regulations, and high schools and colleges had three years to comply. Although Title IX went into law in 1972, it was not until 1978 that most athletic departments were required to act. Even so, throughout the 1970s, Title IX was like a "guillotine in the courtyard," as women's sport advocate Donna Lopiano assessed.[1] The law's presence loomed large and prompted school administrators to add athletic opportunities for girls and women. In 1971, 300,000 American girls—one in twenty-seven—played high school sports. By 2017, on the occasion of Title IX's forty-fifth anniversary, that participation rate had increased tenfold. More than 3 million girls—two in five—counted themselves as high school athletes.

Title IX has also significantly influenced women's participation in intercollegiate sports. In 1971, fewer than 30,000 women played varsity athletics. In 1982, the year that the NCAA took over the governance of intercollegiate women's sports, there were 73,351 college women athletes. As Title IX turned forty-five, that number had grown to 211,862, a sevenfold increase since the pre-Title IX era.

Still, Title IX has not affected all girls and women in the same ways. Girls in less privileged urban and rural areas do not have the same athletic opportunities as those in suburban and affluent schools and school districts. Equity varies according to region. The ten states with the largest inequality gaps (the largest discrepancies between boys' and girls' athletic participation) in public high schools are in the South (the smallest gaps are in Vermont, Hawaii, Maine, and Maryland).[2]

In addition, the National Women's Law Center, working with the Poverty and Race Research Action Council, found that girls and women of color do not reap the same Title IX benefits as their white peers. "In fact," the authors of the study determined, "nationwide, 40 percent of heavily minority schools have large 'female opportunity gaps,' compared to only 16 percent of heavily white schools."[3] College athletics reflect these disparities. The Institute for Diversity and Ethics in Sport's annual survey established that in 2015–2016, white women represented 72.6 percent of NCAA student–athletes across all divisions. In comparison, Latinas represented 5.1 percent of NCAA student–athletes, Asians/Pacific Islanders 2.4 percent, Native Americans 0.4 percent, and, in the authors' words, "Female student–athletes identified as two or more races, 'other,' and non-resident aliens represented 10.2 percent."[4] At 9.3 percent of all NCAA student–athletes, African American women are under-represented in most aspects of college athletics but are over-represented in basketball and track and field—the combined effects of history, tradition, role modeling, social class, and earlier opportunities.

Girls' athletic participation is further influenced by cultural, familial, and religious values. In immigrant families, three-fourths of boys but fewer than half of girls are involved in athletics.[5] There may be cultural pressures for girls to help with household duties, child care, or to earn money in the hours outside of school, thus cutting into extracurricular activities like sport. Financial pressures may be such that families lack the money, time, or transportation required for athletic participation. Still other families may put a premium on education and "intellectual" engagements and may not see much value in sweatier pursuits.

In addition, Title IX has had little application to sports for girls and women with physical, intellectual, or sensory impairments. Approximately nine out of every 100 US families have a child with an impairment that interferes with sports and exercise, yet most elementary and secondary schools lack programs or facilities that address their needs.[6] The same is true with regard to colleges and universities, according to the American Collegiate Society of Adapted Athletics. The Eastern College Athletic Conference (ECAC) is the first and, as of 2017, the only NCAA sanctioned conference to introduce an Inclusive Sport Initiative. According to a 2015 ECAC press release,

> This strategy includes providing reasonable accommodations in existing events and adding adaptive-specific events to existing ECAC Championship sports such as track and field, swimming, rowing, and tennis. Over the coming few years, the ECAC also aspires to add new leagues and championships for adaptive team sports such as wheelchair basketball, sled hockey, goal ball and sitting volleyball. To help [e]nsure the success of this strategy, the ECAC will provide all appropriate and necessary governance, administrative, operations, and sport technical support.[7]

If these sports do become varsity sports, they should comply with Title IX regulations.

How do athletic programs comply with Title IX?

In 1979, the US Department of Health, Education, and Welfare issued its final policy interpretation on "Title IX and Intercollegiate Athletics," which included the "3-Prong Test" for compliance. Today, the Office for Civil Rights (OCR) of the US Department of Education oversees Title IX and maintains that three-part test, which consists of the following:

1. Substantial proportionality: This stipulates that the percentage of male and female athletes in an athletic program must reflect the percentage of full-time male and female students in the school's undergraduate population.
2. History and continued practice of program expansion: A school can show compliance by working to add more participation opportunities for the under-represented sex.
3. Full and effective accommodation of interests and abilities: A school can argue that the under-representation of one sex in an athletic program is not due to discrimination but, rather, to the interests and abilities of the sex in question, which the school has fully and effectively accommodated.

Importantly, schools need only comply with one of the prongs.

The Equity in Athletics Disclosure Act, a federal law passed in 1994, requires post-secondary institutions to report annually to the US Department of Education on athletic participation, scholarship dollars, staffing and average salaries, recruitment expenses, operating expenses, overall expenses, and revenues by men's and women's teams. This information, along with data from other sources, reveals that approximately 80–90 percent of all educational institutions are *not* in compliance with Title IX. Schools that do not comply risk losing federal funding, but that has never happened because the federal government does not actively investigate or enforce the law. An issue usually only comes to light when someone files a complaint, which is unlikely, according to Lopiano. "Who is going to bring the pressure? Just think about that for a while," she told *Vice Sports.* "No. 1, it's an individual institution that is the issue. The coach is probably not going to bring it up, because the coach is afraid of losing their job. The athlete is probably not going to bring it up, because they're afraid of retaliation. It really is an impossible situation." The NCAA does little to rectify the situation. "The best thing to do if the NCAA cared about Title IX at all . . . is to make Title IX eligibility a requirement for the postseason," Lopiano continued.[8] Without structural support for Title IX, either from the NCAA or the federal government, schools continue to get away with failing to provide equitable experiences for male and female athletes.

If athletic departments do not directly receive federal funding, are they exempt from Title IX?

The question of federal funding was a significant stumbling block in the early years of Title IX. In 1984, the Supreme Court provided an answer in the *Grove City College v. Bell* case, in which justices ruled that Title IX only applied to specific programs that received federal funds, thus exempting most athletic departments. Within weeks of the decision, the US Department of Education closed nearly all of its investigations of complaints against college and high school athletic programs.

The interpretation lasted until 1988, after Congress passed the Civil Rights Restoration Act that reversed the *Grove City* decision. As it stands today, if any program or student receives federal funds, the entire institution and all its programs must comply with Title IX. At issue is that federal funds come from taxpayer dollars, which should not be used to discriminate against a class of people. Athletics are considered educational programs and activities, and as such they enjoy tax-exempt status. The argument that college athletics is a business and should be run as such is contrary to its nonprofit, tax-free standing.

Is Title IX to blame when athletic departments cut men's programs?

No. In fact, college men have *gained* athletic opportunities since 1972. Between 1988 and 2015–2016, across all NCAA divisions, the net outcome of added and dropped teams was 98 teams for men and 102 teams for women (Figure 3.1). Since the early 2000s, men's opportunities have grown at a slightly faster rate compared to women's opportunities. However, there have been losses of men's teams at the NCAA Division I level, especially in swimming, wrestling, football, water polo, and baseball, but those losses also occurred between 1984 and 1988, a period during which Title IX was essentially without teeth.

Cutting men's programs is not Title IX's "fault" but, rather, the consequence of those who make decisions about how to allocate resources. Indeed, dropping men's teams to comply

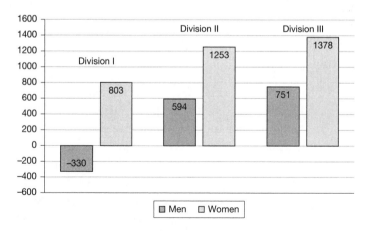

Figure 3.1 Net Outcome of NCAA Added and Dropped Teams.

with Title IX violates the spirit of the law. In 2003, the OCR issued a "Dear Colleague" letter addressing this issue. The document read that "nothing in Title IX requires the cutting or reduction of teams to demonstrate compliance with Title IX" and that this option was a "disfavored practice." Title IX is meant to *provide* opportunities, not take them away.

It is primarily at Division I Football Bowl Subdivision (FBS) or schools with major college football programs that decision-makers have dropped men's sports. The athletic "arms race" is such that in order to stay competitive in football and men's basketball, schools need to spend a lot of money on those sports, particularly on facilities, recruiting, and coaching salaries. FBS schools spend an average of 80 percent of the overall men's athletic budgets on these two sports, leaving all the other men's teams to share the remaining 20 percent. In 2016, FBS athletic departments spent, on average, more than $12 million on football and men's basketball, whereas the average women's budget—for all women's sports—was $9 million.[9]

The counterargument to these statistics is that men's basketball and football are usually the only revenue-producing sports and therefore subsidize women's athletic programs. Again, though, the numbers do not add up. In 2014, only twenty-four of the then 128 FBS schools generated more money than they spent.[10]

What is gender equity?

The NCAA formed a Gender Equity Taskforce in 1992, which formulated a relatively simple definition of gender equity: "An athletics program can be considered gender equitable when the participants in both the men's and women's sports programs would accept as fair and equitable the overall program of the other gender." In other words, if a men's and a women's team were to swap funding, resources, coaching, and all aspects of the other's program, would both sides be satisfied? When the answer is "yes," across all sports, the athletic program is gender equitable.

Do we still need Title IX, as it applies to athletics?

Based on the NCAA Gender Equity Taskforce's definition of gender equity, we still need Title IX. In 1972, 3,666,917 boys played high school sports; forty-five years later, girls have not yet achieved that historic number, and they account for 42 percent of all high school athletes. Of the 3.3 million girls playing high school sports today, approximately 6 percent go on to compete in the NCAA, where they make up 43.5 percent of all intercollegiate athletes—even though they account for 55 percent of undergraduates enrolled at four-year institutions. Simply stated, high school and college sports are still not equitable with regard to sex. In addition, boys' and men's programs continue to receive more funding, attention, and enjoy higher levels of prestige. Women lag behind in positions of power, including coaching and administrative positions (see Chapter 9). And, even after more than four decades of Title IX, the law is constantly under threat. Ideally, Title IX would not be necessary, but until gender equity is uniformly championed, accepted, and achieved, we cannot afford to lose it.

How does Title IX apply to cases of sexual harassment and sexual violence?

Title IX prohibits sexual harassment and sexual violence because they are forms of sex-based discrimination. These crimes can adversely affect students' physical and mental well-being and academic performance, and they can create a hostile or abusive educational environment, thereby disturbing equal access to education and educational activities.

Title IX requires schools to respond promptly, impartially, and effectively to accusations or suspicions of sexual harassment and sexual violence and to take appropriate steps to prevent sexually hostile environments. If an institution fails to adequately prevent, act on, or remedy the effects of a crime, the injured party can wage a Title IX complaint with the OCR. Those who believe that their Title IX rights have been violated can also file a civil lawsuit against the institution and its employees. This typically happens when the litigant believes that the school knew or should have known about the crime and did not act judiciously.

It does not matter if the accused or the accuser is a student or an institutional employee, or whether the misconduct takes place on or off campus. It also does not matter if the accuser or accused has any connection to sport, although a number of high-profile cases have involved athletic programs. For example, in *Jennings v. University of North Carolina*, the courts found in favor of a former member of the women's soccer team, who accused coach Anson Dorrance of sexual harassment, including the use of vulgar language and sexually charged comments. The majority opinion in the case found that Dorrance regularly

> bombarded players with crude questions and comments about their sexual activities and made comments about players' bodies that portrayed them as sexual objects. In addition, Dorrance expressed (once within earshot of Jennings) his sexual fantasies about certain players, and he made, in plain view, inappropriate advances to another.

The university settled the case out of court and levied no sanctions against the coach.[11]

In several Title IX lawsuits, the courts have ruled that school officials acted with "deliberate indifference" in response to allegations of sexual violence. For instance, in *Simpson v. University of Colorado*, the court found in favor of Lisa Simpson, who argued that, since at least 1995, university officials knew that members of the school's football team had a history of sexual violence against female students yet had failed to address the issue. In 2001, several football players and recruits of the program raped Simpson and her roommate. The two women reported the crimes to the University of Colorado's Vice Chancellor for Student Affairs and the director of the Office of Victim's Assistance. Administrators charged several of the players with code of conduct violations but declined to pursue sexual assault charges. None of the accused players even missed a game; the head football coach continued to recruit one of Simpson's assailants. Meanwhile, Simpson, a former honor student, began to struggle academically. Her grades fell, she dropped classes, and she left the University of Colorado without earning her degree.

There have been similar cases involving athletes at the University of Georgia, the University of Notre Dame, Brown University, Florida State University, Michigan State University, Vanderbilt University, and especially Baylor University, where it has become increasingly clear that officials exhibited staggering and continued "deliberate indifference" when dealing with allegations of sexual violence.[12] In particular, a number of women have charged that Baylor officials were aware of a growing problem of sexual assault on campus yet failed to respond or to enact procedural safeguards that might stem the violence. Baylor's football program has been principally embroiled in the charges, and a 2017 lawsuit against the school asserted that between 2011 and 2014—the same time during which the program rose to national prominence under head coach Art Briles—at least thirty-one football players committed more than fifty-two rapes, including five gang rapes.[13] It is likely that the incidence of sexual violence is much higher. As discussed in Chapter 10, an estimated 80 percent of college women do not report sexual assault.[14]

As of 2017, Baylor had settled three of these Title IX cases out of court, including *Jane Doe v. Baylor University,* in which the plaintiff charged that as many as eight members of the football team drugged, kidnapped, and repeatedly and brutally raped her. Doe told multiple Baylor employees about the incident, including a university counselor, her volleyball coach, members of the football program's coaching staff, and the football team's chaplain. No one reported it to Baylor's Office of Judicial Affairs or to law enforcement officials. In Doe's suit, she alleged that gang rapes were part of a hazing and initiation tradition for freshmen football players, who would photograph and record the crimes. Investigators have since found that athletic administrators "affirmatively chose not to report sexual violence" to school and police officials, opting to protect the program's reputation rather than the safety of the accusers and the student body. The report concluded that "institutional failures at every level of Baylor's administration impacted the response to individual cases and the Baylor community as a whole."[15]

Title IX has not been invoked in all the allegations of sexual assault involving Baylor athletes, but perhaps it should be. As more accusations come to light, the public learns that accusers habitually experience lack of support, intimidation, and retaliation. Their physical, emotional, and social well-being suffers, and many ultimately drop out of school. The football program recruited athletes with known histories of violence against women. Coaches and university officials ignored and covered up allegations of abuse, obstructed justice, and disciplined players with little more than a slap on the wrist, when they disciplined them at all. For these reasons, and for many others, we desperately need Title IX. In fact, until there is a major culture shift in US sport, Title IX needs to be even stronger.

4

GENDER AND SPORT

Do the terms "sex" and "gender" mean the same thing?

The terms "sex" and "gender" are often used interchangeably, but there are important differences between them. Sex refers to biological or physiological characteristics that define male and female. As discussed in Chapter 6, sex does not always align neatly according to the male–female binary, but we typically think of it in that way. Gender has to do with the socially constructed roles, understandings, and expectations we have about how boys, girls, men, and women should look, think, and act. Gender, then, relates to masculinity and femininity or, more accurately, masculinities and femininities. It may be helpful to think in terms of gender roles, gender identities, and gender expressions, some of which enjoy greater privilege than others.

Historically, sport and athleticism have been defined by manliness and masculinity and, in turn, manliness and masculinity were defined by one's participation in sport and athletic prowess. Sport was a site at which boys and men could cultivate, perform, and prove culturally sanctioned versions of manhood and therefore viewed as inappropriate for girls and women. Women who adopted so-called manly characteristics or pursued allegedly manly pursuits *transgressed* the established gender norms. In the process,

they challenged and often transformed those norms to re-
define femininity.

How does gender affect girls' and women's participation in sport?

Despite the progress that girls and women have made, there are
still certain sports that we think of as "feminine" and "gender
appropriate." These tend to be individual sports that involve
little physical contact between competitors while emphasizing
grace, beauty, and artistic expression. It has therefore been less
controversial for women to participate in sports such as tennis,
gymnastics, and figure skating.

The sports considered most masculine, such as boxing,
football, rugby, and ice hockey, highlight aggression, collision,
and violence. Even today, research shows that female athletes
in "feminine" sports enjoy more attention from the popular
media, sponsors, and fans compared to women involved in
"masculine" sports. In the same way, boys and men who participate in so-called feminine sports often find themselves targets
of ridicule. Sport, therefore, reinforces gender stereotypes,
which in turn influences participation in sport.

Academic research supports these ideas. In the 1960s,
scholar Eleanor Metheny polled college women to determine which sports they believed were most appropriate for
them. Sports deemed "categorically unacceptable" were the
most masculine sports, while the most feminine sports were
"generally acceptable." In between, Metheny found forms
of competition that "are generally *not acceptable* to college
women in the United States, although they *may be acceptable to
a minority group* within the population," such as the shot-put,
discus, javelin, shorter footraces, low hurdles, and the long
jump. Put differently, Metheny found that what the women
considered acceptable varied according to racial, ethnic, and
social class identities. African American women, she noted,
were "disproportionately represented in track and field
events." Indeed, black women dominated the national track

and field competitions at this time (see Chapter 2). Because of the intertwined histories of slavery, racial segregation, discrimination, and economic necessity, physical activity was not anathema to black women's femininity. In addition, their successes, particularly those won against white competitors, instilled "race pride" and bolstered support for their athleticism. In the same way, women "identified in the lower levels of socioeconomic status," as Metheny put it, could not afford to abide by the myth of female frailty. Accustomed to the strain of working-class life and often shut off from the genteel sports of the elite classes, women of color and working-class women necessarily subscribed to different ideas about gender appropriateness.[1]

As ideas about gender vary according to culture, ideas about gender-appropriate sports also vary. For example, most Americans typically think that field hockey is a sport for girls and women. In the United States, there are no programs for high school boys or college men, although there is a national team, as well as club teams, and a semi-professional league. But in the Netherlands, Argentina, Pakistan, South Africa, China, and other countries, men's field hockey is wildly popular. In fact, it has been an Olympic sport for men since 1908, whereas women first competed on the Olympic stage in 1980. Conversely, soccer has become a gender-appropriate sport for American girls and women, but throughout most of the world, it is a sport associated with manliness and masculinity. Women in countries where men have a long tradition of playing soccer, such as England and Brazil, have had historical difficulties taking the field (see Chapter 2).

The idea of a gender-appropriate sport can also change over time. This has been the case with cheerleading, as examined in Chapter 1. In the same way, figure skating, once the province of upper-class men, as sociologist Mary Louise Adams details in her book *Artistic Impressions: Figure Skating, Masculinity, and the Limits of Sport*, is now considered a feminine-appropriate sport.[2]

What are some examples of gendered differences in sport?

A number of sports have different rules for men and women, and they are "gendered" when the differences relate to dominant ideas about masculinity and femininity. Consider tennis. Initially, men and women both played a best-of-five-sets series, but in 1902 the United States Lawn Tennis Association decided that women could not physically handle the rigors of five sets and reduced their matches to the best-of-three-sets format, which then became the norm (men continued with the five-set structure). The differences between men's and women's tennis are therefore *gendered* because they reflect beliefs about women's physical capabilities.

These same beliefs are evident in the history of basketball. Soon after James Naismith invented the sport in 1891, women physical educators, notably Smith College's Senda Berenson, adapted basketball to limit the mobility and contact between players. Eventually, educators codified a six-player version of basketball with three guards (defensive players) and three forwards (offensive players). No one could cross the half-court line or dribble more than twice, and guards never scored—they didn't even get to take their own foul shots. Some girls and women did play the five-player game in industrial and urban leagues or with the All-American Red Heads (1936–1986), a barnstorming team of red-haired hoopsters that played—and often beat—men's teams. Even into the 1990s, however, girls and women continued to play six-player basketball in certain areas of the United States.

The adaptation of basketball took a slightly different course in the United Kingdom. In the late 1800s, British physical educators created what eventually became netball. Like six-player basketball, the original rules of netball confined players' movement to their designated sections of the court and limited contact between athletes. Throughout the twentieth century, the game spread across the British Empire, and it remains popular for girls and women in many

Commonwealth nations. Just as the six-player game eventually fell by the wayside, so too have some of the antiquated aspects in netball.

Beyond basketball and its derivatives, the contemporary sports world is riddled with gender differences. In badminton, women play to 11 points, but men play to 15. At NCAA cross-country championships, women's races are shorter than those of men. Women typically throw shots, javelins, and discuses that weigh less than the those used by men, and women golf from "ladies' tees" that are closer to the green. Women's National Basketball Association (WNBA) quarters are ten minutes long, but in the men's National Basketball Association (NBA) quarters last twelve minutes. Should we attribute the time difference to beliefs that women cannot handle the extra eight minutes of play, or is it that fans do not want to see women play for the added time? Men's lacrosse and ice hockey permit body checking, but that type of physical contact is illegal for women, presumably because of residual aspects of the frailty myth (see Chapter 2).

Artistic gymnastics also suggests some interesting gender differences. Men compete in six events: the high bar, pommel horse, rings, parallel bars, vault, and floor exercise. Gymnastics experts explain that the men's events are designed to highlight the gymnast's power and upper body strength. Women compete in four events: the uneven bars, balance beam, vault, and floor. Women's events undoubtedly require tremendous strength (three of the four are "leg events," in that they require more leg strength then upper body strength), but they also emphasize balance and grace—ostensibly feminine qualities.[3] Even within the same events, there are significant variations. In the floor exercise, men perform tumbling routines for seventy silent seconds. Women perform to music for ninety seconds and, in addition to tumbling, must incorporate dance elements. This gives them a chance to "express their personalities," as USA Gymnastics describes on its official website—something not required of the men.[4]

How do uniforms express gender differences in men's and women's sport?

On this point, we can continue the discussion about gymnastics, in which women compete in leotards. Men also wear leotards (although they call them singlets or "competition shirts"), but the cut is less revealing and men typically wear pants or shorts over them.

Some sports are marked by the lingering effects of the "skirt theory," built on the idea that the only sports acceptable for women at the turn of the twentieth century were those in which competitors could wear lengthy cumbersome garments, such as golf, archery, and croquet. In fact, the *New York Times* reported that members of the 1914 American Olympic Committee opposed "women taking part in any event in which they could not wear long skirts."[5] This left out "masculine" sports, such as swimming, speed skating, and track and field.

In the 1920s and 1930s, spectators went wild when Norwegian figure skater Sonja Henie shortened her skirt to facilitate her choreography, replete with spins, spirals, and jumps typically performed only by men. Henie won ten consecutive world championships and three Olympic gold medals in her scandalous above-the-knee costume, and her innovations changed both the fashion and the athleticism of the sport. Subsequent figure skaters continued to push the sartorial envelope. At the 1988 Winter Olympic Games in Calgary, Katarina Witt performed in a skirtless, skin-bearing ensemble, and American Debi Thomas wowed the crowd in a one-piece body stocking, or "unitard," much to the dismay of the International Skating Union. The organization consequently decreed that "ladies must wear a skirt," a rule that lasted until 2004. (The use of "lady" in women's sport, such as in the "Ladies Professional Golf Association" or the "Penn State Lady Lions" basketball team, is also gendered, as it implies civility, restraint, and propriety—qualities not typically associated with athleticism.

Men's teams and events are not similarly marked with an analogous term like "gentlemen.")

Skirts continue to be the preferred uniform style in women's field hockey, tennis, golf, cheerleading, and lacrosse. Because of the associations between skirts with femininity, several organizations have tried, unsuccessfully, to require women to wear them, including the International Boxing Association and the Badminton World Federation. Importantly, some sportswomen enthusiastically adopt skirts. Running skirts, for instance, became popular around the same time that Nicole DeBoom wore one in her 2004 Ironman Wisconsin victory. She subsequently launched a successful clothing company, SkirtSports, and big-name retailers have since joined the running-skirt trend.

Of course, uniform differences go beyond the skirt. In some sports, such as volleyball, women's uniforms are more revealing than men's uniforms (think bun-huggers vs. baggy shorts), apparently to add an element of sex appeal. In track and field, elite women competitors typically wear sports bras and short, tight bottoms, whereas male athletes tend to don thigh-length spandex shorts and tank tops. Many women believe that abbreviated clothing provides a competitive advantage. Still others contend that body-conscious clothing helps an athlete's marketability.

The revealing nature of some uniforms has posed a problem for women who observe religious or modest dress customs, though rules are slowly evolving to become more inclusive. Until 2012, for instance, the International Volleyball Federation (FIVB) required women who played beach volleyball to wear bikinis, the bottoms of which could be no wider than six centimeters on the side of the hip. This was an insurmountable problem for observant Muslim women who cover their arms and legs. FIVB has since modified its rules to allow for full-body suits, as have the International Weightlifting Federation and the Fédération Internationale de Gymnastique.

Still, several organizations enforce uniform rules that make it impossible for religiously observant women to compete without compromising their faith. This is perhaps most evident for women who cover their heads. FIFA banned hijabs until 2012, citing both safety issues and a rule that "basic compulsory equipment must not have any political, religious or personal statements." This prevented the Iranian soccer team from playing its 2012 Olympic qualifying match. Until 2017, the International Basketball Federation enforced a similar rule (which also affected Sikh men in turbans and Jewish men in kippot), causing the Qatar women's basketball team to forfeit the 2014 Asian Games. Some organizations rule on head coverings on a case-by-case basis, although the manufacture and sale of sports hijabs should address any lingering, if misguided, safety concerns.[6]

What is the feminine apologetic?

Scholar Jan Felshin coined this phrase in the 1970s to describe women who "apologized" or compensated for their involvement in "masculine" sport by emphasizing traditional ideals of femininity.[7] Compensatory acts included styling one's hair, makeup, and dress to conform to conventional beauty standards; downplaying the importance of sport in one's life; and asserting one's heterosexuality. An apologetic bearing ostensibly softened an athlete's image and assured spectators that sport participation did not threaten her femininity and, in turn, that her participation did not threaten the masculine center of sport.

More recently, scholar–activist Pat Griffin has argued that because women's involvement in sport is no longer a "social anomaly," as Felshin put it in 1974, the feminine apologetic is really a "lesbian apologetic." Women athletes who perform emphasized femininity are not apologizing for their presence in sport but, rather, distancing themselves from the stereotype of the "butch" or lesbian athlete. "Femininity," writes Griffin, "is a code word for heterosexuality" (see Chapter 5).[8] At the same time, research shows that there are many women who are *unapologetic* in transgressing gender norms, whether in their choice of sport or in presenting themselves in ways that the public might interpret as masculine.[9]

Is muscularity a gendered characteristic?

There are historical associations between muscularity, manliness, and masculinity. Strong and noticeably muscular women, then, confuse traditionally gendered ways of thinking. Critics accuse muscular women of taking steroids, of being unattractive, or of being men. As a result, some women employ apologetic strategies to mitigate the supposed incongruity between their brawn and their femininity, and the fear of developing "manly" muscles has long served as a powerful way to dissuade girls and women from pursuing sport or developing their fullest physical potential.

Gendered ideals in bodybuilding illustrate the continued anxieties about muscular women. At the first women's physique competitions in the late 1970s and early 1980s, there were concerns about how to evaluate competitors' builds. While judges had clear ideas about how to rate men's size, development, and symmetry, they had difficulty reconciling these qualities with entrenched ideas about womanhood. As a result, many women hoping to earn high scores avoided "excessive" muscularity and played up their femininity through hair, makeup, facial expressions, costumes, jewelry, nail styles, high-heeled shoes, breast implants or padding, poses, and choreography.

Throughout the 1990s, event organizers instituted a series of "femininity rules" amid growing alarm that women bodybuilders were "too big" to attract fans and sponsors. In 2000, the International Federation of Bodybuilding and Fitness (IFBB) issued judging guidelines that scored women on their face, makeup, skin tone, and grace, as well as on their "symmetry, presentation, separations, and muscularity BUT NOT TO THE EXTREME!." In 2004, the IFBB issued a memo requesting female competitors "decrease the amount of muscularity by a factor of 20%" for "aesthetics and health reasons."[10] Just what those "health reasons" were remains ambiguous.

Over time, the IFBB and other organizations have added alternative competitions to the traditional physique contests, including figure, fitness, bikini fitness, and wellness fitness disciplines, all of which emphasize athletic, toned, and feminine bodies while discouraging sizeable muscularity. In 2014, the IFBB announced the cancelation of the Ms. Olympia contest, established in 1980 and the most prestigious physique competition of its kind, but it continues to host the less controversial figure and fitness competitions.[11]

In other sports, women who do not fit the slim, toned aesthetic find it more difficult to secure endorsements. Weightlifter Sarah Robles struggled to support herself financially while training for the 2012 Olympics. "You can get that sponsorship if you're a super-built guy or a girl who looks good in a bikini. But not if you're a girl who's built like a guy," she told *Buzzfeed*.[12] It may be for this same reason that the Ultimate Fighting Championship (UFC) has balked at adding heavier weight classes for women in mixed martial arts. The UFC initially scoffed at women fighters altogether, but it relented in 2012, creating only the bantamweight class (capped at 135 pounds). Organizers subsequently added a strawweight division (capped at 115 pounds) in 2013 and the 145-pound featherweight class in 2017. Any woman who weighs more than 145 pounds must cut weight, often with drastic, unhealthy consequences (*real* "health reasons"), making it nearly impossible for bigger, more muscular women fighters to enter the octagon. UFC men, it should be noted, have eight weight classes that range from 125 to 265 pounds.

Even women who compete in sports we imagine to be "feminine" face censure for seeming too strong. In figure skating, for example, detractors weighed in on Tonya Harding's and Surya Bonaly's powerful thighs—even though their thighs allowed them to perform incredible, unprecedented feats. Contrasted against their thinner, less overtly strong competitors, Harding and Bonaly were "too athletic," a strange yet somehow effective way to insult a female athlete.

Tennis is another gender-appropriate sport in which muscular athletes experience disapproval. In the 1970s and 1980s, commentators criticized Martina Navratilova's strong physique, suggesting she "must have a chromosomic screw loose somewhere."[13] Consequently, she failed to secure the lucrative endorsement deals won by her primary rival, the appropriately feminine Chris Evert. Still, Navratilova changed the sport. Those who hoped to compete adopted weight-training regimes to add strength and power to their games.

Despite the changes in training programs, women who transgress into "excessive" musculature endure condemnation. Upon losing to Amélie Mauresmo at the 1999 Australian Open, Lindsay Davenport remarked that it had been like "playing a guy." Soon after the match, Mauresmo publicly came out as gay. When Martina Hingis later quipped that Mauresmo was "half a man," it was unclear if she was referring to the French phenom's strength, her sexuality, or, more likely, a combination of both.

Perhaps no woman in tennis has borne the brunt of nasty comments about her body more than Serena Williams. Just as affronts to Mauresmo were tinged with homophobia, the vitriol hurled at Williams has as much to do with race as it does gender (or what queer black feminist Moya Bailey calls *misogynoir* to describe the convergence of racism and misogyny).[14] In spite of it all, Williams has won more grand slam titles than any other player, showing the world the benefits of her powerful frame. Even so, many of Williams's contemporaries disclose that they want to avoid "bulking up." Andrea Petkovic lamented that photographs of her own bulging biceps appear "unfeminine." Agnieszka

Radwanska's coach told reporters that it was important to "keep her as the smallest player in the top 10 . . . because, first of all she's a woman, and she wants to be a woman." In other words, "real" women should not be too muscular. Of course, women have the right to look as they want to look. But it is a problem worth considering when cultural norms keep women from reaching their full athletic potential. When Maria Sharapova says that she "can't handle lifting more than five pounds" during training, we should wonder how her game might transform if she could.[15]

5

SEXUALITIES AND SPORT

What were the historical concerns about women's sexuality in sport?

For the first three decades of the twentieth century, argues historian Susan K. Cahn in *Coming on Strong: Gender and Sexuality in Twentieth-Century Women's Sport*, there were fears that sport would incite women's uncontrollable heterosexual passions. As a result, women physical educators sought to protect the morality of their charges by advocating middle-class notions of modesty and respectability and by discouraging extreme competition. They also kept women's physical activity sheltered from male view and condemned sports promoters for exploiting female athletes' physicality and sex appeal for commercial gain.

Concern for women's unbridled heterosexual desires gave way in the 1930s to worries that sport made women both unattractive and unattracted to men. Either consequence, according to Cahn, signaled "heterosexual failure." This belief paved the way for the stereotype of the "mannish lesbian athlete" as an object of derision in the years after World War II, which further discouraged girls and women from pursuing sport.[1]

In the postwar era of heightened homophobia and gender conservatism, women athletes, especially those who competed in working-class and stereotypically masculine sports, faced new pressures to assert their femininity and heterosexuality.

Women physical educators changed their curricula to emphasize students' personal appearance and comportment. Once fierce guardians of separatism, these same physical educators realized that sex segregation only fueled the discipline's lesbian stereotype and so began to incorporate mixed-sex social events, such as dances and bowling.

Hoping to avoid this very stereotype, sports executives and athletes adopted apologetic strategies (see Chapter 4). Players in the All-American Girls Professional Baseball League (AAGBPL), for example, had to adhere to the league's rules of conduct, which forbade masculine clothing or cutting their hair too short. "Femininity is the keynote of our league," explained AAGBPL executive Philip Wrigley. In his estimation, there was no place for the "pants-wearing, tough-talking female softballer."[2] In the same way, famed Tennessee State track coach Ed Temple insisted his Tigerbelles were "young ladies first, track girls second" who had "no trouble getting boyfriends." In a milieu of homophobia, sexism, and racism, it was important to Temple that the black women on his team embodied respectable femininity. Even after competition, he instructed athletes to wipe the sweat from their faces, apply lipstick and powder, and comb their hair, maintaining that he wanted them to be "foxes, not oxes."[3]

Of course, there were lesbian and bisexual athletes and physical educators during this time, and the growing heteronormativity in physical education and sport undoubtedly caused many women great pain. At the same time, sport also provided a space for women to explore their sexuality and identity, to forge relationships and social networks, and to build communities.

Does "sex sell" women's sport?

Sport media and marketing executives must think that sex sells, because they keep working that angle. In part, they are spurred on by the belief that sex appeal is the only way men will pay attention to women's sport. Lingering beneath the surface are the long-standing presumptions that sport participation threatens women's attractiveness, femininity, and heterosexuality. The commodification and promotion of women's (hetero)sexuality is therefore a powerful mix of sexism and homophobia.

There are several examples of sports organizations that promote the heterosexuality and hypersexuality of conventionally attractive athletes. For years, the running joke has been that the L in the LPGA is not for *Ladies* Professional Golf Association but, rather, for *Lesbian*. To counter the sport's "image problem," executives have repeatedly tried to sex up and "soften" the image of the female golfer. Throughout the 1970s and 1980s, Laura Baugh was the LPGA's pinup girl and biggest celebrity endorser, even though she failed to win a tournament. A 1981 issue of the LPGA's *Fairway Magazine* included a five-page fashion spread featuring four golfers, including the tour's latest "it girl," Jan Stephenson, posed seductively on an unmade bed (fellow golfer Jane Blalock called the shoot "quasi-pornography"). As *Sports Illustrated* later reported, "Stephenson did a lot for the image of women's golf in 1981. That was the year in which Billie Jean King admitted she'd had a lesbian affair and almost knocked a wheel off the apple cart of women's sports."[4] A few months later, the apple cart took another (imagined) blow when Martina Navratilova discussed her relationship with novelist Rita Mae Brown in a *New York Daily News* interview. The implication was that women's sport, an already precarious institution, needed sexy women athletes to counterbalance the lesbian stigma.

The LPGA has continued this trend. In the early 1990s, commissioner Charles Mechem hired an "official image and fashion consultant" to work with athletes on the tour, while using official publications to promote heterosexual players, their husbands, and their families. In 2002, LGPA commissioner Ty Votaw likewise employed experts to school golfers in the finer points of fashion, hairstyles, and makeup as part of a five-point plan to attract more fans to the sport.

Women's tennis similarly banks on players' heterosexual attractiveness. The Women's Tennis Association (WTA) has published calendars featuring athletes in glamorous clothing and decidedly non-athletic poses. "We don't ignore the sexuality part of it," explained WTA spokesperson Chris De Maria in 2002, "It's part of our marketing for sure, because it's a positive part of what we have to offer."[5] Shortly thereafter, members of the All England Club confessed that "physical attractiveness is taken into consideration" when they make Wimbledon court assignments. Specifically, officials assigned lower ranked but conventionally pretty female players to the prestigious Centre Court while relegating higher ranked and less attractive players to outer courts, where there is diminished spectatorship and television coverage.[6]

In the spirit of selling sex, former FIFA president Sepp Blatter once remarked that women soccer players should "play in more feminine clothes like they do in volleyball. They could, for example, have tighter shorts." This was from a man who considered himself the "godfather" of the women's game. Blatter is not alone. Marco Aurelio Cunha, Brazil's head of coordination for women's soccer, chalked the sport's sluggishly burgeoning success to the sex appeal of the athletes. "Now the women are getting more beautiful, putting on make-up. They go in the field in an elegant manner," he told reporters in 2015.[7]

But does sex really sell women's sport? Signs point to no. It turns out that emphasizing athletes' sexuality does little to increase audience interest in or respect for women's sport. Furthermore, as one study determined, the "sex sells" approach also offends women and older men, two core constituents in the fan base for women's sports. In short, the study concluded that "sex sells sex, not women's sports."[8]

What is the Lingerie Football League?

One would be hard-pressed to find a more overt use of sex to sell women's sport than the Lingerie Football League (LFL). It started with advertising executive Mitchell Mortaza, who thought that women playing tackle football in lacy bras, bikini bottoms, and garters (in addition to helmets and pads) would be a good way to fill the halftime of the 2004 Super Bowl. From a financial perspective, Mortaza was correct. Millions of viewers paid $19.95 each to watch a lingerie fashion show followed by the seven-on-seven Lingerie Bowl. In 2009, Mortaza expanded the halftime game into a league, with teams that included the Philadelphia Passion, the Dallas Desire, and the San Diego Seduction. Like-minded entrepreneurs established the short-lived Lingerie Basketball League (2011–2012) and have proposed a frostbite-inspiring Bikini Hockey League.

In 2013, LFL executives rebranded the organization the Legends Football League, but the clothing and, arguably, the mentality behind it did not change very much. What is more, the LFL classifies its players as independent contractors rather than employees. As a result, it does not pay the players (in fact, the players actually pay to play) or offer workers' compensation, insurance, or health care, leaving the women, especially those who become injured, financially strapped.

To be sure, many women in the LFL are exceptional athletes, yet their athleticism is not the selling point. As Mortaza proclaimed, "First and foremost, you have to be beautiful" to join the league.[9] In addition to the obvious sexualization of the athletes, the LFL diverts attention from other women who play serious football in organizations such as the Women's Professional Football League, the Independent Women's Football League, and the Women's Football Alliance.

What is homophobia?

The answer to this question requires a brief explanation of associated terminology. Psychologist George Weinberg coined the term *homophobia* in the late 1960s, and it has come mean negative attitudes, prejudice, or discrimination against gay, lesbian, bisexual, and queer individuals and groups. Critics of the term argue that "phobia" implies an individual's irrational, psychological fear rather than a larger systemic and cultural issue, such as racism or sexism, and have proposed several alternative terms. *Homonegativity* removes the problematic use of *phobia* from anti-gay beliefs and behaviors. *Heterosexism* represents an ideological system that denigrates non-heterosexual behaviors, identities, relationships, and communities. *Heteronormativity* denotes the cultural assumption that heterosexuality is the "natural" and "normal" state of human being rather than one of many possible sexual identities and expressions. Finally, psychologist Gregory Herek recommends the term *sexual prejudice* to represent negative attitudes based on sexual orientation, regardless of what that orientation is.[10]

The prefix *homo* means same or alike. Although homophobia is the most common term used with regard to anti-gay attitudes and behaviors, activists advise against the use of the term *homosexual* to refer to gay/lesbian/queer individuals and their romantic, intimate, social, and sexual relationships. The word has a long clinical history used to pathologize and oppress people as mentally ill or deviant. In fact, the American Psychological Association considered homosexuality a psychological disorder until 1974 and the World Health Organization only declassified homosexuality as a medical diagnosis in 1992. Moreover, anti-gay extremists continue to use the word *homosexual* in the pejorative, implying that one's sexuality is a choice or something to be "cured."

There are many acronyms used to identify sexualities, and the terminology is constantly evolving. Among the most common are LGBT (lesbian, gay, bisexual, and transgender),

LGBTQ (where "Q" stands for queer or questioning), LGBTQIA (where "I" stands for intersex and "A" for either asexual or allied), and LGBT+ or LGBTQIA+, in which the "+" signifies the inclusiveness of gender and sexual identities not otherwise encapsulated by the anchoring acronym. Some advocates have offered LGBTQQIP2SAA as a dizzying abbreviation for lesbian, gay, bisexual, transgender, queer, questioning, intersex, pansexual, two spirit, asexual, and allies. Others have reclaimed the once derogatory use of "queer" and recommend its use as a simplified umbrella term. Yet, as scholar-activist Dennis Altman argues, these terms, in an attempt to be inclusive, become almost meaningless and ultimately hide "the complex interconnections of desire, behaviour and identity in everyday life."[11]

Homophobia in sport takes multiple forms, but it is also important to remember that same-sex relationships and sexual acts are illegal in many places throughout the world. According to the International Lesbian, Gay, Bisexual, Trans and Intersex Association, in May 2017 there were seventy-two countries with criminal laws against same-sex sexual contact. In Sudan, Iran, Saudi Arabia, Yemen, Mauritania, Afghanistan, Pakistan, Qatar, United Arab Emirates, as well as parts of Nigeria, Somalia, Syria, and Iraq, same-sex sexual contact is punishable by death. Still other countries have introduced laws forbidding LGBT "promotion." Russia, for example, banned the "propaganda of nontraditional sexual relations" just one year before it was set to host the 2014 Winter Olympic Games. This led to concerns about the safety of athletes, fans, and allies who attended the games; discussions of protests and boycotts; and rebuke of the International Olympic Committee (IOC), which subsequently rewrote the Olympic Charter's nondiscrimination clause (Principle 6) to include sexual orientation.

Homophobic attitudes and practices exist even in ostensibly progressive countries. In South Africa, for instance, same-sex marriage is legal, and the constitution outlaws discrimination based on sexual orientation. Yet, LGBT South Africans face constant threats. This includes "corrective rape," a hate crime based on the belief that sexual violence will "correct" or cure individuals of their alleged orientation. In 2008, four men abducted, raped, brutally beat, and stabbed to death Eudy Simelane, a former member of the South African women's soccer team and a gay rights activist. Five years earlier, a woman named Phulma accepted a ride home from a group of men after she finished soccer practice. As the men raped her, they repeatedly explained that they were "teaching her a lesson" about her sexuality. "Every day you feel like it's a time bomb waiting to go off," Phulma told *The Guardian*,

> You don't have freedom of movement, you don't have space to do as you please. You are always scared and your life always feels restricted. As women and as lesbians we need to be very aware that it is a fact of life that we are always in danger.[12]

What are some of the ways that homophobia affects women's sport?

In addition to societal fears of violence and discrimination, homophobia in sport affects women in powerful ways. In 1998, sport activist and scholar Pat Griffin published her groundbreaking book, *Strong Women, Deep Closets: Lesbians and Homophobia in Sport*, in which she argued that there are six manifestations of homophobia in sport—all of which still ring true today: silence, denial, apology, the promotion of a heterosexy image, attacks on lesbians, and a preference for male coaches. [13]

Silence refers to lesbian, gay, and bisexual athletes, coaches, and administrators staying closeted for fear of reprisal. For decades, tennis great Billie Jean King kept her relationships with women a secret, fearing that they would hurt the women's tour and her own reputation. Her fears were justified when a former partner outed King in a 1981 lawsuit, and King lost nearly all her endorsement deals within twenty-four hours. Lesbian coaches also remain silent, worried that their sexuality will put their already tenuous jobs in greater jeopardy. In 2016, there were 349 Division I women's basketball programs in the United States, but the University of San Francisco's Jennifer Azzi was the only out lesbian head coach. Experts and basketball insiders know that there are other lesbian coaches at that level, but the silence is almost deafening. Straight coaches contribute to the silence by muzzling gay athletes. Basketball star Brittney Griner revealed that during her time at Baylor University, head coach Kim Mulkey instructed lesbian players not to discuss their sexuality for fear it would hurt the program and recruiting.

In addition to silence, athletes, coaches, and administrators often deny their own sexuality or refute that there a lesbian presence in their sport. One version of denial is what scholar Helen Jefferson Lenskyj calls "coming out straight."[14] Amid rumors that an athlete is gay, she will publicly declare her heterosexuality. During her divorce proceedings, for instance, boxer Laila Ali issued a public statement proclaiming, "Yes, I am in the process of getting a divorce, but I am not dating, nor will I ever be dating a woman, because I am not gay."[15] Regardless of her sexuality, the message is that there is something wrong with being gay, which strengthens both homophobia and individuals' commitments to silence.

Apology refers to the feminine apologetic, discussed in Chapter 4, in which athletes engage in "the protective camouflage of feminine drag."[16] Many softball players, for example, make sure to adorn their ponytails with ribbons, based on the apparently pervasive maxim, "No bow? Lesbo."

The "promotion of a heterosexy image" ups the apologetic ante. Leagues, schools, and organizations sexualize women athletes in promotional campaigns in order to dispel any lesbian stigma. Another strategy is to highlight stories about married coaches and athletes and play up their maternal and domestic roles. While Jan Stephenson smoldered for the LPGA, for example, the league also banked on the wholesome heterosexuality of golfer Nancy Lopez.

Attacks based on sexual prejudice can take a number of forms: intense scrutiny of women's lives, coaches' open and subtle anti-lesbian policies, coaches who lose their jobs because of their sexuality, and lesbian-baiting (taunting, name-calling, and other forms of harassment). Among the most prevalent types of attack is negative recruiting, which involves coaches or administrators who suggest that there are lesbian athletes or coaches on rival teams. In 2011, *ESPN the Magazine* conducted a poll of current and former women collegiate basketball players and found that 55 percent reported that coaches brought up issues of sexuality at some point during the recruiting process.[17]

Basketball coach Rene Portland was unabashed about her "no drinking, no drugs, no lesbians" policy during her twenty-seven-year tenure at Penn State. She resigned in 2007 after a former player filed a lawsuit against Portland for discrimination based on race, gender, and perceived sexual orientation. A university investigation concluded that the coach had created a "hostile, intimidating, and offensive environment." This is evident in the 2009 documentary *Training Rules*, in which former players and assistant coaches detail the stifling, abusive homophobia they experienced during Portland's reign.

Attacks in the form of anti-gay insults continue to plague sport. In 2015, *Out in the Fields,* an international study on homophobia in sports, found that 82 percent of lesbians (and 84 percent of gay men) have heard homophobic slurs in locker rooms. The sting of the insult is compounded by silence from teammates and coaches. Attacks have become even more prevalent and anonymous with the advent of social media, something openly-gay soccer player Jess Fishlock has experienced throughout her professional career. As she explains, social media allows people to "sit behind a computer and say things they wouldn't dream of saying in real life. It's the easiest form of bullying or hate speech there is. They can do it without getting in trouble for it."[18]

Finally, an untold number of coaches have lost their jobs because of their sexuality or perceptions about their sexuality. Belmont University fired soccer coach Lisa Howe soon after she came out to her team. The Baptist institution rationalized that Howe had violated the school's "don't ask, don't tell" approach to sexuality. These types of stories typically come to light only when there is legal action involved, such as when three openly-gay former head coaches at the University of Minnesota–Duluth, including five-time national championship hockey coach Shannon Miller, filed a lawsuit against the school for "blatant discrimination" and creating a hostile work environment. Such allegations can be difficult to prove, a problem that contributes to both silence and denial as ways in which homophobia can manifest in women's sports.

Are there sports opportunities organized specifically for LGBTQ athletes?

There are a number of competitions, teams, clubs, and leagues organized for LGBT athletes at local, regional, national, and international levels. The Gay Games, the largest international event of its kind, is based on the principles of "participation, inclusion, and personal best" and is open to all competitors of all sexual identities. Organizers originally called the competition the Gay Olympics, but just before the first games in 1982, the IOC and the United States Olympic Committee filed a lawsuit claiming exclusive rights to the word "Olympic," a move that many considered homophobic. Controversies within the Federation of Gay Games have led to the formation of the European Gay and Lesbian

Sport Federation's EuroGames and the Gay and Lesbian International Sport Association's World Outgames.

Are things getting better for gay, lesbian, bisexual, and queer athletes?

In many ways, things are getting better. More lesbian, gay, bisexual, and queer athletes are open about their sexuality than ever before. And a number of out lesbian athletes, including Martina Navratilova, Brittney Griner, Amelie Mauresmo, Rosie Jones, Abby Wambach, and Megan Rapinoe, have secured endorsement deals that would have been impossible in the twentieth century. Even so, says Rapinoe, the importance of corporate sponsorship keeps many women in the closet:

> Some athletes have this image to uphold and may feel like sponsors won't want them if they're gay. . . . Maybe they wouldn't discriminate, but you don't know that for sure if you're a player and unsure whether to come out. Otherwise, why wouldn't more people come out?[19]

Part of the attraction of signing lesbian athletes has to do with the lure of "pink dollars" or the purchasing power of the LGBT community. Throughout her storied tennis career, Navratilova had difficulty finding sponsorship deals. It was not until her 2000 Subaru commercial that the corporate world finally recognized her potential, after the car company established that it had a significant lesbian following and launched a campaign specifically aimed at lesbian consumers.

The WNBA took a long time to come around to actively courting pink dollars. Since its inception in 1997, it was clear that the league benefited from an significant lesbian fan base, which executives refused to acknowledge. Frustrated by the lack of recognition from the New York Liberty, the group Lesbians for Liberty organized a "kiss-in" in 2002 as an innovative form of protest. During every time-out of the nationally televised game between the Liberty and the Miami Sol, members of the group locked lips. It was around this time that the league began private discussions about marketing to lesbian fans. Individual teams have slowly embraced the concept, and in 2014, the WNBA began to publicly court gay fans by launching its "Pride" campaign.[20]

Efforts designed to stamp out homophobia have also contributed to progress in sport. At the same time, however, the need for organizations such as Br{ache the Silence, GO! Athletes, the LGBT Sports Foundation, and Ally Athlete, as well as campaigns including You Can Play, the Justin Campaign, and Rainbow Laces indicates that there is still much important work left to do with regard to addressing homophobia in sport.

6

SEX SEGREGATION

Why do we segregate sport on the basis of sex?

In *Playing With the Boys: Why Separate Is Not Equal,* scholars Eileen McDonagh and Laura Pappano argue that there have been "three I's" historically used to justify sex segregation in sport:

> Women's physical differences from men are interpreted to mean that females are athletically *inferior* to men, that women will be *injured* if they "play with the boys," and that sex-integrated sports programs, particularly in contact sports, such as wrestling, are *immoral* by virtue of the close physical contact required or simply by virtue of the damaging results some believe such policies portend for society in general.[1]

There are general physical differences between men and women but, as with any generalization, they do not apply to everyone, and it is important to keep generalities from veering into stereotypes. Many sports favor extreme body types, which also complicates cross-sex comparisons. For instance, although men tend to be taller than women, the average height in the WNBA is just under 6 feet tall, whereas the average height of American men is 5 feet, 9 inches (the average height of men in the NBA is approximately 6 feet, 7 inches, and the average height of the American woman is 5 feet, 4 inches). While we can talk in terms of averages, athletes, especially elite athletes, warrant specific considerations. With these caveats in mind, it is fair to say that the average man is taller and heavier than the average woman. Compared to women, men tend to have more muscle mass, greater bone mass, proportionally larger hearts and lungs, longer limbs relative to their height, narrower hips, more oxygen-carrying red blood cells, and higher levels of circulating testosterone. These attributes generally make men stronger, faster, and more powerful than women. Women typically have a lower center of gravity than men, as well as more body fat, which are attributes that can facilitate balance, buoyancy in swimming, and performance in endurance sports. Even so, as McDonagh and Pappano note, these differences stoke perceptions that women are physically *inferior* to men and, as a result, that women will be *injured* in mixed-sex competition.

The third "I" in McDonagh and Pappano's triad of rationales against sex-integrated sport has to do with the supposed *immorality* of physical and social contact between male and female athletes. A female presence in male sport purportedly violates its sanctity as a masculine preserve and disrupts the traditional gender order on which it stands. A female presence might also incite male arousal. In 2013, school officials forbade twelve-year-old Madison Baxter from playing football because they worried her presence would cause the boys on the team to have "impure thoughts." In 2016, a boys' soccer team from a Christian high school refused to play against an opposing team that included two girls. The decision, explained one administrator, was "based on a religious perspective that God created guys and girls differently. . . . We want to teach our men that honor of ladies is just not in sports." For similar reasons, high school sophomore Joel Northrup refused to wrestle Cassy Herkelman in the 2011 Iowa state tournament.

"As a matter of conscience and my faith," Northrup wrote, "I do not believe that it is appropriate for a boy to engage a girl in this manner." Not everyone feels this way. In 2006, Alaska's Michaela Hutchison became the first girl to win a state title in boys' high school wrestling. Upon losing to Hutchinson, one boy remarked, "I expected it. She's good."[2]

Should we segregate sport according to sex?

Prior to puberty, there are no physical reasons to segregate boys and girls. Youth sports leagues and organizations that insist upon separation typically base the decision on social reasons and misinformation. Even more, experts contend that there are a host of benefits that come from integrated youth sport. It helps boys and girls build friendships, mutual respect, and cooperation, and it guards against sex stereotyping. It is therefore important to also have coaches and adults in leadership positions who do not perpetuate gendered stereotypes. This includes breaking down the sexual segregation of adult labor that too frequently puts men in coaching or leadership positions and women in the role of "team mom." There is nothing wrong with adults serving in these capacities, but if the roles remain strictly segregated by sex, it sends a powerful message to young athletes about what is expected and even possible for them in the future.[3]

After puberty, the answer to segregation depends both on the sport and the individual. In some sports, such as shooting, sailing, equestrian events, or e-Sports, there is no reason for separating female and male competitors. The same is true for sports like automobile racing, yet women drivers encounter tremendous sexism. As Formula One (F1) racing's chief executive, Bernie Ecclestone, told reporters, "I don't know whether a woman would physically be able to drive an F1 car quickly, and they wouldn't be taken seriously."[4] Despite the successes of Janet Guthrie, Shirley Muldowney, Lyn St. James, and Danica Patrick, women in motor sports are few and far between due, in part, to the ignorant attitudes that Ecclestone so baldly expressed.

There are certainly women who could compete in most, if not all, men's sports, if given the chance. And, as with pre-pubescent athletes, adults also benefit from mixed-sex sport. Sociologist Eric Anderson interviewed former high school foot-ball players who went on to become collegiate cheerleaders on integrated squads. He found that the coeducational experience reduced the men's sexist beliefs and promoted their respect for the women as athletes and as individuals.[5]

McDonagh and Pappano's main argument in *Playing With the Boys* is against *coercive* sex segregation—that is, mandating separate teams, leagues, organizations, and competitions for male and female athletes. They are in favor of *voluntary* seg-regation, but they maintain that obligatory, institutionalized segregation perpetuates sex role stereotypes, limits women's opportunities, and relegates women to second-class status in sport and society. Instead, the authors propose a gender-neu-tral view and increased opportunities for coed participation at every level of sport. "There are physical biological differences between the sexes," McDonagh and Pappano concede, "but they are not as great as we have supposed, and the female difference is not necessarily a lacking. Women are not inher-ently weak and in need of protection."[6]

Women's sport advocates agree: Female athletes are not weak, frail, or helpless. But those who argue in favor of sex seg-regation maintain that integration would drastically decrease the number of women in sport. It would reduce opportunities where speed, strength, and power are paramount so that only a few exceptional female athletes could participate. This, in turn, would reduce the number of athletic female role models so important to both boys and girls. Mandating inclusion would create a system of tokenism and lead to resentment of a female presence in sport, which, contrary to the argument for integration, would preserve—not challenge—women's in-ferior standing.

Are women closing the "muscle gap" in sport?

In the 1970s and 1980s, experts began to speculate that women were closing the "muscle gap."[7] They forecast that women's performances were improving at such a rapid rate that they would soon equal, if not surpass, those of their male counterparts. Yet, the precipitous change was largely due to the fact that women were finally gaining access to coaching, training, equipment, sport science, and competitions, and by 1983, women's improvements started to level off. Since then, according to a 2010 study in the *Journal of Sports Science and Medicine*, the average performance gap between the best men's and women's performances has stabilized at about 10 percent. This varies according to the sport. The difference between the best men's and women's performances in the 800-meter free-style swimming event is 5.5 percent, but in weightlifting, the top men outperform the top women by 36.8 percent.[8]

Ultra-distance events in swimming, running, and cycling are one area in which women routinely do well compared to men. We can look back to Gertrude Ederle in 1926 (see Chapter 2) or, more recently, to 2013, when sixty-four-year-old Diana Nyad became the first person to swim the 110 miles from Cuba to Florida without the aid of a shark cage. In fact, women often outperform men in two of the most challenging open-water ultra-distance swimming events—the 20.1-mile Catalina Channel Swim and the 28.5-mile Manhattan Island Marathon Swim. In running, Pamela Reed won the 2002 and 2003 Badwater Ultramarathon, a grueling, 135-mile race through the Mojave Desert. She followed up by becoming the first person—male or female—to run 300 miles straight without sleep. In cycling, Lael Wilcox won the 4,300-mile Trans Am race from Oregon to Virginia, and similar tales of women's prowess in long-distance sport abound.

Even so, women should not have to outperform men to be respected as phenomenal athletes. Tennis great John McEnroe once commented that Serena Williams is the "best female player ever" but that "if she played on the men's circuit, she'd be, like, 700 in the world." Should it matter if Williams can beat the top 699 men in tennis? Can she be a great athlete if she only competes against women? Why do we have to qualify women's accomplishments by comparing them to men? We can turn here to French feminist Simone de Beauvoir, who wrote in her 1949 book, *The Second Sex*, that in sport

> the goal is not to succeed independently of physical aptitudes: it is the accomplishment of perfection proper to each organism; the lightweight champion is as worthy as the heavyweight; a female ski champion is no less a champion than the male who is more rapid than she: they belong to two different categories.[9]

As with so many issues in sport, sex segregation is fraught with a host of important, often contradictory, considerations.

What are some examples of sex-integrated sport?

There is an important distinction between sex-integrated sports, which are open to competitors regardless of sex, and mixed-sex sports that are structured to require both male and female participation. Examples of mixed-sex sports include paired figure skating; ice dancing; mixed doubles in tennis, curling, and badminton; and mixed team events and relays in biathlon, curling, alpine skiing, and luge. As discussed in Chapter 7, the IOC has added additional mixed-sex events to the Olympic program. These competitions are built upon distinguishing between men and women and making sure they are equally represented.

The rules of the International Quidditch Association (IQA), which governs the sport based on J. K. Rowling's *Harry Potter* series, are unique with regard to issues of sex and gender. Seven players from each team take the quidditch field. Of those seven, there must be a maximum of four players "who identify as the same gender in active play on the field at the same time." The rules mandate a sex/gender-integrated sport. In addition, the IQA "accepts those who don't identify with the binary gender system and acknowledges that not all of our players identify as male or female. The IQA welcomes people of all identities and genders into our sport."[10]

Other sports, such as horse racing and dogsledding, are ostensibly gender-neutral, though few women compete at the highest ranks (notable exceptions include jockeys Julie Krone, Rosemary Homeister, and Tammi Piermarini and four-time Iditarod champion Susan Butcher). At the 2016 Olympic Games, women and men only competed against one another in sailing's Nacra 17 and equestrian events. Women have performed especially well in the equestrian discipline of dressage. Anky van Grunsven is the only rider to win gold in dressage in three successive Games (2000, 2004, and 2008), and at the 2016 Games, Charlotte Dujardin, Isabell Werth, and Kristin Bröring-Sprehe swept the event's individual medal count.

Other Olympic sports were integrated in the past but, for various reasons, later segregated. Beginning with the first modern games in 1896, for example, the rifle event was integrated (it still is in American collegiate competitions). In 1976, American Margaret Murdock tied her teammate Lanny Bassham for first place in the three-position small bore rifle event. Officials denied the two athletes a shoot-off and awarded Bassham the gold medal and Murdock the silver. Since the 1984 Los Angeles Games, men and women have competed in separate riflery events. Similarly, China's Zhang Shan won a gold medal in mixed skeet shooting at the 1992 Barcelona Games. Four years later, she was unable to defend her title; it was a male-only event. In 2000, the IOC added a separate women's event to the Olympic program, and the sport remains segregated.

Why do girls and women play softball while boys and men play baseball?

First, many boys and men play softball, and girls and women have always played on baseball teams, clubs, leagues, and in competitions of their own. Examples include the Bloomer Girls, the Dolly Vardens, the Colorado Silver Bullets, the Girls Travel Baseball league, and the USA Women's National Team, which competes in the Pan American Games, the Women's Baseball World Cup, and other prestigious international events. Still, girls are usually directed toward softball for gendered reasons (see Chapter 5). A bit of history is necessary to understand the split.[11]

From 1866 to 1935, according to historian Gai Ingham Berlage, girls and women thrived in amateur, semi-professional, and professional baseball.[12] In the nineteenth and early twentieth century, college women took to intramural baseball with great enthusiasm. Working-class women of all religions, races, and ethnicities enjoyed the sport, and many joined barnstorming teams that toured the country to take on competitors at every stop.

Several women played minor league baseball with men, including seventeen-year-old pitcher Virne Beatrice "Jackie" Mitchell, who pitched for the Chattanooga, Tennessee, Lookouts in 1931. In an exhibition game against the New York Yankees, Mitchell allegedly struck out both Babe Ruth and Lou Gehrig. Days later, Major League Baseball (MLB) commissioner Kenesaw Mountain Landis voided her contract on the grounds that the sport was "too strenuous to be played by women."[13] Major League Baseball's official ban on women lasted until 1992, and although a number of women have played high school, college, and semi-professional baseball with men, none have suited up for a Major League team.

Softball, invented in the 1880s, flourished in the 1930s and 1940s as it firmed its position as the recreational and feminine equivalent to "hard ball." During World War II, while men in the major and minor leagues served in the military, baseball executives organized the All-American Girls Softball Baseball League, which became the All-American Girls Professional Baseball League (AAGPBL). Between 1943 and 1954, more than 600 women played baseball for Midwestern teams as a way to maintain public interest in the sport. This included several Cuban women, who previously played for a similar league, the Cuban Estrellas.[14] Yet league officials refused to sign black women, ignoring a deep reservoir of talent. Since the nineteenth century, as historian Amira Rose Davis notes, African American women played on rural sandlots, segregated leagues and teams, and for the Young Women's Christian Association.[15] In the 1950s, Toni Stone, Connie Morgan, and Mamie "Peanut" Johnson played in baseball's Negro National Leagues, but there were few professional opportunities for talented black women ballplayers.

Just as Major League Baseball closed its ranks to women, youth leagues likewise shut out girls. Organizers established Little League Baseball (LLB) in 1939 to instill "citizenship, sportsmanship, and manhood" in boys ages eight to twelve. In 1950, twelve-year-old Kathryn "Tubby" Johnston became the first girl to play in the league. The following year, LLB established the "Tubby Rule" that officially barred girls from participating. Two decades later, amid a burgeoning feminist movement, girls began to fight the ban. In 1972, eleven-year-old Maria Pepe played with the Hoboken, New Jersey, Young Democrats until league officials threatened to pull the city's charter if she continued. On Pepe's behalf, the National Organization for Women filed a grievance with the New Jersey Division on Civil Rights. The judge ruled in Pepe's favor, arguing that the physical differences between boys and girls were negligible and that "while there are boys who are stronger than girls, there is a great overlap of girls who are stronger than boys."[16] In 1974, Little League's national office announced that it would "defer to the changing social climate" and began registering girls.[17]

At the same time, the organization created Little League Softball. There are at least two ways of interpreting this development. On the one hand, the creation of the new league seemed to meet the needs of a growing legion of athletic girls. On the other hand, the provision of softball can be read as a way of diverting girls from baseball and leaving it the province of boys. LLB does not keep track of how many girls play baseball, but experts estimate the number to be around 100,000. After the age of twelve, girls' participation in the sport drops significantly. According to the 2014–2015 survey of the National Federation of State High School Associations, there were about 500,000 boys and 1,000 girls who played high school baseball and approximately 365,000 high school girls who played softball.

Is there really any such thing as "throwing like a girl"?

The phrase "throwing like a girl" is typically used to insult boys and men by suggesting they lack the ability to throw effectively and, by extension, to impugn their masculinity. In effect, many insults used against boys and men—especially within the context of sport—are designed to wound by implying the target is effeminate or gay, two characteristics supposedly at odds with orthodox notions of masculinity.

Scientists have determined that most of the differences between the ways that men and women throw are due to experience. Boys tend to learn to throw at an early age and are encouraged to practice the skill as they grow up. It is not the same for girls, who are less likely to learn to throw properly when they are young and do not have the same opportunities to cultivate proper throwing techniques.

When researchers ask individuals—male or female—to throw with their nondominant hand, those individuals often "throw like a girl"—that is, their biomechanics are awkward and produce little speed or accuracy. It takes a while to learn to throw with one's nondominant hand, but it does improve over time. In other words, throwing is a learned skill, not a biological one. Of course, there are individuals who naturally throw harder, more accurately, and better. Just ask Mo'ne Davis, who at thirteen years old became the first girl to pitch a shutout in Little League World Series history. Better yet, ask all the boys she struck out what it means to "throw like a girl."

Does Title IX permit girls and women to play on boys' and men's teams?

Yes, provided there is no female equivalent team. This means that if there is a girls' golf team, a girl typically cannot try out for the boys' golf team. It gets trickier in softball and baseball. Some people contend that the two sports are equivalent, but others counter that the differences in field size and dimensions, equipment, balls, rules, and strategies make them two different sports. Those who want to keep girls out of baseball also argue that it is a contact sport (LLB unsuccessfully tried this argument in the early 1970s) and should therefore fall under Title IX's contact sports exemption.

Under the contact sports exemption, which includes "boxing, wrestling, rugby, ice hockey, football, basketball and other sports the purpose or major activity of which involves bodily contact," Title IX allows, but does not require, schools to let a girl or woman try out for a boys' or men's team. If the school allows her to try out and she makes the team, however, she must be treated equally to her male teammates. It was on this stipulation that Heather Sue Mercer won her sex discrimination suit against Duke University. In 1995, Duke football coach Fred Goldsmith invited Mercer, a third-team all-state kicker on her championship high school team, to try out for the squad. He subsequently awarded her a spot on the roster. But Goldsmith then excluded Mercer from preseason practice, subjected her to sexist comments, and refused her a uniform and a spot on the team bench during games. Mercer's legal victory was a milestone in sport history, but the downside may be that fewer girls and women will be allowed to try out for boys' and men's contact sports.

Does Title IX permit boys and men to play on girls' and women's teams?

In terms of athletics, Title IX typically works in favor of the sex that has the fewest opportunities—the "under-represented sex." This is not just about the sport in question but about the overall sports program. A high school boy may lobby to try out for a girls' volleyball team (provided there is no boys' team) on the grounds that boys are under-represented in volleyball at his particular school, but arbitrators would look at the entire athletic program to determine if boys have substantially fewer total sporting opportunities than girls. Still, there are boys who have successfully fought to play girls' high school volleyball, tennis, swimming, gymnastics, soccer, and especially field hockey.

High school sports in the United States are governed at the state level, not the national level, and different state organizations have ruled differently with regard to boys on girls' teams. Michigan and New Jersey, for instance, prohibit boys from playing on girls' teams, but Massachusetts allows it because of the Equal Rights Amendment to the state constitution. (As a confusing aside, the rules of the Massachusetts Interscholastic Athletic Association stipulate that a girl on a boys' team can help win a team title but cannot win an individual title or play in the individual state tournament. Thus, when high school junior Emily Nash won a 2017 divisional boys' golf tournament—playing from the same tees as the boys—officials barred her from receiving the title and trophy and from advancing to the state tournament.)

In some states, administrators leave it to conference or school officials to decide on a case-by-case basis. Advocates for allowing boys on girls' teams contend that it is an issue of fairness and that it is a double standard to allow girls on boys' teams but not the reverse. On the other side are those who assert that allowing boys on girls' teams takes opportunities away from girls (the historically under-represented sex) and presents safety concerns, particularly with stronger or bigger boys in contact sports.

The NCAA does not allow men to compete on women's teams because it technically makes the sport coed. One area of contention has been women's teams that practice against "scout teams" made up primarily of non-varsity, male athletes. Although the routine pushes the varsity athletes to prepare and improve, some women's sports advocates worry that it also relegates talented, second-string women to the sidelines, costing them precious occasions to practice, progress, and compete. Also, occasionally, athletic departments have tried to fudge their Title IX compliance numbers by illegally claiming male practice members as varsity *female* athletes.

What are "sex tests" in women's sport?

In the 1930s, skeptics voiced concerns about "masculine"-looking women athletes, especially in track and field. Observers worried that competitors might either be men in disguise or athletes with differences of sex development (what they then called "hermaphrodites," a term now considered outdated and inappropriate), and so the International Association of Athletics Federations (IAAF; track and field's governing body) and other sports authorities asked for sexual verification. At first, it was up to national governing bodies to check athletes prior to international competitions. In the 1940s, the IAAF and IOC required women athletes to produce affidavits from physicians that affirmed their sex. Men, it should be noted, have never had to prove that they are men. There are two assumptions here: (1) that women who record superlative performances are "too good" to really be women and (2) that "real" women could never compete against men.

Anxieties about "manly" women grew in the post-World War II era, especially with the success of Soviet and East German competitors. The specter of powerful Communist women, not bound by the same dictates of Western (white) femininity, ruffled the sensibilities of cynics who already worried about sport's masculine character. In 1966, the IAAF initiated its first standardized, pre-competition sex test by asking women at the British Empire and Commonwealth Games in Kingston, Jamaica, to undergo gynecological examinations. The women did not expect the ensuing "grope," as pentathlete Mary Peters described it in her autobiography, which amounted to what she called "the most crude and degrading experience I have even known in my life."[18]

Later, at the European Athletics Championships in Budapest, Hungary, the IAAF ordered all female athletes to submit to visual inspections or "nude parades" before a panel of three female physicians. As *Time* reported,

> The examination, as it turned out, was perfunctory. Lined up in single file, the 234 female athletes paraded past three female gynecologists. "They let you walk by," said one competitor afterward. "Then they asked you to turn and face them, and that was it."[19]

IAAF officials next turned to a laboratory-based chromosomal assessment for the 1967 European Cup in Kiev, and the IOC adopted the procedure the following year, making it the standard sex test for more than two decades. Specifically, officials swabbed the inside of women's cheeks or harvested a hair root for chromosomal analysis. Women with XX sex chromosomes (men typically show XY) successfully passed the test and were awarded "certificates of femininity"—licenses they could produce at subsequent competitions to avoid further testing. Anything other than XX became grounds for disqualification.

Polish sprinter Ewa Klobukowska, who passed the visual inspection at the 1966 European championships, "failed" her sex test the following year for having what authorities determined to be "one chromosome too many."[20] At twenty-one years old, Klobukowska could no longer compete in the sport to which she had devoted her life. "It's a dirty and stupid thing to do to me," she said at the time, "I know what I am and how I feel."[21]

Throughout the years, there have been a number of women whose test results complicated the qualification standards. Spanish hurdler María José Martínez Patiño originally passed her sex test but forgot her certificate of femininity for the 1985 World University Games in Kobe, Japan. She submitted to retesting and two months later received a letter informing her that her test results showed XY sex chromosomes. This was a shock to Martínez Patiño, who never questioned her femaleness—she looked, acted, and identified as a woman. Upon further testing, doctors determined that she also has androgen insensitivity syndrome, a condition that makes her unable to utilize the testosterone in her body. As such, she cannot develop the strength or body type associated with male levels of testosterone; neither can she benefit from the use of anabolic steroids. Martínez Patiño challenged her disqualification and the IAAF ultimately restored her license, finding her condition conferred no athletic advantage.

In recognition of the complications brought about by the chromosome test, the IOC altered its sex-testing procedures in 1992 to first search for the presence of Y chromosomal material and, if found, a specific gene (SRY or sex-determining region Y) believed to lead to embryonic testicular development and determine an individual's sex. Nevertheless, there were too many problems associated with the analyses, and the 2000 Sydney Games marked the end to comprehensive sex tests for women Olympians, though IOC and IAAF policy left the possibility of sex testing open if an athlete seemed "suspicious" or if there was a "challenge" to her sex. In 2011, the IAAF announced that it had "abandoned all reference to the terminology 'gender verification' and 'gender policy' in its rules."[22] Instead, the federation adopted a policy on hyperandrogenism (discussed later).

It is impossible to know how many women have been disqualified by the results of sex-testing procedures. After Klobukowska, the IOC and other organizations refused to comment on any test results. Experts estimate that the examinations have barred one or two women at each Olympic Games, but most competitors who do not align with the sporting parameters of femaleness are likely ruled out at the local, regional, or national level and do not make it to the international stage. Even women not directly affected by the tests might avoid sport if they suspect they might not pass. As the history of sex testing demonstrates, assigning sex is not as easy or straightforward as one might expect, which further complicates the issue of sex segregation.

What is hyperandrogenism?

Hyperandrogenism is a condition in which an individual's body naturally produces high levels of androgens, or "male" hormones, notably testosterone. Both men and women produce testosterone, but women typically produce between 0.35 and 3.0 nanomoles of testosterone per liter of serum (nmol/L), whereas men produce from 10 nmol/L to 35 nmol/L. Hyperandrogenism affects men and women, but athletic authorities are only concerned with women who have "too much" testosterone—not men.

South African runner Caster Semenya seems to have been the catalyst for the IAAF's 2011 policy on hyperandrogenism, although the athlete has never confirmed she has the condition. Just before the 2009 IAAF World Championships in Athletics in Berlin, Germany, Semenya was a victim of suspicion-based testing—an official, coach, or fellow athlete questioned her sex, and authorities forced her to undergo analysis. She was allowed to race and retained her subsequent 800-meter victory, but the IAAF requested Semenya withdraw from the sport while a panel of experts reviewed her case.

It took nearly a year for officials to reinstate Semenya. She was significantly slower upon her 2011 return to the track, causing observers to speculate that she had undergone some type of intervention designed to lower her testosterone levels. The IAAF fueled those speculations by subsequently releasing its policy on hyperandrogenism, which affects any woman athlete with a functional testosterone level in serum of 10 nmol/L or greater. This is at the low end of what is considered the "normal" male range and above the "normal" female range. Women diagnosed as hyperandrogenic can submit to testosterone-suppression treatments to bring them below the 10 nmol/L threshold before applying for readmittance to women's athletics. The IOC passed the same regulations in 2012.

Based on this policy, the Sports Authority of India disqualified sprinter Dutee Chand in 2014. Chand fought back, taking her case to the Court of Arbitration for Sport, where adjudicators ruled that until the IAAF produced conclusive evidence linking high testosterone to enhanced athletic performance, it could not enforce its policy on hyperandrogenism. This decision allowed Chand and other hyperandrogenic women to compete in the 2016 Olympic Games and left the IAAF scrambling to defend its position. Chand failed to qualify for the 100-meter semifinal, but Caster Semenya won the gold in the 800-meter race.

Individuals who support restoring the IAAF's policy on hyperandrogenism maintain that the condition poses a health risk to athletes if left undiagnosed and untreated and, even more, that hyperandrogenic women have an "unfair" advantage over female competitors with lower levels of functioning testosterone. Those who oppose the policy argue that there is no confirmed connection between elevated testosterone and superior performance and that even if there is a connection, there is nothing unfair about a naturally occurring condition. Elite sport is inherently unequal. Some athletes have greater means, access, and opportunities to train and compete. Others enjoy biological, physiological, and genetic gifts that predispose them to athletic excellence. Physicians diagnosed the great Nordic skier Eero Mäntyranta, for example, with polycythemia. Because of a genetic variation, Mäntyranta's body naturally produced approximately 50 percent more oxygen-carrying red blood cells than his average competitor—a huge advantage in endurance sports. Scientists have identified at least twenty genetic variations (or polymorphisms) that contribute to athletic excellence, so to single out hyperandrogenism as a disqualifying condition should give pause. Although authorities explicitly maintain that testing for hyperandrogenism is not sex testing, it serves the same purpose: to define and defend a particular version of femaleness in order to uphold sex segregation in sport.

What policies do organizations follow with regard to transgender athletes?

Transgender is a broad adjective used to describe people whose sex or gender identity does not match their sex assigned at birth (the term *cisgender* refers to individuals whose gender identity corresponds with their sex assigned at birth). A transgender woman (or trans woman) is an individual assigned male at birth but who identifies as a woman; a transgender man's (or trans man's) original birth certificate indicates female, but he identifies as a man. Alternative terms include "affirmed females" for those who identify as women but were assigned male sex at birth and "affirmed males" who identify as men but were assigned female sex at birth, "MTF" for individuals who transition from male to female, and "FTM" for individuals who transition from female to male.

Not everyone agrees on the terminology, however. Some women, including former cyclist Kristen Worley and retired professional golfer Mianne Bagger refer to themselves as "XY women." Bagger is cautious of the use of "trans," particularly for women who have surgically transitioned, because "of the 'othering' of people that it tends to lead to."[23] Many transgender people, however, opt not to undergo gender confirmation surgery and/or hormone therapies. Additionally, some individuals identify as neither men nor women, as a combination of sexes, or as shifting among multiple identities, and promote terms that include nonbinary, genderqueer, gender nonconforming, gender fluid, agender, or with plural pronouns such as "they" and "them."

Because sport is usually organized according to the male–female binary, authorities have fumbled over how to include trans athletes. The United States Tennis Association used a sex test to bar Renée Richards, born Richard Raskind, from the 1976 US Open (although Richards produced "gynecological affirmation that she is a woman," she has XY sex chromosomes). Richards took her case to court and, just days before the 1977 tournament, a judge ruled in her favor (Richards lost in the first round). As pundits debated whether her male genetics presented an unfair *biological* advantage, sport scholars Susan Birrell and C. L. Cole argue that a greater inequity resulted from the *social* advantages Richards received as Raskind, which included attending a boys' preparatory school, captaining the Yale tennis team, and greater overall access to competitive sport.[24]

The use of the sex test for establishing trans athletes' eligibility was short lived. As an alternative, some organizations insist that athletes compete as the sex assigned at birth. This was the situation for high school wrestler Mack Beggs. Designated female at birth, Beggs began his transition, including hormone therapy, at age fifteen. He wanted to compete as a boy, but Texas state athletic legislation forbade it. Beggs went on to win the 2017 Class 6A 110-pound girls' state wrestling championship. In addition to the overtly transphobic insults he endured, detractors took issue with his use of testosterone, a banned substance unless prescribed by a doctor, as it was for Beggs as part of his transition.

Contrary to Texas high school protocol, USA Wrestling recognizes Beggs as a boy and allows him to wrestle as such. The organization worked with Beggs on its 2017 transgender policy, which stipulates that prior to puberty, wrestlers can compete as the sex with which they identify. After puberty, athletes who transition from female to male can wrestle in the boys' division "without restriction." Athletes who transition from male to female must keep their testosterone level in serum below 10 nmol/L for at least twelve months prior to their first competition, echoing the IAAF's policy on hyperandrogenism.[25]

Again, however, high school rules vary from one state to the next. In 2016, trans athletes in Nebraska had to follow the state's complicated "Gender Participation Policy." In addition to other provisos, the policy stipulated that a student must submit proof of a "consistent gender identity" to the Gender Identity Eligibility Committee, including documentation from friends, family, or teachers, as well as written verification from a physician, and the committee must rule unanimously on the student's eligibility.[26] The American Civil Liberties Union criticized Nebraska's policy for setting up too many barriers for transgender students to participate in sport.

Still other states, including California and Washington, have enacted inclusive laws that allow student–athletes to compete as the sex with which they identify. In this spirit, USA Soccer became the first major sports organization to adopt a policy of self-determination, although it does not apply to members of the US national teams, which must abide by FIFA's rules. Jaiyah Saelua is thought to be the first transgender athlete recognized by FIFA, though it is worth noting that Saelua is not called transgender in her native American Samoa but, rather, someone of a third gender called *fa'afafine*, or "the way of women," for those born male but who identify as female.

This reminds us that the sex/gender systems are culturally specific, not universal.

As an international federation, FIFA will likely align its regulations for transgender athletes with the IOC, which, in 2015 issued a statement titled "Consensus Meeting on Sex Reassignment and Hyperandrogenism." Transgender athletes no longer have to undergo "surgical anatomical changes," as an earlier recommendation stipulated. Instead, an athlete who transitions from male to female "must demonstrate that her total testosterone level in serum has been below 10 nmol/L for at least 12 months prior to her first competition." This effectively (and problematically) defines femaleness in terms of testosterone. Conversely, those who "transition from female to male are eligible to compete in the male category without restriction."

On the surface, the question of whether we should segregate sport on the basis of sex seems to be fairly simple. Upon further consideration, it is much more complicated than a simple yes or no. In addition to factoring in the sport, the athlete, and the rules of engagement, we must also take into account how, why, and in what circumstances we distinguish between male and female.

7

THE OLYMPIC AND PARALYMPIC GAMES

How is the Olympic Movement organized and what role do women play in its organization?

The Olympic Movement includes organizations and individuals who comply with the rules, guidelines, and fundamental principles defined in the Olympic Charter. There are three main constituents of the Olympic Movement: The International Olympic Committee, International Sports Federations, and National Olympic Committees.

The IOC is the "supreme authority" of the Olympic Movement.[1] Established in 1894 by French aristocrat Pierre de Frédy, Baron de Coubertin, the original IOC was made up of fourteen upper-class Anglo-Saxon men. The committee has since diversified its membership to include up to 115 people, including a maximum of 70 individual members, 15 athlete members, 15 International Federation presidents, and 15 National Olympic Committee presidents.

For nearly a century, only men led the IOC. It was not until 1981 that Finland's Pirjo Haggman and Venezuela's Flor Isava-Fonseca became the first female IOC members; in 1990, Isava-Fonseca became the first women elected to the IOC executive board. Anita DeFrantz became the first women elected IOC vice president (1997–2001). In 2016, twenty-three women served as members of the ninety-two-member IOC. No woman has ever served as IOC president.[2]

The IOC staged the Games of the 1st Olympiad in 1896, with each subsequent Games scheduled every four years. The IOC canceled the Games in 1916, 1940, and 1944 because of war. In 1924, the IOC established a separate Winter Olympic Games, and until 1992, the Summer and Winter Games occurred during the same calendar year. Since 1994, the IOC has staggered the Summer and Winter Games to alternate every two years. In 2010, the IOC added the Summer Youth Olympic Games and, two years later, the Winter Youth Olympic Games.

As the second constituent of the Olympic Movement, International Sports Federations (IFs) are nongovernmental organizations officially recognized by the IOC as the highest authorities of their respective sports. IFs organize competitions, establish and enforce rules, develop athletes, and administer one or more sports on a global scale. Examples include the International Judo Federation, FIFA, and the World Curling Federation. Some IFs monitor sports that include multiple disciplines. For instance, the International Swimming Federation administers swimming, diving, synchronized swimming, and water polo, and the International Skating Union oversees figure skating (a branch that includes single and pair skating, ice dance, and synchronized skating) and speed skating (long and short track). As of 2016, there were twenty-eight Summer Olympic IFs (women held approximately 13 percent of all IF executive board positions) and seven International Olympic Winter IFs (women held 19 percent of all executive board positions).

The third arm of the Olympic Movement is the National Olympic Committees (NOCs), which are affiliated with the IFs. Members of these committees are responsible for organizing, developing, and governing high-performance sport in their respective nations. NOCs also supervise the preliminary selection of cities bidding to host the Games. In addition to member states recognized by the United Nations, the IOC also recognizes NOCs from Palestine (an observer state), the Cook Islands (a free state associated with New Zealand), and nine dependent territories including four US territories (American Samoa, Guam, Puerto Rico, and the US Virgin Island), three British Overseas Territories (Bermuda, British Virgin Islands, and the Cayman Islands), Aruba (a territory of the Kingdom of the Netherlands), and Hong Kong (a special administrative region of China).

Athletes representing 206 NOCs from five continents competed at the 2016 Summer Olympics. This included the Refugee Olympic Team, made up of ten athletes from Syria, South Sudan, Ethiopia, and the Democratic Republic of the Congo. Women made up 10.4 percent of leadership positions within those 206 NOCs. Significantly, there were 162 NOCs (80 percent) that did not have any women serving in leadership capacities. Women are similarly under-represented at the Winter Olympic Games. A record high number of ninety-three NOCs competed in the 2018 Winter Olympics in Pyeongchang, South Korea with the notable absence of the Russian Olympic Committee, which the IOC banned after allegations of state-sponsored doping, although athletes who could prove they were "clean" were allowed to compete under a neutral flag as an additional delegation of "Olympic Athletes from Russia."

There have been several initiatives to increase women's involvement in the Olympic Movement. Since 1991, any sport seeking inclusion on the Olympic program must include women's events. In 1995, the IOC established the Women and Sport Working Group, which in 2004 became a commission to advise the president and executive board on policy. In 1996, the IOC initiated its first World Conference on Women and Sport, to be held every four years; however, there was no conference in 2016, and it is unclear whether the IOC will revive the meeting in the future. The IOC has also amended the Olympic Charter to affirm its commitment "to encourage and support the promotion of women in sport at all levels and in all structures, with a view to implementing the principle of equality of men and women."[3]

How long have women been competing in the Olympic Games?

Only men participated in the ancient games, both as athletes and as spectators. Coubertin and his nineteenth-century compatriots romanticized the ancient Panhellenic festival and revived the modern games as a means to promote global peace and understanding and to glorify the amateur male athlete. The role of women, the Baron maintained, was to cheer on the competitors. As he remarked in 1912,

> The Olympic Games must be reserved for men. . . . We have tried and must continue to try to achieve the following definition: the solemn and periodic exaltation of male athleticism with internationalism as a base, loyalty as a means, art for its setting, and female applause as reward.[4]

Coubertin fought against women's Olympic participation for more than thirty years. The "indecency, ugliness and impropriety" of women in the Games, he believed, could only result in "destroying their feminine charm and leading to the downfall and degradation of sport."[5]

Initially, the organizing committees of the host cities selected the program of events. This allowed women to compete in golf, tennis, croquet, sailing, and archery, although there is some debate as to whether the women were "official" Olympic athletes. These early women competitors came from privileged backgrounds, possessing the means and time to train and travel to the games. Their sports were not only the sports of the upper class but also sports considered to be "gender appropriate" (see Chapter 4).

On the eve of the 1928 Games, three years after retiring as IOC president, Coubertin continued his disapproval: "I am personally opposed to women's eligibility in the Games. It has been adopted against my wish, and women sport demonstrations are increasing in number."[6] With nearly 300 women set to compete, the 1928 Games marked a significant increase in female Olympians, although it was not until the 1952 Helsinki Games that women made up more than 10 percent of all athletes, and the 1988 Seoul Games marked the first time that more than one-fourth of all participants were women. Women comprised 45 percent of all 2016 Summer Olympians and 43 percent of all 2018 Winter Olympians. (Tables 7.1 and 7.2)

What Olympic sports have been the most difficult for women to gain access?

For the most part, it has been team sports, long-distance events, and disciplines associated with strength and hypermasculinity to which Olympic executives resisted including women (Table 7.3).

The 1964 volleyball tournament marked the first time that women competed in an Olympic team sport and, it is worth noting, it is a sport that minimizes bodily contact by separating competitors with a net. There are considerable gaps between the dates that the IOC included opportunities for men and women in water polo (men 1900, women 2000), soccer (men 1908, women 1996), field hockey (men 1908, women 1980), ice hockey (men 1920, women 1998), handball (men 1936, women 1976), and basketball (men 1936, women 1972).

The IOC added women's athletics (the European term for track and field) relatively early to the Olympic program, although not without great controversy. In the first part of the twentieth century, athletics had the reputation as a masculine sport. In 1919, Alice Milliat, a French athlete and organizer,

Table 7.1 Women's Participation in Olympic Summer Games

Year	Sports	Women's Events*	Total Events	% of Women's Events	Women Participants	% of Women Participants
1900	2	2	95	2.1	22	2.2
1904	1	3	91	3.3	6	0.9
1908	2	4	110	3.6	37	1.8
1912	2	5	102	4.9	48	2.0
1920	2	8	154	5.2	63	2.4
1924	3	10	126	7.9	135	4.4
1928	4	14	109	12.8	277	9.6
1932	3	14	117	12.0	126	9
1936	4	15	129	11.6	331	8.3
1948	5	19	136	14.0	390	9.5
1952	6	25	149	16.8	519	10.5
1956	6	26	151	17.2	376	13.3
1960	6	29	150	19.3	611	11.4
1964	7	33	163	20.2	678	13.2
1968	7	39	172	22.7	781	14.2
1972	8	43	195	22.1	1,059	14.6
1976	11	49	198	24.7	1,260	20.7
1980	12	50	203	24.6	1,115	21.5
1984	14	62	221	28.1	1,566	23
1988	17	72	237	30.4	2,194	26.1
1992	19	86	257	33.5	2,704	28.8
1996	21	97	271	35.8	3,512	34.0
2000	25	120	300	40	4,069	38.2
2004	26	125	301	41.5	4,329	40.7
2008	26	127	302	42.1	4,637	42.4
2012	26	140	302	46.4	4,676	44.2
2016	28	145	306	47.4	~4,700	~45

*Including mixed events.

Source: International Olympic Committee. "Factsheet: Women in the Olympic Movement." January 2016. https://stillmed.olympic.org/Documents/Reference_documents_Factsheets/Women_in_Olympic_Movement.pdf.

Table 7.2 Women's Participation in Olympic Winter Games

Year	Sports	Women's Events*	Total Events	% of Women's Events	Women Participants	% of Women Participants
1924	1	2	16	12.5	11	4.3
1928	1	2	14	14.3	26	5.6
1932	1	2	14	14.3	21	8.3
1936	2	3	17	17.6	80	12
1948	2	5	22	22.7	77	11.5
1952	2	6	22	27.3	109	15.7
1956	2	7	24	29.2	134	17
1960	2	11	27	40.7	144	21.5
1964	3	14	34	41.2	199	18.3
1968	3	14	35	40.0	211	18.2
1972	3	14	35	40.0	205	20.5
1976	3	15	37	40.5	231	20.6
1980	3	15	38	39.5	232	21.7
1984	3	16	39	41.0	274	21.5
1988	3	19	46	41.3	301	21.2
1992	4	26	57	45.6	488	27.1
1994	4	28	61	45.9	522	30
1998	6	32	68	47.1	787	36.2
2002	7	37	78	47.4	886	36.9
2006	7	40	84	47.6	960	38.2
2010	7	41	86	47.7	1,044	40.7
2014	7	49	98	50.0	~1,120	40.3

*Including mixed events.

Source: International Olympic Committee. "Factsheet: Women in the Olympic Movement." January 2016. https://stillmed.olympic.org/Documents/Reference_documents_Factsheets/Women_in_Olympic_Movement.pdf.

asked the IOC to introduce women's track and field events at the 1920 Antwerp Games. Frustrated by the IOC's lack of cooperation, Milliat established the Fédération Sportive Féminine Internationale (FSFI) in 1921 and hosted the First Women's World Olympic Games the following year (after the IOC objected to the use of the word "Olympic," the event became the Women's World Games). A reported 20,000 spectators

Table 7.3 Introduction of Olympic Women's Sports

Year	Sports
1900	Tennis, golf
1904	Archery
1908	Tennis,* skating
1912	Aquatics
1924	Fencing
1928	Athletics, gymnastics
1936	Skiing
1948	Canoe-kayak
1952	Equestrian
1964	Volleyball, luge
1976	Rowing, basketball, handball
1980	Hockey
1984	Shooting, cycling
1988	Tennis,* table tennis, sailing
1992	Badminton, judo, biathlon
1996	Football, softball
1998	Curling, ice hockey
2000	Weightlifting, modern pentathlon, taekwondo, triathlon
2002	Bobsleigh
2004	Wrestling
2012	Boxing
2016	Golf,* rugby

*Sports that were reintroduced to the Olympic Program.

Source: International Olympic Committee. "Factsheet: 3Women in the Olympic Movement." January 2016. https://stillmed.olympic. org/Documents/Reference_documents_Factsheets/Women_in_ Olympic_Movement.pdf.

cheered on seventy-seven women from five countries who competed in eleven track and field events. Between 1922 and 1930, the FSFI hosted four games that grew to include athletics, basketball, and hazena (Czech handball). At its peak, FSFI members represented thirty nations.[7]

Threatened by the success of the FSFI and the Women's World Games, the IAAF assumed control over women's athletics and subsequently convinced the IOC to add five women's events to the 1928 program, including the 800-meter race—then the longest allowable distance. The top three finishers in that event (Germany's Lina Radke, Japan's Kinue Hitomi, and Sweden's Inga Gentzel) all broke the existing world record, yet journalists misrepresented the race in the popular press. Acclaimed sportswriter John Tunis claimed that he had witnessed "11 wretched women, 5 of whom dropped out before the finish, while 5 collapsed after reaching the tape." The *Chicago Herald-Tribune* called it a "pitiful spectacle."[8]

Contrary to these reports, existing footage shows that just one 800-meter contender, who had been injured a week earlier, fell at the end of the race. Even so, the distance made "too great a call on feminine strength," lamented the *New York Times*.[9] The IOC cut back on the number of women's track and field events, and the 800-meter race remained absent from the program until 1960. Yet, the IOC and IAAF seemed to have little concern when men faltered in long- and middle-distance races. In fact, officials and spectators regularly applauded men who bravely stumbled across the finish line in various states of distress. Following the 800-meter men's race at the 1904 Olympics, for example, one runner was "carried to his training quarters helpless. Another was laid out upon the grass and stimulants used to bring him back to life," as the *St. Louis Globe-Democrat* reported. Yet, no one suggested that two laps around the track was too taxing for male athletes. They just agreed that the race had been "a good one." [10]

Long-distance races for women advanced at a sluggish pace, and it was not until 1984 that the IOC added the 26.2-mile marathon to the women's program, an event in which men have competed since 1896.[11] The IOC has also been slow to add distance events for women in cross-country skiing, speed skating, the biathlon, and swimming. The Olympic 50-kilometer race walk is still only for male competitors, even though the IAAF allows women to race that distance in other competitions.

In 2012, boxing became the last Summer Olympic sport to include women, although not all NOCs supported its inclusion. Cuba, for example, has won more medals in men's boxing than any other country, but the Cuban government bans women from the ring. Government officials explain that they require medical studies that confirm the sport is safe for women, while a former top coach told reporters that "Cuban women are meant to show the beauty of their face, not receive punches."[12]

As of the 2018 Winter Games, women did not compete in the Nordic combined, which includes a 10-kilometer cross-country ski and ski jump events. In fact, women only gained entry into the Olympic ski jump in 2014 after a long campaign, including a lawsuit, against some antiquated ideas related to the medical and social rationales against women in sport (see Chapter 2). In 2005, for example, Gian-Franco Kasper, president of the International Ski Federation and a member of the IOC, commented that the sport "seems not to be appropriate for ladies from a medical point of view." Nine years later, just a week before the 2014 Games, Russian ski jumping coach Alexander Arefyev worried that the sport might injure women who "have another purpose—to have children, to do housework, to create hearth and home."[13] Ski jump champion Lindsay Van once suggested that women might challenge men in a sport that favors light, flexible bodies with a low center of gravity. "If women can jump as far as men, what does that do to the extreme value of this sport?" Van asked in a *New York Times Magazine* interview.[14]

Do women compete in the same Olympic sports as men?

At the 2012 London Olympic Games, for the first time in history, women competed in all twenty-six sports in which men competed. There were two disciplines reserved for female competitors only—synchronized swimming and rhythmic gymnastics—even though there are men who compete in both sports and hope to one day prove themselves on the Olympic stage.

Although women competed in the same sports as men again at the 2016 Games, they did not compete in the same events. Specifically, women competed in 136 events (making up 45.6 percent of all Olympians), while men competed in 161 events. There were also nine mixed-sex events. The participation differences came from sports that offered more weight classes for men, such as boxing (ten weight classes for men and three for women) and weightlifting (eight for men and seven for women). Other tournaments included a greater number of men's teams than women's teams, such as in water polo and soccer. The IOC added women's freestyle wrestling to the program in 2004, but men compete in both the freestyle and Greco-Roman disciplines.

Sex disparities should improve at the 2020 Olympic Games in Tokyo with the introduction of new sports and events that will make the program "more youthful, more urban, and will include more women," as IOC President Thomas Bach announced in 2017.[15] New sports include sport climbing, skateboarding, surfing, karate, three-on-three basketball, and BMX freestyle cycling. Baseball and softball return to the program after the IOC dropped them in 2008. Some events designated only for men will be open to women, including canoe and the 1500-meter swim. The Olympic program committee has also added mixed-sex events in swimming, track, triathlon, archery, judo, and table tennis. Experts project that women will make up 48.8 percent of the athletes at the 2020 Games, edging them closer to the IOC's goal of 50 percent female participation, as outlined in its Olympic Agenda 2020. The Winter Games are also inching closer to equality. The IOC added six events to the program of the 2014 Winter Games in Sochi, Russia: ski half-pipe (men and women), women's ski jumping, figure skating team event, and coed relays in biathlon and luge. The 2018 Games in Pyeongchang, South Korea, saw the additions of mixed-doubles curling and coed alpine team skiing, although women were still in the minority.

Still Olympic critic and scholar Helen Jefferson Lenskyj cautions that the goal of equal opportunity for women sets a "low bar" for reform and fails to address fundamental flaws in the Olympic industry. The liberal approach of gender parity, she argues, leaves intact problematic aspects of the Olympic Movement—issues of corruption, commercialism, athlete exploitation, and the health risks associated with high performance sport. This approach also imagines "universal woman" and assumes that "what is good for western women and men is good for all women and men," thereby perpetuation global systems of colonialism and oppression.[16]

Are there any negative consequences to adding new sports and events to the Olympic program?

In order to control the size and cost of the Games, the IOC eliminates some sports and events in order to make room for new additions. This has devastating consequences for athletes, particularly those who compete in sports that do not offer professional options. The Olympics may be their one chance to show the world just how good they are and to reap any financial benefits from the sports to which they have devoted so much of their lives.

The 2020 Tokyo program includes thirty-three sports but 285 fewer athletes than competed in Rio. Track and field and weightlifting lost 105 and 64 spots, respectively. In the IOC's terminology, sports such as boxing, canoe, and judo must "transfer" participation spots "from men to women" in order "to reach gender balance." Other sports, including sailing, rowing, and shooting, face a "reduction" of athletes for the same reason.[17] In other words, to create space for women, the IOC will take away men's participation opportunities, which may have the unfortunate effect of making people less receptive, perhaps even hostile, to women's sports.

Do all National Olympic Committees send female athletes to the Games?

At the opening ceremony for the 2012 London Olympic Games, IOC president Jacques Rogge proudly announced, "For the first time in Olympic history, all the participating teams will have female athletes."[18] He was incorrect. Barbados, Nauru, and the Federation of Saint Kitts and Nevis failed to send any female competitors. The 2016 Rio Olympics seemed to be another triumph for women, yet five nations (Iraq, Monaco, Nauru, Tuvalu, and Vanuatu) included no female athletes (Bhutan's team included two female athletes and no male athletes).

Financial resources and population size play significant roles in who participates in the Olympic Games. Simply put, larger, wealthier nations have more resources to devote to athletic development, training, infrastructure, and travel. Smaller and less developed nations are likely to bring small delegations. Combined, the NOCs of Nauru, Tuvalu, and Vanuatu sent just eight athletes (all men) to the 2016 Games.

Some federal governments subsidize elite sports. In the 1960s and 1970s, Soviet bloc countries institutionalized their talent identification and development programs and Olympic-caliber athletes trained in specialized sport schools. The Chinese government adopted a similar model, and the Australian Institute of Sport and the Norwegian Olympiatoppen have borrowed some of these ideas to centralize their athletic efforts. After the United Kingdom's poor showing at the 1996 Atlanta Olympics, the government revamped its priorities to create UK Sport, which receives funds from government coffers and the national lottery. As a result of a strategic, and often controversial, performance-based funding program, the United Kingdom finished second in the 2016 medal count. However, the use of federal funds for performance sport may shortchange non-Olympic citizens who desperately need money for health and welfare issues, including opportunities for physical activity.

A country's prevailing gender norms also matter. Scholars Jennifer Berdahl, Eric Luis Uhlmann, and Feng Bai compared the medal counts from the Summer 2012 and Winter 2014 Olympic Games with each country's gender gap score— a measure of economic, political, health, and educational equality between men and women. The researchers found that the most successful Olympic nations were those with higher levels of gender equality.[19] Similarly, political scientist Danyel Reiche has studied what contributes to a country's Olympic success and finds that the promotion of women's sport is crucial.[20] Quite simply, the medal count does not discriminate, and so countries that restrict the rights of women do not fare well at the Games.

The promotion of women's sport remains difficult in nations governed by religious or gender-conservative regimes. There is a noticeable shortage of women on Olympic delegations from Muslim or Muslim-majority countries, although Muslim women have competed in the games since at least 1936 (Turkish fencer Halet Cambel). Until 2012, for example, the Saudi Arabian government banned women from competing at Olympics, as well as from participating in state-organized sports leagues, official sports clubs, national tournaments, and, until 2017, from physical education classes. Just before the 2012 Games, the Saudi Arabian Olympic Committee (SAOC), under threat of expulsion from the IOC, added runner Sarah Al-Attar and judoka Wojdan Ali Seraj Abdulrahim Shahrkhani to its delegation. The SAOC doubled its number of female Olympians in 2016, but without early sports experiences for girls, the country lacks a talent pool from which to draw. Bahrain has found a way to circumvent developing native-born talent—for both men and women. The nation's 2016 Olympic track and field team was made up primarily of runners from Kenya, Ethiopia, Jamaica, Morocco, and Nigeria, who became naturalized citizens in order to compete for the oil-rich country.

Geography and climate also effect participation, especially in the Winter Olympics, in which athletes from African, Caribbean, and South American nations are historically underrepresented. The 2018 Winter Olympics marked the first time any Nigerian athletes competed in the Winter Olympic Games, and the first time for any African team in the bobsled, after Seun Adigun, Ngozi Onwumere, and Akuoma Omeoga qualified for the event.

What are the Paralympic Games?

The world's third-largest sporting event (behind the Olympics and the FIFA Men's World Cup), the Paralympic Games is an elite sporting competition for athletes with impairments. The *para* prefix is for *parallel*, as they are meant to run alongside the Olympic Games. Since the 1988 Summer Games of Seoul, South Korea, and the 1992 Winter Games of Albertville, France, the Paralympic Games have taken place weeks after the Olympic Games and utilize the same venues.

The Paralympic Games began at Stoke Mandeville Hospital in Aylesbury, England, where Dr. Ludwig Guttmann ran the Spinal Injuries Centre for soldiers and civilians injured during World War II. Guttmann introduced sport as a type of rehabilitation, which developed into competitions between patients. In 1948, Guttmann organized the Stoke Mandeville Games, which took place on the same day as the London Olympics' opening ceremonies. Fourteen men and two women, representing teams from Stoke Mandeville and the Star and Garter Home for Injured War Veterans, competed in wheelchair archery. The following year, Stoke Mandeville hosted sixty athletes from five hospitals. In 1952, a team from the Military Rehabilitation Centre in the Netherlands participated to establish the first International Stoke Mandeville Games, in which more than 130 athletes competed in archery, table tennis, darts, and snooker. In 1960, the first official Paralympic Games took place in Rome, hosting 400 athletes from twenty-three countries. Organizers added a Winter Paralympic Games in 1976, held in Örnsköldsvik, Sweden, which included fifty-three athletes from sixteen countries who competed in Alpine and Nordic skiing.[21]

Originally for wheelchair athletes with spinal cord injuries, the Paralympic Games have grown to include athletes with ten eligible impairments types. There are events for athletes with visual and intellectual impairments, as well as those for athletes with impaired muscle power, impaired passive range of movement, limb deficiency, leg length difference, short stature, hypertonia, ataxia, and athetosis.[22] Paralympic sports are further organized into sport classes, which are designed to equalize competition by grouping together athletes of similar limitations. Some sports have one sport class, such as ice hockey and powerlifting, whereas track and field has forty-nine classes to accommodate different impairments and abilities. Although sport classes help to level the playing field, there are some problems with the system, including classifier error and athletes who intentionally misrepresent the severity of their impairments. In addition, a complicated classification scheme can be difficult for spectators and journalists to follow, which may work against generating greater interest in parasport.

At the 2016 Summer Paralympic Games in Rio, 4,328 athletes from 159 nations competed in twenty-two different sports and 528 medal events. The Winter Paralympic Games have also grown. The 2018 program for Pyeongchang, South Korea, included six sports (Alpine skiing, biathlon, Nordic skiing, ice sledge hockey, snowboard, and wheelchair curling) and eighty events for athletes representing forty-two National Paralympic Committees.

Sports for athletes with impairments have existed since the nineteenth century, including Berlin's Sports Club for the Deaf, established in 1888. By 1924, six countries sent teams to the First International Silent Games, which became the World

Games for the Deaf and then, in 2001, the Deaflympics, officially recognized by the IOC. Other major disability sport competitions are the Invictus Games and the Warrior Games (for injured military personnel), the Asian Para Games, the Parapan Games (which run parallel to the Pan American Games), the International Blind Sports Federation Games, Disability World Cups and Championships, the Disability Commonwealth Games, the Extremity Games, as well as competitions for individual sports and those held at local, regional, national, and international levels. The IOC also recognizes the Special Olympics, the world's largest sports organization for children and adults with intellectual impairments. Established in 1968, the competition has grown to include the Special Olympics World Games, held every two years and offering more than thirty individual and team sports.

How is the Paralympic Movement organized and what role do women play in the organization?

In order to manage the expanding scope of parasport, organizers established the International Sports Organization for the Disabled in 1964, which gave way to the International Coordinating Committee of World Sports Organizations in 1982 and became the International Paralympic Committee (IPC) in 1989. The IPC is made up of a general assembly, governing board (20 percent women), management team (55 percent women), eleven committees (40 percent women), eight sport technical committees (23 percent women), and the Athletes' Council (64 percent women). No woman has ever served as IPC president.

The general assembly is the IPC's highest governing body, made up of IFs, National Paralympic Committees (NPCs), Regional Organizations, and the International Organization of Sport for the Disabled, which represents specific impairment groups to the IPC. These include the Cerebral Palsy International Sport and Recreation Association, the International Blind Sports

Federation, the International Sports Federation for Persons with Intellectual Disability, and the International Wheelchair and Amputee Sports Federation.

In 2002, the IPC established the Women in Sport Commission (now a committee). The following year, the IPC General Assembly adopted a policy on gender equity, including a 2009 target of women holding at least 30 percent of leadership positions in all entities belonging to the Paralympic Movement—a target that is nearing achievement. The Agitos Foundation, established in 2012, is the developmental arm of the Paralympic Movement designed to increase global opportunities for athletes with impairments. One of the initiatives of this foundation has been its "WoMentoring" program, which matches businesswomen in sport with potential Paralympic coaches, leaders, and board members to help meet its this goal.

The IPC recognizes fifteen IFs, which serve the same functions as the IFs associated with the IOC. In addition, the IPC acts as the IF for ten sports. Of the 170 NCP presidents listed on the IPC website in 2016, there were 26 women (15 percent), and women hold 24 percent of the positions on the boards of Paralympic governing bodies.[23]

Do men and women compete equally at the Paralympic Games?

Female athletes comprised approximately 39 percent of competitors at the 2016 Rio Paralympics, a slight increase from the 2012 London Games (Table 7.4). There were twenty-two Paralympic summer sports in 2016, and women competed in all but two: five-a-side soccer and seven-a-side soccer that together account for 176 participation opportunities. There were 264 events for men and 226 events for women, as well as 38 mixed-sex events. Half of all events were open to women, but female competitors were significantly under-represented in the mixed sports of wheelchair rugby (2.1 percent of competitors) and sailing (just under

Table 7.4 Evolution of the Paralympic Summer Games

Games	Year	Athletes	Nations	Men	Women	% of Women
Rome, Italy	1960	400	23	ND	ND	ND
Tokyo, Japan	1964	375	21	ND	ND	ND
Tel Aviv, Israel	1968	750	29	ND	ND	ND
Heidelberg, Germany	1972	1,004	43	798	210	20.9
Toronto, Canada	1976	1,657	40	1,404	253	15.2
Arnhem, Netherlands	1980	1,973	43	1,614	359	18.2
New York, US/Stoke Mandeville, UK	1984	1,800	45	1,561	535	25.5
Seoul, Korea	1988	3,059	61	2,379	680	22.2
Barcelona, Spain	1992	3,001	83	2,301	700	23.3
Atlanta, US	1996	3,259	104	2,470	791	24.3
Sydney, Australia	2000	3,881	122	2,891	991	25.5
Athens, Greece	2004	3,810	135	2,645	1,165	30.6
Beijing, China	2008	4,011	146	2,628	1,383	34.5
London, UK	2012	4,302	164	2,776	1,510	35.1
Rio, Brazil	2016	4,317	159	2,648	1,669	38.7

ND, not determined.
Source: Adapted from Simon Darcy and David Legg, "Brief History of the Paralympic Games: From Post-WWII Rehabilitation to Mega Sport Event." September 7, 2016. http://www.abc.net.au/news/2016-09-07/brief-history-of-the-paralympic-games/7819772, with data from WSF report.

19 percent). At the 2018 Paralympic Winter Games, there were 670 total athletes (43 percent were female athletes).[24] Of the six winter sports, wheelchair curling was the only mixed-sex event; ice sledge hockey allows integrated teams, but Norway's Lena Schroeder was the only woman to compete in the sport.

Women with impairments are affected by both sexism and ableism (discrimination against those with disabilities), which accounts for some of the discrepancies in their athletic participation. According to the IPC Women in Sport Leadership Toolkit, "Women in Paralympic sport have reported that social factors, shortened sport careers, cultural implications of both gender and disability, and limited 'grassroots' opportunities are factors limiting their participation in sport."[25]

Do all National Paralympic Committees send female athletes to the Games?

Of the 159 NPCs at the 2016 Games, forty-two failed to include any female athletes in their delegations (seven NPCs did not include any male athletes), and only eleven NPCs had delegations of at least 50 percent women athletes. Larger nations, which generally offer more services for citizens with impairments, typically sent the most female athletes to the Paralympic Games in 2016. The cost for equipment for some sports, such as specialized wheelchairs and prosthetics, put para sport out of reach of most people with impairments.

With 1.3 million citizens, India is the second most populous nation in the world, ranking just behind China. Yet without a strong sport system or continuous funding, India's performances at the Olympic and Paralympic Games have fallen short. Recent initiatives are helping. Nineteen athletes represented India at the 2016 Rio Paralympic Games and won four medals, including a silver medal in the shot-put for Deepa Malik, the country's first woman Paralympic medalist. The growth in India's Olympic and Paralympic programs is the result of a corporate social responsibility law, the government's "Target Olympic Podium Scheme," and the efforts of the GoSports Foundation.

Do the Paralympic Games receive the same amount of media coverage as the Olympic Games?

Although India sent its largest ever delegation to the 2016 Paralympic Games in Rio, neither the Indian government nor any private Indian sports channel bought the broadcast rights for the event. This is an extreme example of the lack of media coverage, but across the board, the media fails to give parasport much time or consideration.

Women athletes generally receive less media attention than men, but every four years, viewers can count on a boost to women's sport coverage during the Olympic Games. There is not, however, a similar spike during the Paralympic Games. According to journalism professor John Affleck, there were 400 accredited American journalists and photographers in Rio to cover the Olympic Games but just twenty-nine at the Paralympics.[26] China, which won the 2016 Paralympic medal count, similarly failed to provide much media coverage of the games. Singapore public broadcasting showed full live coverage of the Olympics but opted to air only select highlights of the Paralympics. In every country, the media either marginalizes or ignores the accomplishments of male and female Paralympians.

There is some evidence that media coverage is improving. In 2016, NBC announced that it would show 66 hours of the Games, a 60.5-hour increase over the paltry coverage it gave to the London 2012 Paralympics.[27] With an audience of more than 4.1 billion people, the 2016 Paralympic Games were the most viewed in history and were broadcast in a record-setting 154 countries, with more live broadcasts and total hours of broadcast than ever before.[28] Yet, according to the 2016 report commissioned by the Women's Sport Foundation, there was a "clear absence of media coverage of the Paralympics on ESPN, ESPNW, NBC, *New York Times*, *Sports Illustrated* and *USA Today*."[29]

Even with the problematic, often deficient, coverage of women in the Olympic and Paralympic Games (as discussed in Chapter 8), it cannot be denied that they represent the very best athletes the world has to offer. Few athletes will ever compete in the Olympic or Paralympic Games (New Zealand archer Neroli Fairhall and a few others have competed in both and there are proposals to integrate the two events). In

2012, statisticians estimated the odds of becoming a Summer Olympic athlete. For women, their best chance was in handball; serious competitors had a 1 in 40 chance of making it to the Olympic stage (at 1 in 67, men found their highest probability in equestrian events). Basketball presented the toughest challenge for both male and female elite athletes; just 1 in 45,000 top basketball-playing women ultimately represented their nation.[30]

Although the odds are slim, this is undeniable progress, both in the sense that so many women compete at the elite level and in the sense that there are growing opportunities for women to compete in the Games. In fact, every year, the IOC and IPC have added participation spots for sportswomen, thus inching closer to gender equity in that regard. Yet, too many nations fail to provide, develop, and support sport for girls and women in ways that manifest so clearly at the Games, and Olympic and Paralympic governance remains male dominated. True equity will only come when all nations fully integrate and equally represent women in all aspects of the Olympic and Paralympic Movements.

8

WOMEN, SPORT, AND
THE MEDIA

*Do male and female athletes receive the same amount
of coverage in sport media?*

Studies conducted in North America, Europe, Australasia,
Canada, Africa, and parts of Asia have all yielded similar
results: Women are significantly under-represented in sport
media. Dependent on the culture, sportswomen receive between 1.8 and 10 percent of coverage across all media platforms,
including newspapers, magazines, radio, television, and new
or electronic media.[1] Scholars call this inattention "symbolic
annihilation."[2] When we do not see female athletes represented
in the media, the message is either that they do not exist or that
they do not matter.

In the United States, 40 percent of all sport participants are
girls and women, yet they appear in just 4 percent of all sport
media.[3] In their 2015 study, Cheryl Cooky, Michael A. Messner,
and Michaela Musto surveyed televised sport media and found
that women's status had not improved in the past twenty-
five years. Network news programs devoted just 3.2 percent
of newscasts to women's sport, opting instead to focus on the
"big three" American men's sports: football, basketball, and
baseball. ESPN's flagship program *SportsCenter* dedicated
2 percent of its hour-long highlight show to women.[4] Upon
analyzing the content of these programs, the authors dub

them "dude time" and a "mediated man cave," made up by "a configuration of three intertwined patterns: (1) almost entirely men's sports content, (2) delivered almost entirely by men commentators, and (3) deploying an amplified excited style of delivery" when covering men's sports. Conversely, journalists discussed women's sports in what the authors describe as a "'matter of fact' style of commentary" that did little to stimulate viewers' excitement or interest.[5]

It is important for girls to see media representations of sportswomen. One survey determined that nearly seven out of ten girls in the United States believe that there are not enough female role models in sport. As Jen Welter, a sports psychologist who became the first female coach in the NFL, asked, "Why would you think that a girl would feel like she belongs in sports if she doesn't see girls in sports in the same amount and degree as the boys do?"[6] This is especially true for girls and women of color, as the limited reportage of American women's sport centers white, conventionally feminine, heterosexual, and able-bodied athletes. And for all media consumers—male and female—proportionate coverage of women athletes acknowledges that sport is a *human* activity and not just something for and about men.

Isn't this difference in coverage based on consumer interest?

This is a common response—that men receive the lion's share of sport media because that is what the audience cares about. Decision-makers, such as editors, producers, programmers, journalists, and sponsors, are just giving people what they want. Although this is undoubtedly true, there is another way to think about it. As Cooky, Messner, and Musto argue, "Broadcasts build audiences for men's sports while positioning women's sports as unimportant and less interesting than men's sports."[7] The media's symbolic annihilation of women's sport makes it difficult to generate interest and build an audience, which keeps demand low.

How does the coverage of women's sport differ from the coverage of men's sport?

In 2016, experts at Cambridge University Press analyzed decades of English language news articles, academic papers, social media, and Internet forums to examine how language indicates "our gendered attitudes to sport." The researchers found that men were mentioned within a sporting context almost three times more often than women. The only exception was that women were mentioned more often in ways that marked their sports as "other." Thus, the discourse of sport establishes men as the norm and positions women as different from and inferior to that norm.[8]

The Cambridge study found that the primary mechanism for "othering" was through asymmetrical gender marking, that is, identifying women's sports as *women's* sports but not similarly marking men's sports (most men's sports become the "unmarked category"). For example, when we read about the "World Cup" in the newspaper, we assume the article refers to the *men's* tournament, even though the term is not "marked" as such. On the contrary, women's events are almost always qualified by the sex of the participants—it is the "Women's World Cup" (or the NCAA Women's Final Four, or Wimbledon's Ladies' Final, or the HSBC Women's World Rugby Sevens Series). One way to fix this problem is to *symmetrically* mark all events, a rhetorical shift that implies equality.

Asymmetrical gender marking also occurs when commentators emphasize an athlete's sex, even in the context of paying her a compliment. The implication that she is a good *female* athlete—not simply a good athlete. As Serena Williams wrote in a 2016 open letter, women athletes

are constantly reminded we are not men, as if it is a flaw. People call me one of the "world's greatest female athletes." Do they say LeBron is one of the world's best male athletes? Is Tiger? Federer? Why not? They are certainly not female. We should never let this go unchallenged. We should always be judged by our achievements, not by our gender.[9]

In much the same way, women who perform well are said to "play like a man." *The Daily Mail* referred to swimmer Katie Ledecky as "the female Michael Phelps." Journalists have called Jackie Tonawanda "the female Ali"; Sheryl Swoopes, Candace Parker, and Maya Moore the "female Michael Jordan"; and Barbara Latorre "the female Messi." The remarks may seem flattering, but they remind us that men are the standard by which we judge excellence.

Beyond these othering tendencies, there is an extensive body of research that details persistent inequalities in the ways that sport media portray women. Women who compete in "gender appropriate" or "feminine" sports receive more attention (see Chapter 4). Photographs of athletes typically show men actively engaged in their sport, whereas women are more likely to be pictured in passive, non-sporting poses. Journalists also disproportionately attend to women's personal lives and physical appearance. There is no shortage of examples. Guests on the Fox News' program *Sports Court* debated whether female Olympians should wear makeup. At the 2015 Australian Open, a journalist asked Canadian tennis star Eugenie Bouchard to "give us a twirl and tell us about your outfit?" It is difficult to imagine men athletes fielding the same sort of question, which is precisely the point of the #CoverTheAthlete campaign. If journalists were to ask hockey player Sidney Crosby who he would like to date, or to ask Michael Phelps if shaving his body helps his love life, or if male athletes are concerned about their hairstyles or maintaining their figures, it would seem ridiculous.[10] Yet these are the very questions with which female athletes regularly contend.

In addition, studies have found that journalists unduly attribute women's success to the support and guidance of fathers, male partners, and male coaches. Several incidents during the 2016 Olympics illustrate this point. Following Hungarian swimmer Katinak Hossuz's world-record performance, NBC announcers turned their attention to her husband and coach and explained to viewers, "there's the man responsible." The *Chicago Tribune* celebrated American trap shooter Corey Cogdell-Urein's performance with the headline, "Wife of Bears' Lineman Wins Bronze Medal Today in Rio Olympics." Yes, she is married to a man who plays for the NFL's Chicago Bears, but the description not only diminishes her accomplishments but also does not even mention her name. Newspapers editors also failed to name Simone Manuel after she became the first black woman to win a gold medal in swimming. Instead, as the *San Jose Mercury News* thoughtlessly put it, "Michael Phelps Shared Historic Night With African-American."

The most conventionally attractive women athletes have always received incommensurate media attention, from tennis great Helen Wills to swimmer Eleanor Holm and "Gorgeous Gussy" Moran, who competed at the 1949 Wimbledon tournament in what was then considered "shocking" lace panties. Anna Kournikova serves as a classic example in this regard. Despite having never won a major singles tournament, the Russian beauty enjoyed unprecedented endorsement deals, media attention (including a 2000 cover story in *Sports Illustrated* with a title reading, "She Won't Win the French Open, But Who Cares? Anna Kournikova Is Living Proof That Even in This Age of Supposed Enlightenment, a Hot Body Can Count as Much as a Good Backhand"), and became the Internet's most searched athlete in 2008, even though she had already retired from the game.[11] The "Kournikova syndrome," as pundits call it, privileges the most conventionally attractive women athletes on the basis of their looks rather than their talents.[12]

Representations of women athletes also include "hetero-sexy" or hypersexualized imagery. Perhaps the most obvious examples include women athletes who pose for soft-porn layouts in men's magazines such as *Playboy* or *Maxim;* the

Lingerie Football League (see Chapter 5); or teams that resort to selling nude or semi-nude calendars to fund their programs, as the Australian women's soccer team did in 2000. But even mainstream publications rely on sexed-up images of women athletes to sell copy.

NASCAR driver Danica Patrick has posed for these types of pictorials, yet she also struck back against the tendency to reduce athletes to their sex appeal, telling reporters, "I don't quite understand why, when you're referring to a girl—a female athlete in particular—that you have to use the word 'sexy.' Is there any other word you can use to describe me?" In response to her question, Fox 5 San Diego sports anchor Ross Shimbuku quipped, "Oh, I got a few words. . . . Starts with a B and it's not beautiful."[13] Shimbuku implied that Patrick is a "bitch" for capitalizing on her sex appeal while criticizing those who comment on it. Just the same, an athlete has every right to be taken seriously in the context of her sport, regardless of what she does outside it.

It is also important to remember that sportswomen are not (always) coerced into these types of depictions. Many athletes actively choose to present themselves in provocative ways, arguing that they are empowered by controlling their own image and are proud of the bodies for which they have worked so hard. As it currently stands, sport media provides few opportunities for women athletes to promote themselves. Rather than chastise individuals for appearing in provocative ways, it is important to examine the system that leaves these types of representation among sportswomen's few opportunities.

Are sportswomen of color treated differently in sport media?

When considering media representations of women athletes, sport sociologist Katherine M. Jamieson reminds us that "gender is never the only appropriate category of analysis, nor can it be the most significant, because it is always mediated by other systems of inequality."[14] When women of color make up a minority or marginalized segment of the population, "mainstream" journalists tend to represent non-white women differently—that is, when they represent them at all. Sometimes the differences are pronounced, and other times the differences are subtle.

For most of the twentieth century, the mainstream American media overlooked the accomplishments of women of color. Jim Crow segregation facilitated this neglect, but it also occurred in the coverage of ostensibly integrated sports. Women's track teams from Tuskegee Institute and Tennessee State University, both historically black colleges, registered phenomenal performances on national and international cinders (see Chapter 2). Yet, the media virtually ignored the exploits of Alice Coachman, Mae Faggs, Wilma Rudolph, and their talented teammates, opting instead to feature articles on white teams such as "Flamin' Mamie's Bouffant Bells" and the "uncommon beauty of its girls, who compete in dazzling uniforms, elaborate makeup and majestic hairdos." The Bells, the 1964 *Sports Illustrated* cover story continued, had "done more to promote women's track in the U.S. than if its members had, say, won the national AAU championships." Tuskegee and Tennessee State, teams that actually *had* won champions (along with a slew of Olympic medals), went virtually without notice.[15] Indeed, the magazine ignored women of color for far too long. In 1957, Althea Gibson became the first black sportswoman to appear on the cover of *Sports Illustrated*; it took another three decades for the magazine to feature a second, the incredible heptathlete Jackie Joyner-Kersee.

Although white sport media paid scant attention to women of color, many of these women became heroes in their local communities and earned great acclaim in specialized publications. Linda D. Williams found that black newspapers regularly sang the praises of black sportswomen and celebrated a wider range of activities for women than did white mainstream papers. This included considerable coverage of women in segregated sport, such as athletic programs at segregated schools, the United Golf Association, and the American Tennis Association. Black newspapers also sponsored women's leagues or teams in basketball, softball, and bowling. Perhaps the most famous of these was the *Philadelphia Tribune* Girls, a team that dominated amateur basketball in the 1930s and 1940s playing by "men's rules" (the five-player game; see Chapter 4).[16]

Allowing that mainstream publications have since increased their attention to black sportswomen, some of this attention unfortunately contributes to racial stereotypes. In basketball, for example, commentators perpetuate the myth of African Americans as "natural" athletes, which implies physical giftedness and de-emphasizes hard work, dedication, and intelligence.[17] Other problematic comments include those that highlight racialized physical differences, particularly those that do not align with white, Western feminine ideals. Women of color who conform to these ideals are more likely to receive media attention, corporate sponsorship, and commercial endorsements than women who do not. Journalists have critiqued—often in derogatory terms—the strong, muscular physiques of women such as Florence Griffith Joyner, Surya Bonaly, and Serena Williams. Black women's hair is another topic about which journalists believe they have a right to comment, whether it is the beaded braids of the Williams sisters, radio shock jock Don Imus referring to the Rutgers' women's basketball teams as "nappy-headed hos," or the scrutiny of Olympic gymnast Gabrielle Douglas's ponytail.[18]

The popular media also stereotypes Asian American sportswomen even though, as scholar Yomee Lee reminds us, there are many ethnic and cultural differences within the broad construction of "Asian."[19] Newspaper editors either forgot the complexity of this racialized category or overlooked the accomplishments of Filipina American diver Victoria Manalo Draves, who in 1948 became the first Asian American to win an Olympic gold medal. When Korean American diver Sammy

Lee died in 2016, the press feted him with that particular accolade.[20] Journalist Devin Israel Cabanilla criticized the neglect of Draves as both sexist and racist. Cabanilla interviewed psychologist E. J. R. David, who "pointed out that while Filipinos and South Asians compose half of all Asian Americans today, articles on 'Asian American' often only include people with East Asian ancestry—those with Chinese, Japanese and Korean ancestry."[21]

Another stereotype that has plagued Asian Americans is that they are "forever foreigners" who regardless of their time or birth in the United States can never fully assimilate. Media commentary during the 1992 Winter Olympic Games, highlighted the "foreignness" of US-born, fourth-generation Japanese American figure skater Kristi Yamaguchi by suggesting she shared "bloodlines" with Japan's Midori Ito.[22] This same type of ignorance manifested at the 1998 Winter Olympics when Michelle Kwan, a third-generation Chinese American figure skater, finished second to teammate Tara Lipinski. An MSNBC headline reported, "American Beats Out Kwan." Four years later, when Sarah Hughes edged out Kwan for the gold at the Salt Lake City Games, the *Seattle Times* declared, "American Outshines Kwan."[23]

As with athletes of Asian heritage, the popular press routinely homogenizes the tribal, national, ethnic, and cultural affiliations of Latina and Native American sportswomen. At the 2002 Winter Olympics, for example, NBC Sports' Tom Hammond referred to Karuk ice dancer Naomi Lang as the first Native American Olympian since Jim Thorpe, thus erasing the noteworthy performances of a number of Native American Olympians, including twin sisters Sharon and Shirley Firth, who competed in cross-country skiing at the 1972, 1976, 1980, and 1984 Games, and the 1904 women's "World Basketball Champions" from the Fort Shaw Indian Boarding School (see Chapter 2).

In the absence of overt stereotypes, elements of colorblind racism, subtle slurs, and the erasure of race and ethnicity abound, as Jamieson found in the coverage of Mexican American golfer Nancy Lopez.[24] Media scholar Cynthia M. Frisby likewise discovered a journalistic increase in microaggressions—indirect, pervasive insults that demean or denigrate an individual based on her social identities—directed toward sportswomen in general, but especially toward sportswomen of color.[25]

Are Muslim women treated differently in sport media?

As with any group, it is important not to overgeneralize Muslim sportswomen. As fencer Ibtihaj Muhammad explains, "We are conservatives and we are liberals. There are women who cover and women who don't. There are African-American Muslims, there are white Muslims—there are so many different types of Muslims."[26]

Nevertheless, sports activist Shireen Ahmed notes the media's disturbing tendency to homogenize Muslim sportswomen. Reporters fall back on recurring tropes, including mentioning the athletes' "country of origin, their father's opinion of sport, and any particular incident of violence against women that was unrelated to the said athlete but mentioned anyway due to similar faith or culture." In addition, journalists cannot seem to resist commentary on women who dress in identifiably Muslim clothing, including headscarves and modest sportswear. As Ahmed notes, "We don't refer to any other athlete who observes a faith by a religious accessory, be it a necklace or tattoo featuring a cross, the Star of David, or a 'Karma' symbol." Identifying an athlete as a "hijabi sportswoman" not only takes away from her athleticism but also perpetuates what Ahmed calls "gendered Islamophobia." Finally, Ahmed reminds readers that "Muslim women are completely capable of writing about themselves."[27] For example, Iranian journalist Solmaz Sharif founded *Shirzanan* ("female heroes" in Persian), an online media and advocacy platform for and about Muslim women in sport.

Are there any significant themes that emerge in the media
coverage of parasport or female athletes with impairments?

There are online outlets and journals devoted to disability sport, such as *Ability, Challenge, Deaf Sports Review, New Mobility, Palaestra,* and *Sports n' Spokes,* but there is very little coverage of disability sport in the so-called mainstream media. Even the Paralympic Games receive relatively limited attention. To date, few studies have addressed sex and gender differences in parasport, contributing to the invisibility and symbolic annihilation of sportswomen with impairments.[28] Media exposure is important because it not only highlights phenomenal athleticism and competition but also helps breakdown stereotypes of people with impairments as weak, frail, or dis-abled. Yet, what little coverage there is too often reinforces stereotypes through ableist frameworks and "othering" processes.

According to disability sport scholars Andrew Smith and Nigel Thomas, para athletes "tend to be portrayed as 'victims' or 'courageous' people who 'overcome' the 'painful' experience of disability in order to participate in sport."[29] Celebrating personal triumphs is not necessarily harmful, but it can imply that anyone—with enough pluck and determination—can succeed. This not only neglects the historical and systematic barriers to achievement, but also blames individuals for their own "failures."

Another problematic representation is when media stories frame para athletes as "supercrips," a term defined by sociologist Ronald J. Berger as "individuals whose inspirational stories of courage, dedication, and hard work prove that it can be done, that one can defy the odds and accomplish the impossible."[30] This reinforces the athletes' status as "other," creates a standard that most individuals with disabilities cannot meet, and fails to acknowledge the social barriers with which individuals with impairments must contend.

Disability activists are also critical of depictions that verge on "inspiration porn," which scholar Jan Grue explains in three parts:

> (a) An image of a person with visible signs of impairment who is (b) performing a physical activity, preferably displaying signs of physical prowess, and is (c) accompanied by a caption that directs the viewer to be inspired by the image in question.[31]

Finally, the limited media coverage of parasport tends to favor "aesthetically pleasing" athletes, finding them more marketable and telegenic than athletes with "severe impairments." Such favoritism marginalizes certain competitors and impairments and shapes public perceptions about parasport.[32] The inclusion of more people with impairments within the media—as journalists, photographers, editors, and producers, as examples—may make a difference in reportage.

To improve some of these issues, the International Paralympic Committee created a guide to help journalists report on athletes with *impairments* (the IPC advises against the term *disabilities*). The guide recommends the use of "people-first language" to identify the person before the impairment, as in "an athlete with an impairment" instead of an "impaired athlete." Other recommendations include avoiding emotional wording such as "tragic," "victim," or "confined to a wheelchair," which emphasize an athlete's limitations as opposed to her abilities. Conversely, referring to athletes with impairments as "extraordinary" or "superhuman" suggests that "the original expectations were not high."[33] And of course, everyone, journalists included, should avoid ableist language—that is, terminology (e.g., "stupid," "moron," "crippled," "lame," "maniac," "spaz," and "retarded") that denigrates and perpetuates prejudice.

Has new and electronic media changed the coverage of women's sport?

Traditional media forms devote more feature articles to sportsmen and prioritize the placement, scheduling, and production of men's sport. As alternatives, there have been multiple attempts to create media outlets dedicated to women's sport, all of which are now defunct (including *womenSports, The Sports Woman, Sports for Women, Real Sports,* and *Sports Illustrated for Women*). New media has succeeded where earlier attempts have failed, and it has provided unparalleled capacities to democratize and globalize sport. Those wanting to watch women's sports can seek out live streaming and other online outlets if they cannot find coverage on television. Women bloggers, argue sport media scholars Dunja Antunovic and Marie Hardin, "offer an alternative approach and, thus, may challenge the masculine understanding of performance-oriented institutionalized sports."[34] To be brief, new electronic media has fundamentally changed the sporting landscape.

In 2010, ESPN, Inc. launched espnW as a blog and, the following year, converted the blog to a website "to serve, inform and inspire today's female athlete and fan." There are two ways to think about this. On the one hand, researchers have determined that espnW portrays women athletes as serious and competent competitors and provides an alternative to the sexism of mainstream outlets.[35] On the other hand, sites such as espnW may create a niche market that further segments sports media; absolves ESPN from increasing its attention to women fans, athletes, and sports; and positions "today's female athlete and fan" as separate and different from today's male athlete and fan.[36]

Social media has also changed the tenor of sport communication. Observers declared the 2012 London Olympics to be the "first social media games," as athletes took to Twitter and Facebook in significant numbers. Sportswomen use these platforms for personal brand development, money-making opportunities, to connect with fans, to engage in

self-representation and promotion, and to subvert traditionally mediated themes. One refreshing outcome of the sexism in
2016 Olympic coverage (see Chapter 7) was that social media
gave critics an immediate and public way to denounce it.

Video games are another form of commercial sport media
that significantly privilege male athletes. Slowly, however,
women are starting to appear in virtual competitions in
volleyball, hockey, tennis, golf, and the Ultimate Fighting
Championship. In 2015, Electronic Arts' soccer video game,
FIFA 16, included women's national teams for the first
time since its 1993 debut. Still, most games are "a sea of
maleness," as one reporter described them. The only women
in Madden 16, a popular NFL game, were cheerleaders. Even
the computer-generated spectators were all men, despite the
fact that women comprise nearly half of the NFL's real-life
audience.[37]

What is the status of women in sport journalism?

Sport and the media joined together in the nineteenth century
in a mutually beneficial relationship. There have always been
women sport journalists, albeit in decidedly small numbers.
As sport journalism grew throughout the twentieth century,
the number of women in the business remained low.

In the early 1970s, the Associated Press estimated that
there were only twenty-five women writing about sport for
American newspapers and just five women in sport television broadcasting.[38] Women made headway during this time,
earning spots as beat writers (newspaper journalists assigned
to a specific sport), sideline reporters, and broadcast analysts.
Still, they faced overwhelming discrimination. Many organizations and fellow male journalists did not allow women entry
in the press box. Owners and athletes worked hard to keep
women out of men's locker rooms. Athletes refused to take the
women seriously.

Although things have improved for women journalists, they remain the minority in virtually every country in the world. According to the 2017 Women's Media Center report, women make up just 11.3 percent of all American sport columnists and 12.6 percent of sport reporters. Women of color are especially under-represented in these positions. The study identified 0.6 percent of sport columnists as African American women, 0.3 percent as Latina, and 0.3 percent as Asian. In terms of sport reporters, the study identified 1 percent as African American, 0.3 percent as Latina, and 0.5 percent as Asian.[39]

The numbers are not much better with regard to television. In the network news and highlight shows that Cooky, Messner, and Musto analyzed, 95 percent of anchors and co-anchors were men. Men also made up 96 percent of sports analysts, whereas women's highest representation ranked in at 14.4 percent of ancillary reporters.[40]

What types of challenges do women sport journalists face?

Studies show that women sport journalists have to deal with specific types of prejudice that their male colleagues do not. One survey determined that 85 percent of women in sport media reported that sex discrimination is a problem in the profession, 87 percent believed they had a tougher job than male journalists, and 60 percent believed that sport fans and media consumers did not take women journalists as seriously as men journalists.[41] It is rare for television networks to hire women as play-by-play or color analysts in big-time sport. More likely, producers assign women to sideline reporting, short feature segments, or to cover non-revenue sports. Research finds that women have to work harder for promotions that rarely materialize and are typically paid less than their male counterparts.

Women must also repeatedly prove their credibility because of the assumption that they lack the necessary sports knowledge for the job. In 2002, *60 Minutes* correspondent Andy Rooney remarked, in an interview with Larry King,

The only thing that really bugs me about television's coverage [of football] is those damn women they have down on the sidelines who do not know what the hell they are talking about. I mean, I am not a sexist person, but a woman has no business being down there trying to make some comment about a football game.

Rooney's supporters dismissed the remark as characteristic of his curmudgeonly persona, or his age, or that he was just trying to be funny. Unfortunately, Rooney gave voice to what many men felt: Keep women out of football and men's sports in general.

This sentiment reared its ugly head in 2017 when Beth Mowins became the first woman in thirty years to call an NFL game. While her performance earned high praise from her peers, social media lit up with comments from men who simply hated the sound of her voice. As veteran NFL reporter Andrea Kremer assessed, "I have no doubt that 'hating the sound of her voice' is code for 'I hate that there was a woman announcing football.'"[42] At the same time, journalist Kavitha Davidson had a different reaction to Mowins's voice—a "visceral feeling of hearing someone who sounded like me occupying the booth." Drawing attention to just a few of the countless girls and women who rejoiced in the moment, Davidson continued, "If something as seemingly unassuming as a woman calling a nationally televised NFL game can at once anger and inspire at the level it did last night, she's absolutely doing something right."[43]

Jessica Mendoza must also be doing something right. In 2015, the Olympic gold medalist and former professional softball player became Major League Baseball's (MLB) first female analyst on national television. But despite her credentials and obvious baseball acumen, critics just did not want a woman commenting on the national pastime. "No lady needs to be on espn [sic] talking during a baseball game specially Mendoza sorry," tweeted a minor league player. One radio personality dismissed Mendoza as "Tits McGhee," as if her breasts undercut any authority she might have. The pressure is high for minorities in any field. Responding to the vitriol, Mendoza commented, "You can't say, 'This is not a big deal,' because it is. Not just for me, but for my entire gender. If you screw this up, Jess, this door is gonna close."

Women reporters face further discrimination when it comes to their physical appearance. Television network executives frequently hire women based on their looks and sex appeal rather than their knowledge and experience, which adds fuel for those who already doubt women's credibility. The same is true for men's magazines and websites that publish lists of the "hottest" and "sexiest" women sports reporters. Because of this type of attention, older women, despite their capabilities, lose their jobs to younger women as networks attempt to cater to their key demographic: 18- to 34-year-old men. In 2014, Fox Sports demoted 53-year-old African American Pam Oliver from her NFL sideline gig and replaced her with a white 36-year-old, Erin Andrews. Critics alleged both racism and ageism in the decision. As Oliver later remarked, "Some asked, 'Do you think it had something to do with your race?' No. I definitely do not. Others asked, 'Does it have something to do with your age?' Well, maybe." As she rightly points out, "It's not difficult to notice that the new on-air people there are all young, blond and 'hot.'"[44]

Women reporters must additionally contend with sexual harassment and sexual violence. Male colleagues, athletes, coaches, agents, and sports executives have catcalled women reporters and made sexual comments, innuendos, and advances. During a television interview, for example, Jamaican cricketer Chris Gayle asked reporter Mel McLauglin out for drinks, telling her "don't blush, baby." Gayle later defended his actions, stating, "But you're a woman in an environment with men. You're good-looking. What do you expect?"[45] The following year, tennis player Maxime Hamou repeatedly tried to grope and kiss Eurosport journalist Maly Thomas during a live televised interview. The French Tennis Federation revoked Hamou's accreditation for the remainder of the French Open, but Thomas's in-studio colleagues laughed and clapped as she dodged his advances. It is as if men forget that these are professional women in the workplace. Maybe they just don't care.

These sorts of stories, many of which women do not report for fear of reprisal, happen too frequently. Journalists Julie DiCaro and Sarah Spain devised a unique way of confronting the barrage of misogynistic remarks directed to them on Twitter, Facebook, and Reddit. They filmed a public service announcement titled "#MoreThanMean," in which they sat across from men who read aloud comments the women had received. The men in the video did not write the words, but they still had difficulty repeating them in the presence of the women. When the men got to statements such as "I hope you get raped again" and "I hope your boyfriend beats you," Spain wrote, "Their hands shook, they began to sweat and they squirmed in their seats. Every single one apologized to me after reading the comments, wondering aloud how anyone could possibly think such awful things, never mind type and send them." Yet these are the types of messages that women journalists receive with alarming regularity.[46]

Are women journalists allowed in men's locker rooms?

Yes, primarily due to the efforts of several pioneering women in the 1970s. *New York Times* reporter Robin Herman convinced the National Hockey League (NHL) to allow women in the locker room following the 1975 All-Star Game. Not long after that, however, MLB Commissioner Bowie Kuhn formally opposed the practice. In 1977, baseball executives denied entrance to *Sports Illustrated* reporter Melissa Ludke and instead brought individual players into the hallway to talk with her. Time, Inc., the parent company of *Sports Illustrated*, filed a lawsuit against Kuhn. A federal judge in New York ruled that MLB's policy violated the Equal Protection Clause of the 14th Amendment to the US Constitution, a decision that opened the locker room door to Ludke and other women.

Yet, even after the Ludke case, women reporters found that the supposed sanctity of men's locker rooms seemed to license bad, bullying, and sometimes criminal behavior. Players cursed at Jane Gross, the first female reporter to enter a men's basketball locker room, and poured a bucket of water over her head during an interview. Athletes have groped and manhandled women journalists in attempts to intimidate and humiliate them. Women recount athletes picking them up and carrying them out of space, verbally and sexually harassing them, and refusing to talk with them.[47] Most athletes, coaches, and team owners conduct themselves with decorum and professionalism when it comes to female reporters, yet too many remain silent, and therefore complicit, in the face of bad behavior.

In one of the more egregious incidents, members of the NFL's 1990 New England Patriots exposed themselves and fondled their genitals in front of the *Boston Herald*'s Lisa Olson as they threatened her with vulgar and sexually explicit language. After the incident went public, and rather than condemning the players' behavior, Patriots owner Victor Kiam dismissed Olson as a "classic bitch," adding, "No wonder the players can't stand her." NFL commissioner Paul Tagliabue subsequently levied fines against the accused Patriot players after an investigation determined that they had indeed "degraded and humiliated" her. Still, public reactions to the case were appalling. Attackers besieged Olson with hate mail and death threats. Vandals slashed her tires and burglarized her apartment. Olson, fearing for her safety, relocated to Australia.[48]

Despite the progress women reporters have made over the years, the men's locker room continues to be a source of controversy. In 2013, Canadian hockey commentator Don Cherry stated emphatically that he did not "believe that women should be in the male dressing room." Two years later, an usher tried to stop three credentialed women journalists from entering the locker room following an NFL game. The crux of the issue is that if men journalists are allowed in the locker room and women are not, then women do not have the same access to athletes and their reporting will suffer by comparison. If men can enter changing rooms, talk with players, and file their stories by deadline, but women cannot do the same, why would any editor hire women sports reporters? Women are already the minority in sport journalism, and denying them entry into men's locker rooms would exacerbate the problem.

There are other solutions. Journalist Jason Whitlock suggests that the locker room is no place for any reporter, male or female. ESPN's Suzy Kolber advocates for a neutral spot outside the changing area for all post-game interviews. And, for the record, male reporters are allowed in some women's locker rooms. The WNBA, for instance, has the same rules as the NBA, which opens the space to reporters at designated times. NCAA institutions can make their own access rules for collegiate basketball during the regular season. There are women's teams and leagues with media policies that do not grant reporters locker room access, but those policies extend to all journalists, regardless of sex.

Even so, rules and policies designed to ensure sex equality in sport media are few and far between. Because of the coverage of women athletes and women's sport, in terms of both quantity and quality, they remain the "other"—different from and inferior to men athletes and men's sports. The othering process is further compounded by issues of race, ethnicity, religion, and impairment, along with "other systems of inequality," as Jamieson states. The same power dynamics play out in sport journalism, such that consumers grow not only accustomed to a male voice of authority but also intolerant of any deviation from that norm. Until all women are represented fairly and equitably in all aspects of sport media, it will remain, as critics have characterized it, "a sea of maleness" or, more simply, "dude time."

9

PROFESSIONAL OPPORTUNITIES

What is the status of women in coaching positions?

Before the passage of Title IX in 1972, women coached more than 90 percent of women's intercollegiate teams. In 2016, just over 40 percent of those programs had a woman at the helm. According to the 2017 report "Gender, Race, and LGBT Inclusion of Head Coaches of Women's Teams," 88 percent of the coaches for NCAA Division I women's teams were white, 7 percent were African American, less than 3 percent were Latina/o, and 2 percent were of Asian descent.[1]

The coaching situation for women is even worse in the lower levels of sport. Only 27.5 percent of all American high school coaches are women.[2] And more than 6.5 million adults coach youth sport teams up to the age of fourteen years, yet only 27 percent of those coaches are women, according to the 2016 Aspen Institute's Project Play survey.[3] In no uncertain terms, women are significantly under-represented in all coaching ranks in the United States.

In a strange turn, women coaches have become victims of the success of girls and women in sport. The growing prestige and money in distaff athletic programs made them attractive opportunities to male coaches. Studies show that homophobia, gender bias, and sexism also play a role in limiting the number of women coaches. These attitudes come from both men and women, and research finds that the majority of female athletes express a preference for male coaches.[4] Other factors contributing to the relatively low percentage of women coaches include the power and exclusivity of the "old boys" network, the difficulties associated with women striking a work–life balance, the responsibilities of motherhood, and the lack of networking and mentorship opportunities. Women coaches report that they are paid substantially less than men, have more difficulty negotiating salary increases and promotions, and worry that speaking out against these practices will have negative repercussions on their careers.[5]

The deficit in women coaches matters. Girls and women who do not have women coaches are less likely to think that coaching is a viable profession for them.[6] It also matters to boys and men, very few of who have opportunities to play for female coaches. In college sport, across all divisions, women are the head coaches in just 3 percent of men's programs. There have been some high-profile stories of women coaching high school boys' programs (journalists seem to especially like it when women coach boys' football teams), but this rarely happens. "Boys are denied the ability to see women operate in leadership roles that males most respect," explains Tom Farrey, the head of the Sports and Society Program at the Aspen Institute, "This has deep implications for our society as boys grow into adulthood, work with, and decide whether to empower, women."[7]

There is a clear double standard: It is culturally acceptable—even preferred—for men to coach women, but the inverse is not true. As Stanford University women's basketball coach Tara Vanderveer asked, "Anytime someone hires a male coach and says, 'Coaching is coaching,' well, why aren't more women in men's basketball?"[8] Yet, when CBS Sports reporters polled a group of anonymous coaches about whether a woman will ever coach an NCAA Division I men's basketball team, 42 percent responded no. "A big part of being a college coach is molding boys into successful men," answered one of the respondents, "Obviously a woman can't do that. I just don't see a place for it." Men's programs that do not consider women coaches put themselves at a disadvantage, reasons economist David Berri: "If only men are considered for jobs coaching male teams, then half the population has been excluded. And that means the odds of finding the best possible coaches are lower than they have to be."[9]

It is particularly rare to find a woman coach in professional men's sports. Becky Hammon, a former WNBA standout, became the first full-time woman coach in any of the major US men's sports when she joined the staff of the NBA's San Antonio Spurs in 2014. The Spurs named Hammon the head coach of the Spurs' summer league team, which she led to the 2015 Las Vegas Summer League title. That same year, the NFL's Arizona Cardinals hired Jen Welter to coach inside linebackers during training camp and preseason, making her the first woman coach in the league. The following season, Kathryn Smith became the NFL's first full-time female coach when she joined the Buffalo Bills as special teams' quality control in 2016, the same year that the NHL's Arizona Coyotes hired Dawn Braid as a skating coach. Katie Sowers joined the San Francisco 49ers' staff in 2017, making her both the NFL's second full-time woman coach and the first openly gay coach in any men's professional team sport. As she explained to *Outsports*,

> There are so many people who identify as LGBT in the NFL, as in any business, that do not feel comfortable being public about their sexual orientation. The more we can create an environment that welcomes all types of people, no matter their race, gender, sexual orientation, religion, the more we can help ease the pain and burden that many carry every day.[10]

Tennis pro Andy Murray is one male athlete who believes in hiring the best coach, regardless of sex. He grew up under the tutelage of his mother, Judy Murray, a well-respected coach. Still, many tennis insiders (and outsiders, it stands to reason) criticized his choice to hire former champion Amélie Mauresmo in 2015. As Murray told *The Telegraph*,

> Some argue, "Oh, well, she's a woman, so she can't understand the men's game." But then how can a man understand the women's game? I obviously grew up getting coached by my mum, so I didn't see any issue. But even when I came on the professional tour, there were no men coached by women, so looking for a coach, you assume you're looking for a man, but when you get older you realize, "well, no, it doesn't have to be that way."[11]

What is the status of women in other positions of authority in sport?

In 2013, *Sports Illustrated* published its list of the "50 Most Powerful People in Sports." Forty-eight of the entries were men, including team owners, CEOs, executive directors, anti-doping authorities, entrepreneurs, league commissioners, sportscasters, and media moguls. There were just three women on the list: Coca-Cola marketing executives Alison Lewis and Sharon Byers shared a spot and Cindy Davis, who held a similar position with Nike golf (Nike has since discontinued its golf line).

Indeed, women are under-represented at all levels of leadership as Women on Boards determined in its 2016 "Gender Balance of Global Sport Report."[12] There is a shortage of women in Olympic and Paralympic leadership positions and in major International Sport Federations (see Chapter 7). Few women own professional teams, represent professional athletes as agents, serve as president or CEO of major sports leagues, or serve as athletic directors in scholastic or intercollegiate sport. Nationwide, an estimated 15 percent of all high school athletic directors are women.[13] In the 2016–2017 academic year, there were 1,135 athletic directors in all divisions of college sport; just 222 (approximately 20 percent) were women, and 87 percent of those women identified as white. At Football Bowl Subdivision schools (Division I programs characterized by "big time" college football), women accounted for less than 7 percent of athletic directors, and until the University of Nevada, Las Vegas hired Desiree Reed-Francois in 2017, there were no women of color. [14]

Umpires, referees, and officials represent other authority figures in sport. It is becoming more common for women to officiate girls and women's sport, although data are lacking to speak in terms of definitive numbers. Youth and high school administrators frequently decry a shortage of qualified officials, yet women seem to remain an untapped resource.[15] Slightly more is known about women officiating men's sport, primarily because these occasions strike journalists as unusual and therefore newsworthy. Sadly, among these stories are extreme incidents of sexism. In 2008, for example, St. Mary's Academy, a private Catholic school in Kansas, refused to let basketball referee Michelle Campbell on the court. Her role "would have put a woman in a position of authority," speculated *Athletic Business*, "which apparently runs contrary to the school's philosophy."[16]

A woman on the court seemed to run contrary to coach LaVar Ball's personal philosophy as well. At the AAU's Adidas Uprising Summer Championships in 2017, a female official, who also calls Division I women's games, gave Ball a technical foul for complaining about a call. Ball pulled his team off the court and threatened to forfeit unless tournament administrators replaced her. After a ten-minute, on-court deliberation, an Adidas representative complied, substituting a man her place. Another (male) official later gave Ball another technical foul and ejected him from the game, but Ball still went on a misogynistic postgame rant about "girl refs," calling the slighted official "a woman trying to break into the game" who "needs to stay in her lane."[17] The Court Club Elite, which provided officials for the tournament, condemned "the agenda and lack of courage to do the right thing by Adidas leadership" and terminated its five-year affiliation with the company.[18]

Yet, for every extreme, overt incident of sexism, there are countless subtle affronts that chip away at women's authority and their desire to pursue officiating. In professional sports, neither the NHL nor MLB has ever employed a woman official. Women have refereed spring training games and minor league baseball games, including Bernice Gera, a forerunner in this regard. In 1967, Gera enrolled in the Florida Baseball School, where she reportedly excelled. In 1969, unable to secure work, she filed a sex discrimination case against the National Association of Baseball Leagues. Three years later, she won her suit and became the first woman to umpire a men's professional baseball game—a class A minor league doubleheader. Discouraged by the sexist reactions from coaches, her fellow referees, and others, Gera resigned between games.

The NBA has been slightly more progressive than other organizations by hiring referees Violet Palmer and Dee Kanter in 1997, but it was not until 2014 that the league hired a third female official, Lauren Holtkamp. NFL administrators have unveiled a Women Officiating Now program as part of the NFL's Football Officiating Academy and in 2015 hired Sarah Thomas as the first female official in professional football.

In addition to officiating initiatives, NFL commissioner Roger Goodell announced that the league would initiate a type of "Rooney Rule" that requires interviewing women for all executive positions. Established in 2003, the Rooney Rule, named for former Pittsburgh Steelers owner and chairman of the NFL's diversity committee Dan Rooney, requires teams to interview racial and ethnic minority candidates when searching for head coaches and senior football operations positions. Since then, other leagues and industries have adopted similar policies. If enacted, these sorts of statutes will not ensure that sports organizations hire women in positions of authority, but they will give women a foot in the door—something they have lacked for too long.

Are there any professional sports in which women earn the same amount of money as men?

Yes. As just a few examples, the World Squash Championships, International Volleyball Federation beach volleyball, the World Surf League, and several World Marathon Majors have started awarding equal prize money to male and female champions. Before that, tennis was among the first sports to equalize pay, at least at Grand Slam events (Australian Open, Roland Garros/ French Open, Wimbledon, and the US Open) and a few major tournaments. Equality, however, did not come easily. Before 1968, these tournaments were only open to amateur players. Tennis's subsequent "open era" allowed professionals to compete as well, which drew attention to the staggering inequalities in prize money. At major tennis tournaments, men outearned women by a ratio of 2.5 to 1. At lesser events, that ratio grew to 5, 8, and even 12 to 1. At the 1970 Italian Open, Ilie Nastase, the men's singles champion, won $3,500, whereas the women's champion, Billie Jean King, received just $600. That same year, the Pacific Southwest tournament offered $12,500 and $1,500 to the male and the female winner, respectively.

In response, nine women (King, Peaches Bartkowicz, Rosemary Casals, Kristy Pigeon, Judy Tegart Dalton, Julie Heldman, Kerry Melville Reid, Nancy Richey, and Valerie Ziegenfuss) decided that they had had enough. The "Original 9" took their grievances to Gladys Heldman, a former player and the founder, publisher, and editor of *World Tennis*. Heldman organized a separate event, which the United States Lawn Tennis Association (USLTA) refused to sanction. By breaking away from their parent organization, the women risked "career suicide," as King characterized it, and yet they persevered. More women joined what became the Virginia Slims Tennis Circuit, and the players worked tirelessly to make the tour a success. They later unionized to establish the Women's Tennis Association and, together, negotiated for higher pay before realigning with the USLTA. As a result, the 1973 US Open was the first major tennis tournament to equalize prize money.

Still, it took another twenty-eight years for the second Grand Slam, the Australian Open, to bestow men and women the same awards. In 2006, the French Open followed suit, but Wimbledon lagged behind, which understandably grated on the sensibilities of many players, including Venus Williams. The day before Williams won the 2005 Wimbledon title, she addressed the board of the All England Lawn Tennis and Croquet Club (AELTCC), which runs the tournament. "Close your eyes," she told those in attendance,

> Imagine you're a little girl. You're growing up. You practice as hard as you can, with girls, with boys. You have a dream. You fight, you work, you sacrifice to get to this stage. You work as hard as anyone you know. And then you get to this stage, and you're told you're not the same as a boy. Almost as good, but not quite the same. Think how devastating and demoralizing that could be.[19]

It was a moving speech, but still the AETCC did not balance the prize money.

The following year, Williams published an op-ed in the *London Times*, arguing that pay disparity had repercussions outside of the sport: "The message I like to convey to women and girls across the globe is that there is no glass ceiling. My fear is that Wimbledon is loudly and clearly sending the opposite message."[20] She kept fighting until AELTCC conceded, and in 2007, Venus Williams won her fourth Wimbledon championship to earn $1.4 million—precisely the same amount earned by the men's champion, Roger Federer.

Despite the changes at these major tournaments, pay inequality persists at tennis's smaller events. For instance, at the

2015 Western & Southern Open in Mason, Ohio, the fourth-largest tennis tournament in the United States, Federer, the men's champion, won $731,000; women's champion Serena Williams made $495,000 for her victory. To that end, *New York Times* journalist Ben Rothenberg analyzed the top 100 earners on the men's and women's tours and found that women netted roughly 80 percent of what men earned (the same pay gap, incidentally, found in the American workplace).[21] In addition, men consistently reap greater financial rewards off the court through sponsorships and endorsement deals.

In what sports are pay disparities between men and women athletes the widest?

In 2017, BBC Sport released a global study that analyzed forty-four prize-money sports, finding parity in beach volleyball, windsurfing, figure skating, judo, wheelchair tennis, cross-country skiing, and several other sports.[22] In point of fact, thirty-five of the sports analyzed in the study (83 percent) paid male and female champions equal prize money, although the governing bodies for ice hockey and basketball did not respond to the survey, and researchers did not consider wages, bonuses, or sponsorships in their calculations—all of which significantly skew the numbers. *Forbes'* annual list of the Top 100 World's Highest Paid Athletes filled in the gaps by taking into account the salaries, prize money, and bonuses of athletes from twenty-one countries in eleven sports. The 2017 list included 99 men. Ranking number 51, Serena Williams was the only woman.[23]

Some of the largest pay gaps are found in professional cricket, cliff diving, cycling, ski jumping, golf, soccer, hockey, and basketball. The total prize money for the 2014 PGA tour was over $340 million, for example, more than five times as much as the 2015 LPGA tour. The winner of the 2015 US

Women's Open, Chun In-gee, won $810,000; Jordan Spieth, the winner of the men's Open, won $1.8 million.[24]

There are similar disparities in professional soccer. The men's German national team netted $35 million for winning the 2014 World Cup. In comparison, the US women, who won the title in 2015, received just $2 million. What is worse, the US men received four times that amount—for losing in the first round of the 2014 tournament. In the United Kingdom, Steph Houghton was the best-paid female player of 2015, earning approximately £65,000 (just over $85,000 USD) a year, while the best-paid male player, Wayne Rooney, received £300,000 (nearly $400,000) *per week*.[25]

Meanwhile, Marta Vieria da Silva (or Marta, as she as known) was the FIFA World Player of the Year an unprecedented five times in a row (2006–2010). Yet, she has struggled to find a stable professional league to showcase her talents. Seven of the eight professional teams on her resume have folded for financial reasons. The owners of one of those teams, Santos Futebol Feminino, ceased operations so that the men's Santos Futebol Club could raise the salary of its star player, Neymar da Silva Santos Júnior. The women's entire operating budget had been $667,000. Neymar made $447,000 a month.[26]

Throughout the world, women soccer players have registered their opposition to pay inequalities. Norwegian women have been the most successful. The Norwegian Football Association announced that, as of 2018, the women would earn the same as the men, but only after members of the men's national team players agreed to forfeit 550,000 kroner ($69,000 USD) a year in marketing payments to the women's national team.

Other teams have not been so fortunate. The Danish Women's National Team went on strike in 2017, missing a World Cup qualifying match with the Netherlands, after almost a year of stalled negotiations with the Danish Football Association. The Matildas, Australia's national team, similarly boycotted its 2015 training camp and canceled a sold-out

US tour after Football Federation Australia refused to raise salaries that were well below the national minimum wage. On the professional stage, Australian women reached a collective bargaining agreement in 2017 that increased the W-League's minimum salary, provided income protection for injured players, and granted a new maternity policy.

Similar lobbying took place on American soil when five players on the Women's National Soccer Team filed a wage discrimination suit against the US Soccer Federation. The women pointed out that their team generated nearly $20 million more revenue than the men's team during the previous season, yet the federation paid women approximately one-fourth of what the men received. The women's team had won three World Cups since FIFA first held the tournament in 1992; American men have never advanced past the quarterfinals.[27]

After more than a year of negotiating, the US Soccer Federation agreed to increase women's pay and bonuses and to improve their travel accommodations, although the terms do not bring them up to par with the men. Inspired by the case, the US Women's Hockey Team successfully threatened to boycott the 2017 International Ice Hockey Federation Women's World Championship, forcing USA Hockey to improve its financing of female athletes. Still, they are vastly outearned by men on the US national hockey teams, who also typically play in the NHL, in which the minimum salary is more than $500,000. Women can play in the National Women's Hockey League, established in 2015, but salaries are low: They ranged between $10,000 and $26,000 until the middle of the 2016 season, when league officials announced they would slash all wages in half due to low attendance.[28]

Conversely, players in the National Women's Soccer League (NWSL) saw their minimum salaries *double* from $7,200 in 2016 to roughly $15,000 in 2017 (incidentally, there were ten NWSL teams in 2017, only one of which had a female head coach). Playing for the Orlando Pride, Marta made the league maximum of $41,000, but most players do not make a living wage and are forced to take on other jobs, live with host families, or play in overseas leagues to supplement their meager incomes. The salary issue influenced Marta's former Pride teammate, Maddy Evans, to retire from the NWSL. "I've made it work for the past five years," Evans told the *Philadelphia Inquirer,* "I'm thankful that I was able to be paid, albeit not a huge amount, to do what I love—I'm very thankful for that—but it is difficult."[29] In comparison, the men's professional organization in the United States, Major League Soccer (MLS), pays a minimum salary of $60,000. At just over $7 million, Marta's Brazilian compatriot, Ricard Izecson dos Santos Leite (who goes by Kaká) of Orlando City, is MLS's highest paid player.[30]

Women in the WNBA also have to be creative about making ends meet. In 2015, the minimum salary was $38,913; the NBA minimum, by comparison, was $525,093. The *average* WNBA salary is $77,000, compared to $5.8 million in the NBA (of the twelve WNBA head coaches in 2017, there were five women and the league president was Lisa Borders). Men must be one year removed from high school to be NBA draft-eligible, but women must be at least twenty-two years old and have no remaining collegiate eligibility to enter the WNBA draft. There are positive and negative aspects to this stipulation, but it does hinder women's lifetime earning potential in professional sport. Moreover, professional opportunities are few and far between. NCAA data show that of the 16,593 women playing collegiate basketball in 2016, 3,687 were eligible for the draft. The WNBA draft picked up just 35 (3.2 percent) of those players.[31]

Those who go undrafted can take their talents overseas to the approximately twenty professional women's leagues operating in more than eighteen countries. Even WNBA players, whose season runs from June to September, take advantage of the global marketplace. Phoenix Mercury star Diana Taurasi, who became the WNBA's all-time leading scorer in 2017, made the WNBA's maximum salary—just over $100,000. In 2015, the Russian Premier League team UMMC Ekaterinburg, for which

Taurasi plays in the winter, paid her $1.5 million to sit out the WNBA season.

How do the WNBA and other professional women's leagues survive?

The WNBA is not the first women's professional basketball league in the United States. That distinction belongs to the Women's Professional Basketball League that lasted from 1978 to 1981. In 1996, following the success of the US Women's Olympic basketball team, the American Basketball League (ABL) began operations. It lasted just over two seasons. Unable to secure television exposure, sponsorship deals, and to compete with the WNBA, ABL executives folded shop in 1998. The WNBA might have met a similar fate if not for its partnership with the NBA.

Established in 1996, the WNBA is the longest continuously running professional league for women's team sports. The success of the US women's national team at the 1996 Olympic Games convinced NBA commissioner David Stern and his board of governors to introduce a women's division. Val Ackerman, a woman who moved on to become the commissioner of the NCAA's Big East Conference, served as the WNBA's first commissioner. Originally, the NBA owned the eight WNBA charter teams, all of which were located in cities with an NBA franchise. That arrangement changed in 2003 to allow for individual team ownership. As a result, some WNBA teams are owned independently and exist in cities without an NBA presence, and some teams have formal partnerships with NBA counterparts.

Despite support from the men's league, the WNBA has struggled financially. As a result, teams have folded, relocated, and dropped roster spots. Half of the twelve WNBA teams lose money and attendance is low—regularly registering well below 10,000 spectators per game (an NBA game draws almost 18,000). Revenue is the primary factor in dictating players' salaries. The NBA netted $5.18 billion in 2015, whereas the WNBA earned an estimated $35 million.[32]

Rather than directly compare the two leagues, however, it may be more instructive to weigh them based on where they stood at the time of their respective twentieth anniversaries. Founded in 1946, the NBA started with eleven teams, few of which survive today in their original form. Initial salaries were low, and players took on additional jobs in the offseason. For decades, the NBA struggled with sponsorship, media coverage, and prejudice. At the dawn of its twentieth season, the league drew an average audience of just 6,000—approximately one-third of what it does today and considerably less than the average WNBA draw.[33] Without question, the WNBA could not survive without the subsidies and support from the NBA, but it may be just a matter of time before the WNBA can stand on its own.

In many of the same ways, women's soccer has had difficulty digging its cleats into the turf of professional sports. Following the popularity of the 1999 Women's World Cup, organizers launched the Women's United Soccer Association. It lasted just three seasons (2001–2003) and lost $100 million. A new league, Women's Professional Soccer, debuted in 2009. It also folded after three seasons. The next year, the US Soccer Federation introduced the National Women's Soccer League (NWSL). Similar to the WNBA–NBA arrangement, teams in the NWSL are affiliated with the MLS, which organizers hope will make this iteration of women's professional soccer more stable and viable. The league also has arrangements with the US Soccer Federation, the Canadian Soccer Association, and the Mexican Football Federation to subsidize the NWSL salaries of their respective national team players.

English women's soccer has also benefited from partnering with established men's teams. In 2011, the English Football Association (FA) established the Women's Super League, which includes a number of teams linked to the men's Premier League. In 2014, the FA added a second division league for women. Three years later, the Lewes Football Club (FC) announced that it would become the first to pay its women's and men's teams the same (it is worth noting that, at the time, the men played in England's eighth tier and the women in the premier league). According to the women's club director, Jacquie Agnew,

> By committing to paying our women's and men's teams equally, and providing equal resource for coaching, training and facilities, we hope to spark a change across the UK that will help put an end to the excuses for why such a deep pay disparity has persisted in our sport. Together with our owners, donors and sponsors, Lewes FC can show that equal pay can be implemented to the benefit of both women and men in sport and beyond.[34]

Despite these important milestones, it seems that most professional sportswomen cannot financially support themselves by their sport alone. Of course, a professional sports career is a privilege—a luxury at which many people would jump. Yet, scraping together a living while playing professional sport means that athletes are unable to focus solely on their sporting careers. This diverts their time and energy elsewhere and keeps them from reaching their full athletic potential. National Pro Fastpitch is softball's third attempt at establishing a women's professional league in the United States. Players make an average of $5,000 to $6,000 for the three-month season and must find second and off-season jobs to earn a living wage. This is true for many women's "professional teams," some of which offer no salaries at all, such as the women's professional football league, and the Legends Football League (see Chapter 5). Similarly, the United Women's Lacrosse League, established in 2016, could not afford to pay its athletes in its first year of operation. During that time, executives of a second organization, the Women's Professional Lacrosse League, announced that it would begin play in 2018. One wonders if the sports world can sustain both.

There is some hope, however. Women throughout the world are demanding and receiving more respect and better compensation. Partnerships with profitable men's leagues have, to date, stabilized women's soccer leagues in Australia, the United Kingdom, and the United States. And there are new opportunities on the horizon. As just one illustration, the United World Sports company announced that it would inaugurate a North American Super 7's Rugby League in 2018 and grant men and women equal pay.

Why aren't women's professional sports more successful?

Many women's leagues are still in their infancy, and history tells us that any organization, including the NFL, NBA, and MLB, takes significant time to establish. As "Title IX babies" have babies of their own, women's sport will continue to develop. And as parents raise athletic daughters, they understand the value of women's athletics and question why those daughters should not have the same opportunities as their sons.

For now, most professional women's sports have yet to achieve consumer, media, and commercial success. Part of this stems from fans who harbor sexist and antiquated attitudes about women's sport as uninteresting, unexciting, or as a poor approximation of the men's standard. *Sports Illustrated*'s Andy Benoit stoked this fire by tweeting "women's sports in general not worth watching." Advocates ask that potential fans give women's sport a chance, maintaining that the physicality, beauty, drama, and competition rival those found in any men's game.

Finances are perhaps the biggest problem for women's professional sport. Leagues and teams have small operating budgets, with little money to compensate players, coaches, and staff; rent prominent venues; or advertise their products.

Investors, wary of the history of instability in women's professional sport, are reluctant to take a gamble. Sponsorship and media go hand-in-hand, such that it is nearly unthinkable to have one without the presence of the other. Why would a corporate sponsor advertise if no one is watching or, more accurately, if no one *can* watch?

Without the visibility that media exposure provides, it is almost impossible to build an audience for women's sport. Although the NBA brokered a deal with ESPN to cover the WNBA, these relationships are rare, as the history of women's soccer demonstrates. The first US professional women's league, the WUSA, was unable to secure a deal with network television and turned instead to the cable network PAX TV to broadcast the games. "You say you've never heard of PAX?" asked Jeanette Howard of the *Chicago Tribune*, "That's the point."[35]

The second league, Women's Professional Soccer, streamed most of its games on team websites and through its YouTube channel. Viewers had to actively seek out these options; the casual channel-surfing sports fan would miss the games entirely. In 2017, the third league, the NWSL, announced a three-year deal with Lifetime Network as an official sponsor and broadcast partner. Consequently, Lifetime will air a Game of the Week each Saturday, as well as the playoff semifinals and the championship game. This is an encouraging prospect, but we should wonder why the deal is with a niche channel built around "women's programming" instead of with a major sports channel.

It is difficult for anyone to make a living in sport, whether as an athlete, coach, executive, administrator, official, owner, or agent. But it is especially difficult for women, who remain the minority in all sporting careers. As discouraging as the state of affairs may seem at times, perhaps there is some solace, perhaps some encouragement, in a quotation from tennis star Andy Murray, cited previously in this chapter: "It doesn't have to be that way."

10

THE SPORT–HEALTH CONNECTION

Is sport healthy?

Sport can be a healthy pursuit associated with a variety of physical, psychological, and social benefits, as mentioned in Chapter 1. It is therefore important that everyone has access to sport and other forms of physical activity. Yet too many girls and women experience barriers to participation related to impairment, geography, race, ethnicity, religion, sex, gender, sexuality, and social class. The lack of access and opportunity to facilities, teams, coaching, and competition, compounded by transportation and safety issues, influences girls' and women's potential to play sports.

Even those girls privileged with athletic opportunities turn away from sport. Statistics show that by age fourteen, American girls drop out of sport at twice the rate of boys, with seven out of ten girls reporting that they felt they did not belong.[1] By age seventeen, more than half of all girls quit sport, 67 percent of whom explain that society does not encourage their participation.[2] This is not just a matter of sport but also a matter of health. Adolescents who play sport are eight times more likely to be active at age twenty-four than their nonsporting peers. More than three-fourths of adults older than thirty played sport as children, while just 3 percent of active adults did not.[3] Simply put, physically active children are more likely to be physically active adults.

Those who stay in the game may discover that sport, especially when taken to extremes, can actually become unhealthy. In the quest to be the best (or in just trying to keep up), athletes may engage in harmful practices, including overtraining, unhealthy eating habits, substance abuse, overuse injuries, and doping. The long-term health effects of high-performance sport can include anemia, arthritis, fertility issues, and problems of the heart or kidneys. As Sally Jenkins wrote in a 2007 *Washington Post* article, "Most people don't realize it, but training at the elite level is actually the antithesis of a healthy lifestyle. . . . The definition of peak performance means that you are constantly at or near a state of physical breakdown."[4]

There are also mental and emotional health issues to consider. For all the psychological benefits outlined in Chapter 1, sport can also contribute to anxiety, stress, and insomnia. A 2016 study found that almost 30 percent of collegiate women student–athletes show signs of depression, compared with 18 percent of men student–athletes.[5] Depressive symptoms increase in elite athletes, particularly in response to performance failure.[6] Athletes can also become obsessive about their sport and training in ways that affect social relationships and their non-sporting lives.

Children require special considerations. Athletes who specialize in one sport at an early age are at an increased risk for injury, psychological stress, and burnout. For these reasons, experts recommend sport diversification, especially for athletes younger than twelve.[7] In fact, studies show that, contrary to popular belief, today's top athletes developed their talents playing multiple sports rather than developing a singular focus. One survey found that 88 percent of NCAA athletes played several sports as children, and 70 percent did not specialize in one sport until after the age of twelve.[8] *USA Today* examined the careers of American women on 2015 World Cup championship soccer team and found that, collectively, they played at least fourteen sports growing up.[9] Since then, the US Tennis Association, NFL, MLB, NHL, NCAA, the US Olympic Committee, and three dozen other leading sports organizations have joined together to campaign for athletic diversification. There are a few sports in which early specialization may be advantageous, including figure skating, gymnastics, and diving, where peak performance typically occurs before full physical maturation.[10] However, the long-term physical and emotional tolls this training takes on young athletes warrant greater attention.

Do female athletes have health concerns that are different from those of male athletes?

In general, women have health concerns both similar to and different from men. Athletes are no different. Some concerns are biological, others are cultural, and most are a combination of both.

There are two specific types of injuries that women seem to sustain at higher rates than men: anterior cruciate ligament (ACL) tears and concussions. The ACL is one of the major ligaments in the knee, and it is most often sprained or torn in sports that involve contact from a collision, quick changes of direction, jumping, pivoting, and sudden stops, such as soccer, basketball, and volleyball. Studies find that relative to male athletes, female athletes are 3.5 times more likely to sustain a non-contact ACL injury—a discrepancy that does not manifest until after puberty.[11]

Researchers have developed multiple theories to account for sex differences in ACL damage, including the following:

- Women tend to have wider hips than men, which affects knee alignment.
- Women's knees may be more flexible than men's knees, making them more prone to hyperextension.

- Strength imbalance between women's hamstring and quadriceps.
- Ligament laxity due to estrogen levels at certain stages of the menstrual cycle.
- Biomechanical differences in running and jumping.
- Women have a smaller intercondylar notch, through which the ACL connects to the femur.

ACL tears can be season- and even career-ending for athletes and treatment typically requires surgery and intensive rehabilitation. Physicians recommend girls and women receive better instruction in running and jumping techniques and warm-up activities and also engage in strength training, balance, and neuromuscular regimens to help prevent these types of injuries.

Concussions are the second type of injury that girls and women sustain more often than boys and men. Although headlines attend more often to brain injury in men's sports, particularly football, women may actually be at greater risk. Studies of college athletes show that female ice hockey players experience nearly three times as many concussions as male football players. The concussion rate of college softball players is double that of baseball players. In high school soccer, girls are twice as likely to suffer a concussion compared to boys.[12]

Researchers speculate that girls and women have relatively weaker necks (perhaps because they are not encouraged to strengthen them as boys and men often are), which increases the likelihood of head trauma. Others propose the differences may be hormonal. Then again, it may be that girls and women are more likely to admit that they have suffered some type of injury or that athletic trainers and physicians may be more cautious with female athletes. And because concussions have been such a hot topic in men's sport, there is less attention paid to the phenomenon in women's sport, leading to less research and general knowledge about how traumatic brain injuries particularly affect female athletes.

Repeated concussive and subconcussive brain injuries can lead to chronic traumatic encephalopathy (CTE), a degenerative brain disease caused by repeated blows to the head. CTE can only be definitively determined upon autopsy. So far, it seems to be most common in male athletes who compete in contact sports (boxing, hockey, football, and rugby), although doctors have found the condition in those who played baseball, soccer, and basketball. To date, no woman athlete has been diagnosed with CTE, but this should not allay concerns. Soccer stars Cindy Parlow Cone and Brandi Chastain have both pledged to donate their brains to CTE research. As Chastain remarked,

> Having played soccer since I was little, I can't even attempt a guess at how many times I've headed the ball. It's a significant number. It's scary to think about all the heading and potential concussions that were never diagnosed in my life, but it's better to know.[13]

Does menstruation influence women's sport participation?

The research on menstruation and sport is limited and contradictory, and so, speaking practically, it seems that the answer to this question depends on the individual athlete. Some women experience pain, cramps, headaches, low energy, and fatigue during their periods, which can affect performance, but many athletes do not experience these symptoms. Few athletes publicly broach this seemingly taboo subject, which further complicates our understanding. One exception is Chinese swimmer Fu Yuanhui, who confessed during the 2016 Olympics, "My period started last night, so I'm feeling pretty weak and really tired. But this isn't an excuse. At the end of the day I just didn't swim very well."[14] Then again, marathoner

Paula Radcliffe broke the Chicago Marathon world record during her period. Radcliffe has called for more study on the connections between the menstrual cycle and athletic performance, and she is critical of sport physicians who prescribe women norethisterone and other drugs to delay their periods for competitive reasons.

Historically, physicians and physical educators cautioned girls and women not to exercise during menstruation. We now know that regular exercise can decrease dysmenorrhea (painful menstruation) and may help regulate women's cycles. Just the same, intensive training can delay menarche and contribute to menstrual cycle irregularities. There is provisional evidence to suggest that spikes in estrogen levels, which accompany the menstrual cycle, can contribute to tissue and ligament injuries, but there has not yet been enough definitive study of the subject.

What is the female athlete triad?

As first described at the 1993 meeting of the American College of Sports Medicine, the female athlete triad referred to three interrelated conditions: disordered eating, amenorrhea (the loss of menstruation), and osteoporosis (porous bones). That definition has since evolved to include energy deficiency (with or without disordered eating), menstrual dysfunction, and low bone mineral density.

In brief, the problem starts with athletes who expend more energy than they consume. Low energy availability can be advertent or inadvertent in athletes who burn more calories exercising than they take in by eating and drinking. Chronic low energy availability can lead to menstrual irregularities, including amenorrhea. Missed periods can mean lower estrogen levels, which affects bone density and bone strength, potentially increasing an athlete's risk of fractures. Experts caution that education, prevention, early diagnosis, and intervention are critical with regard to the female athlete triad.[15]

In what sports are female athletes most
susceptible to disordered eating patterns?

Disordered eating includes a spectrum of problematic eating attitudes and behaviors, as well as body image distortions, all of which can affect one's physical, psychological, and social well-being. Types of disordered eating patterns include chronic dieting, fasting, binging, and purging through the use of laxatives, diuretics, self-induced vomiting, or saunas. Mental health professionals also refer to anorexia athletica (sometimes called hypergymnasia or sports anorexia), a condition characterized by excessive and obsessive exercise.

Male and female athletes in all sports are more susceptible to disordered eating patterns compared to their non-sporting peers, but studies show that athletes in "lean" sports that favor low body weight are at the greatest risk. This includes sports that are organized by weight classes, such as wrestling, boxing, and martial arts. When espnW researchers surveyed Division I college women athletes, they found that 32 percent of rowers reported having an eating disorder at one time in their lives; 54 percent said they had teammates with eating disorders. In rowing's lightweight division, the average weight for everyone in the boat cannot exceed 125 pounds, including a coxswain who must weigh at least 110 pounds, and many high-caliber athletes struggle to meet these criteria.[16]

Lighter boats can travel at faster speeds. The same is true for bodies in endurance sports, such as long-distance running and cycling, and in sports in which athletes must hoist their own body weight, such as climbing. Athletes in aesthetic sports are similarly vulnerable to unhealthy eating practices. It is easier for lighter bodies to flip, turn, and twist and turn in the air for sports such as diving, gymnastics, cheerleading, and figure skating. Sports in which athletes compete in revealing uniforms also show a higher prevalence of eating issues due, in part, to the added pressures of having one's body on display for spectators to judge and evaluate. Recall the 2016 Olympics when 99-pound Mexican artistic gymnast Alexa Moreno found herself in the crosshairs of Twitter trolls who chided her as too "fat."

Ski jumping technique also favors lighter bodies because they tend to stay aloft for longer distances. As Norway's Oevind Berg, the 1993 world champion, explained to a reporter, "I jumped one meter [3.3 feet] farther for each kilogram [2.2 pounds] I lost."[17] As such, there have been widespread and well-justified concerns about athletes who reduce their weight to unhealthy extremes. The International Ski Federation responded in 2004 with a rule that ties the maximum length of a jumper's skis to her or his body mass index (BMI; a formula based on one's height and weight). Skiers who fall below the minimum BMI must jump using shorter skis, which places them at a competitive disadvantage. Preliminary data show that the rule has motivated some skiers to maintain healthier body weights.

Disordered eating patterns are not just about denying the body energy. Some athletes may develop compulsive overeating or binge-eating disorders. These issues are understudied, although experts postulate that they are both prevalent and dangerous.

Is it OK to compete in sport while pregnant?

Physicians used to tell pregnant women to stay off their feet and rest as much as possible. Strenuous exercise, especially sport, was considered off limits. There were women who bucked convention to compete during and after pregnancy in the first part of the twentieth century, including the Netherland's Fanny Blankers-Koen, the thirty-year-old mother of two who won four gold medals in track and field at the 1948 Summer Olympics in London. Yet, it was not until 1985 that the American College of Obstetricians and Gynecologists published its first guidelines for exercise during pregnancy, which advised women to keep their heart rates low and to stop exercising after 15 minutes.[18]

Times have changed. The dominant message is that moderate levels of sport and physical activity provide many benefits to the mother and unborn child, including a reduction in gestational diabetes, preeclampsia, and hypertension, and can help the mother with her weight management, posture, low back pain, endurance, muscular fitness, cardiovascular fitness, mood, and mental health. Women who were active before pregnancy can maintain physical activity. Women who were relatively inactive before pregnancy are counseled to consult with their physicians before starting any exercise regimen. Most guidelines continue to recommend that women watch for specific contraindications and advise against contact or collision sports and sports such as cycling and downhill skiing that might result in a fall.[19]

In 2015, the IOC convened leading experts for its first meeting on exercise during pregnancy and after childbirth for elite athletes. With few studies on the topic, the group determined that, in general, "Profound anatomical and physiological changes accompany pregnancy but there are few reasons that pregnancy should preclude healthy women from regular exercise."[20] In the absence of conclusive research, there are numerous anecdotes of elite athletes who successfully balance pregnancy and their careers. Alysia Montaño, a two-time 800-meter American record holder, competed in the 2014 USA Track and Field Outdoor Championships when she was eight-and-a-half months pregnant. Three years later, clad in a Wonder Woman sports bra and five months pregnant with her second child, Montaño ran again. As she told reporters, she hoped her appearance would inspire others. "This isn't to pressure women to run during pregnancy. That's not the point at all," she said, "We're just different and that's the point."[21] In other words, there is no single exercise prescription that applies to all pregnant women.

What performance-enhancing drugs do women use and what are the effects?

Athletes have always used performance-enhancing drugs (PEDs) to gain a competitive edge. Athletes in ancient Greece used hallucinogenic mushrooms, sesame seeds, alcoholic concoctions, and animal hearts and testicles in their efforts to boost performance. Throughout history, athletes of all ages, at all levels of sport, have doped.

For the first part of the twentieth century, there were no laws prohibiting the use of PEDs. A mix of brandy, egg whites, and strychnine sulfate propelled Thomas Hicks across the finish line to take the gold medal in the 1904 Olympic marathon (after officials disqualified top finisher Fred Lorz for riding in an automobile for 11 miles of the race). In 1928, the International Association of Athletics Federations (IAAF) became the first international organization to ban doping, even though, at the time, officials lacked testing procedures.

It was not until the 1960s, following the amphetamine-related deaths of cyclists Knud Jensen (1960) and Tom Simpson (1967), that sports authorities began to wage serious anti-doping efforts. The IOC established its Medical Commission in 1967 with the dual purposes of testing for drugs and to verify the sex of female competitors (see Chapter 4). Faced with the ever-increasing prevalence and sophistication of doping techniques, in 1999 the IOC established the World Anti-Doping Agency (WADA) as an independent, international organization involved in research, education, and the development and monitoring of anti-doping codes.

Each year, WADA updates its list of prohibited substances. The most common PEDs athletes take are stimulants, anabolic–androgenic steroids, human growth hormone (hGH) and growth factors, erythropoietin (EPO), diuretics, and beta blockers. WADA's 2016 data showed that more than four times as many male athletes tested positive for PED violations than female athletes, but doping remains a significant problem in women's sport.

Stimulants affect the central nervous system to speed up the brain and increase heart rate, blood pressure, body temperature, and metabolism. Athletes take stimulants to reduce fatigue, increase aggressiveness and alertness, improve endurance, increase aerobic performance, and to suppress their appetites in order to lose weight. At the turn of the twentieth century, competitors ingested strychnine, nitroglycerine, and cocaine. As pharmacology advanced, they experimented with any number of drugs, including Benzedrine, bromantane, ephedrine, and Adderall, which is prescribed for patients with attention-deficit/hyperactivity disorder and related conditions. The use of stimulants is associated with several risks, including irritability, insomnia, dehydration, heart palpitations and rhythm abnormalities, heatstroke, circulatory problems, stroke, and heart attack.

Anabolic–androgenic steroids (AAS) are synthetic derivatives of testosterone that promote the growth of skeletal muscle. They can increase strength and muscle mass, reduce body fat, and help athletes train harder and recover more quickly from strenuous workouts. For women, the side effects of AAS can include menstrual irregularities, deepened voice, acne, increased facial hair, male pattern baldness, small breasts, clitoromegaly (enlargement of the clitoris), sterility, high blood pressure, liver damage, heart attack, and stroke. Some of these side effects may be irreversible even after an athlete stops taking AAS.

Male athletes, notably weight lifters, began experimenting with steroids in the 1950s, and female athletes followed soon after. In the 1960s and 1970s, observers noted the strong physiques of Eastern Bloc women who dominated international swimming and track and field competitions. These athletes were particularly conspicuous at the 1976 Summer Olympics, as East German women won eleven of the thirteen swimming events, although all women passed their drug tests. It was not until after the fall of the Berlin Wall that the world learned of the East German government's massive doping program, which affected an estimated 10,000 athletes. Competitors as young as age twelve, often unbeknownst to them or their parents, received the anabolic steroid Oral Turinabol. German officials specifically targeted girls and women for the drug because it had a more dramatic effect on their bodies than it did for boys and men. The doping program rocketed East Germany to the upper echelon of the Olympic medal count, but it has had significant and long-lasting consequences to the athletes' health. According to one advocacy group, 90 percent of the athletes recognized as doping victims currently have serious health issues, including cancer, heart enlargement and heart attack, malfunction of lungs and kidneys, infertility, ovarian cysts, joint and bone problems, and psychological trauma.[22]

The Russian government was similarly embroiled in a state-sponsored doping scandal, as a WADA-commissioned report detailed in 2016. Attorney Richard McLaren determined that between 2011 and 2015, more than 1,000 Russian athletes were involved in an institutionalized, systematic conspiracy to conceal positive drug tests. The fallout from this has been severe, resulting in a ban of the Russian track and field team from the 2016 Summer Olympic Games, and bans of the entire Russian delegation from the 2018 Winter Olympic Games and the 2016 and 2018 Paralympic Games, although "clean" athletes can compete under a neutral flag as "Olympic Athletes from Russia" (see Chapter 7).

Another high-profile doping scandal occurred in 2003 when journalists Lance Williams and Mark Fainaru-Wada revealed that the Bay Area Laboratory Co-Operative (BALCO) had developed a powerful and, at the time, undetectable steroid called tetrahydrogestrinon (THG or "The Clear"). The BALCO scandal implicated numerous high-profile male and female athletes, including cyclist Tammy Thomas and track and field athletes Regina Jacobs, Zhanna Block, Kelli White, and Marion Jones.

With effects similar to AAS, hGH poses yet another problem for anti-doping authorities. The pituitary gland produces the hormone, which stimulates the growth of muscle, bone, and cartilage. Natural production peaks in adolescence and declines with age. Initially, athletes doped with hormones extracted from human cadavers. In the 1980s, scientists synthesized hGH through genetic engineering, and the IOC banned its use in 1989. Potential side effects of hGH include muscle, joint, and bone pain; accelerated osteoarthritis; and excessive growth of hands, jaw, liver, kidneys, and heart, putting individuals at greater risks for heart disease and certain types of cancer.

Athletes similarly seek ways to boost their bodies' production of red blood cells, which carry oxygen to the muscles to delay fatigue, making it popular in endurance sports. As with hGH, the body naturally produces EPO, which stimulates the production of red blood cells, and scientists have also synthesized the hormone in the laboratory. EPO is most often associated with cycling, but a number of top women distance runners have also been caught using it, including Liliya Shobukhova, Rita Jeptoo, and Jemima Sumgong, winner of the 2016 Olympic marathon. Athletes can achieve similar effects through blood doping, a process that involves drawing and storing one's blood while the body naturally regenerates red blood cells. Just before competition, athletes re-inject the stored blood into their bodies for a rush of the oxygen-carrying cells. The risks associated with EPO and blood doping include thickened blood, and can lead to heart disease, stroke, and cerebral or pulmonary embolism, and both practices are banned by WADA and other authorities.

Diuretics, which increase urination, also fall under the category of banned substances. Athletes take them to lose weight and to mask other drugs in their urine. Yet another type of doping involves the use of beta blockers, which impede the effects of adrenaline to reduce blood pressure, heart rate, muscle tremors, and anxiety. These responses are useful in sports that require a calm and steady hand, such as pistol shooting, billiards, and archery.

It is difficult to keep up with the constantly evolving development and use of PEDs in sport. Detection typically involves reactive tests—that is, first identifying a particular drug in a laboratory and then looking for its presence in an athlete's blood, urine, or both. As an alternative, testers have developed an Athlete Biological Passport, which establishes an athlete's baseline of biological markers and then searches for variances in that baseline. The passport is effective, but it is also expensive and not yet widely used.

Further complicating the issue of doping is that WADA and other organizations allow "therapeutic use exemptions" for athletes with illnesses or conditions that require medical treatment with a banned substance. Soon after the 2016 Olympic Games, a Russian cyber espionage group hacked into WADA's database, likely in retaliation for the ban of Russian Olympians and Paralympians. The group, which went by the name "Fancy Bear," publicized information that several American athletes, including Serena Williams and gold medal gymnast Simone Biles, had tested positive for banned substances. Both women subsequently revealed that WADA had granted them therapeutic use exemptions and they were therefore not in violation of anti-doping policy.

WADA's list of prohibited substances and methods includes anything that meets two of the following three criteria:

1. It has the potential to enhance or enhances sport performance;
2. It represents an actual or potential health risk to the athlete;
3. It violates the spirit of sport (this definition is outlined in the Code).[23]

Based on these principles, sport organizations must further deal with issues of "technology doping," which refers to sports equipment (e.g., hydrodynamic swimsuits, motors hidden in bicycles, and cutting-edge prosthetic limbs) that may provide an unfair advantage. The criteria also spurred parasport officials to ban "boosting," which involves intentionally injuring a part of the body in which an athlete with an impairment has no feeling. Examples include breaking a toe, the use of electric shock, allowing one's bladder to overfill, or overtightening one's leg straps. These techniques "boost" the athlete's blood pressure and heart rate, potentially dangerous responses believed to improve athletic performance. Finally, gene doping is a significant concern for authorities, particularly because the manipulation of one's genetic makeup may be impossible to detect. WADA first banned gene doping in 2003 and amended its policy in 2018 to include "The use of gene editing agents designed to alter genome sequences and/or the transcriptional or epigenetic regulation of gene expression."[24] This refers to tweaking an athlete's existing genes (through methods such as CRISPR, which stands for Clustered Regularly Interspaced Short Palindromic Repeats), in addition to introducing new genes, as was the procedure with earlier technologies.

Does sport put girls and women at risk for sexual violence?

The World Health Organization asserts that sexual violence is a public health and human rights problem with long-term consequences on victims' physical, mental, reproductive, and sexual well-being.[25] Sexual violence refers to a variety of behaviors, including non-contact crimes such as sexual harassment, exhibitionism, and exposure to sexually explicit language and imagery, as well as crimes that involve physical interaction, such as sexual contact or touching, sexual exploitation, sexual assault, and rape. The National Sexual Violence Resource Center offers the following definition:

Sexual violence means that someone forces or manipulates someone else into unwanted sexual activity without their consent. Reasons someone might not consent include fear, age, illness, disability, and/or influence of alcohol or other drugs. Anyone can experience sexual violence including: children, teens, adults, and elders. Those who sexually abuse can be acquaintances, family members, trusted individuals, or strangers.[26]

Unfortunately, the culture of sport does put girls and women, as well as boys and men, at risk for sexual violence. Sport often involves interpersonal closeness, intimacy, and physical contact. There are many situations—in training, locker rooms, athletes' residences, social gatherings, doctors' offices, examination and treatment rooms, travel, and competition—that leave athletes vulnerable in unsupervised settings. Organizations and institutions may prioritize performance, results, and reputation over the health and well-being of athletes, all of which contribute to unsafe conditions.

Moreover, coaches and other authority figures wield tremendous power over athletes. Sport, especially elite sport, is built on a cycle of rewards and punishments that disempower athletes and foster a culture of silence. Athletes may be reluctant to question a coach's authority for fear of retribution. According to Nancy Hogshead-Makar, a civil rights attorney, women's sport advocate, and former Olympian,

An authoritarian style doesn't allow kids to say no, to say they have an injury, aren't ready to do a trick or need to eat more calories. If you can't say no to an injury, you can't say no to sexual abuse by someone who has power over you.[27]

Fierce competition for team positions and funding exacerbates the problem, as athletes may refuse to jeopardize their standing.

Coaches may also act as parental figures or gain an athlete's trust through "grooming," which involves strategies to convince or coerce an athlete to engage in sexual behavior. "Grooming is important," researchers maintain, "because it brings about the appearance of co-operation from the athlete, making the act of abuse seem to be consensual."[28] In the same way, inappropriate relationships between athletes and authority figures can be manifestations of "athlete domestic violence," which refers to

> an athlete in a (perceived) "relationship" with a coach and can involve consenting age or not. The dynamics develop regardless of age. Professional standards maintain that a "romantic relationship" is never appropriate as the coach always has a structural power advantage over a competing athlete.[29]

Girls and women are also at risk of sexual violence from male athletes and within the context of men's sports. Because of sport's vaunted status, particularly as a masculine domain, male athletes often enjoy a sense of privilege and entitlement. Team culture, characterized by male bonding, pressure, competitiveness, and aggression, can develop into "rape culture." Although the vast majority of male athletes do not sexually assault women, studies show that athletes, relative to their non-athletic peers, are over-represented in sexual assault cases.[30] Male intercollegiate athletes tend to be more accepting of "rape myths," or the "beliefs and situational definitions that excuse rape or define assaultive situations as something other than rape."[31] In one study, 54 percent of male student–athletes admitted to committing at least one "sexually coercive" act in their lives.[32] At the same time, as mentioned in Chapter 3, the US Department of Justice determined that a staggering 80 percent of college women do not report sexual assault.[33] Those who do report these crimes may find their character and credibility impugned, or that coaching staffs and athletic departments cover up or discount their accusations, or that athletes convicted of these crimes receive lenient consequences. Additionally, there are a growing number of reports that major sporting events foster human sex trafficking. Watchdog groups have been expressly concerned with the FIFA Men's World Cup, the Super Bowl, and the Olympic Games. Investigations into this phenomenon are contradictory, but advocates argue that a large gathering of people in one area may boost the illicit sex market.

There is a lot in the news concerning sexual abuse scandals in sport: Is this a new phenomenon?

The global sports world has been rocked by stories about the sexual abuse of athletes. Just a smattering of related scandals involves executives, scouts, physicians, and coaches in Flemish judo, Dutch cycling, Danish orienteering, Penn State football, USA Swimming, English para-archery, and the English soccer system, in which the widespread abuse of boys appears to have occurred from at least 1972 to 2005. Although this may seem a recent phenomenon, it is not. "In sport," writes child protection expert Celia Brackenridge, "far from being a new problem, sexual abuse almost certainly has been around for centuries but, until recently, has been ignored."[34]

Determining the rate of sexual abuse in sport is difficult. Definitions vary, and experts assess that many victims remain silent out of fear or shame, thereby making sexual abuse a significantly under-reported crime in all aspects of social life, including sport.

Unfortunately, too many sports organizations are complicit in the sexual abuse of athletes by ignoring the problem, failing to properly check employees' backgrounds, failing to adopt or enforce an appropriate policies, doubting accusers, or by "passing the trash," which allows an employee suspected of sexual misconduct to resign rather than undergo investigation. Without a record of inappropriate or illegal behavior, that person is free to find work elsewhere. In 2016, the *Indianapolis Star* reported that in the past twenty years, more than 360 gymnasts had accused coaches, gym owners, and other adults in USA Gymnastics (USAG) of sexual misconduct. The journalists "uncovered one example after another of coaches who were not only suspected of abuse, but actually convicted of molesting children, yet they did not show up on the banned coaches list for years—even decades—after that conviction."[35]

After reading the *Star*'s exposé, former gymnast Rachel Denhollander emailed the authors to tell them that, more than ten years earlier, she had been "molested by Dr. Larry Nassar, the team doctor for USAG. I was fifteen years old, and it was under the guise of medical treatment for my back." Denhollander's disclosure initiated what the judge in Nassar's subsequent criminal trial characterized as a "tidal wave" of survivors to come forward with similar charges.[36] Starting at least as early as 1997, Nassar used his position with USAG, as well as his work with athletes at Michigan State University, the USOC, and the Twistars gymnastics club in Dimondale, Michigan, to abuse girls and women. It now seems that each organization prioritized their reputations over the well-being of their athletes. As of January 2018, 265 girls and women had accused Nassar of assault and there are undoubtedly many more who choose to remain silent.

How could this happen to so many athletes over such a long period of time? There are a number of mitigating circumstances. Nassar groomed athletes by acting as a confidante, soothing and supporting them as they recovered from physical injuries and dealt with psychological damage inflicted by abusive coaches, parents, peers, judges, and a hyper-competitive sport. "It is a clear that in an environment like Twistars, a monster like Nassar should thrive," explained Bailey Lorencen in her victim-impact statement at Nassar's sentencing. "He just had to be the nice guy so that all these little girls would look at him as a savior and that safe place at the gym."[37]

When accused of misconduct, as he was several times, Nassar explained that the molestation was a type of therapeutic massage. Authorities believed him. MSU gymnasts told their coach that Nassar had fondled and vaginally penetrated them during "treatment." The coach dismissed their concerns and vouched for Nassar's character. So did the track coach when an athlete on the team relayed a similar story. So did several athletic trainers when a MSU softball player likewise confided in them. It may be that, for more than two decades, at least fourteen members of the MSU staff heard allegations against Nassar, yet he continued on at the school until 2015.

As a respected physician, Nassar seemed to be unassailable. In 2004, a seventeen-year-old girl and her mother went to local police to accuse Nassar of assault. Officers dropped the case after Nassar offered a Powerpoint presentation to explain that while he had touched the girl between her legs, it was a legitimate therapeutic technique. Ten years later, another woman went to MSU officials and university police with related charges. The school launched a Title IX investigation that ultimately cleared Nassar of any wrongdoing, finding that the accuser did not understand the "nuanced difference" between sexual assault and appropriate medical procedure. Conversely, the MSU police submitted an arrest warrant for Nassar for fourth-degree criminal sexual conduct, but prosecutors denied the charges on the grounds that the doctor's procedure seemed to be "a very innovative and helpful manipulation."[38] Even some of the athletes he assaulted trusted his authority. It wasn't until years later that gold medal gymnast Aly Raisman realized that Nassar had molested her, though she always felt their was something "weird" about her visits with him. "What people don't get is that he was a doctor," Raisman explained to *Time*. "I would never have imagined that a doctor would abuse me or manipulate me so badly."[39]

Former gymnast Annie Labrie testified that Nassar did things to her that "made her skin crawl," but the adults she told dismissed her accusation because of his strong reputation.

Labrie went on to explain that there is a specific culture in gymnastics, dance, and other activities in which girls learn at a young age not to question authority: they are "conditioned for years to obey at all costs." This mentality creates a breeding ground for sexual predators like Nassar, Labrie insists that it is "imperative we as society do not view this as an isolated incident."[40]

In November 2017, Nassar pleaded guilty to seven counts of first-degree criminal sexual conduct. At his sentencing hearing two months later, 156 women, over the course of seven days, delivered their victim-impact statements, articulating what he had done to them and the devastating effects of his abuse. Rachel Delhollander spoke last, telling Nassar and those in attendance, "Women and girls banded together to fight for themselves because no one else would do it." Judge Rosemarie Aquilina applauded the survivors' courage and sentenced Nassar, who was already serving a 60-year sentence for possessing 37,000 images of child pornography, to another 40 to 175 years in prison. In February 2018, he received an additional sentence (40 to 125 years) after a second sexual assault trial.

What is being done to address and prevent sexual abuse in sport?

As the USAG and Nassar scandals bring into sharp relief, sports organizations have been far too slow to develop policies to prevent and protect athletes from sexual misconduct. Former federal prosecutor Deborah Daniels investigated USAG and assessed that "the athlete protection function is, at best, secondary to the primary focus: winning medals." In her 114-page report, Daniels urged "complete cultural change" in USAG and proposed seventy recommendations, all of which the organization's board of directors unanimously accepted (the entire board later resigned). The recommendations included creating and requiring annual training in abuse policies; implementing procedures and reporting mechanisms; regular education for parents and athletes on abuse prevention;

a greater "independent" presence on the board of directors and USGA staff, whose livelihoods are not dependent on gymnastics; and requiring that the adults who work at the 3,500 member clubs, which together enroll 121,000 children, become USAG members and undergo criminal background checks and abuse-education training. Daniels further advised

> strict requirements for the reporting of physical, emotional and sexual abuse. Failure by a club owner, a professional member, or any other person under the jurisdiction of USA Gymnastics to report misconduct as outlined by the revised reporting guidelines (of USA Gymnastics and the US Center for SafeSport) should be punishable with sanctions ranging up to the revocation of membership.[41]

To that end, the US Senate passed the Protecting Young Victims from Sexual Abuse and Safe Sport Authorization Act of 2017, requiring amateur athletics governing bodies, such as USAG, to immediately report sex-abuse allegations to local or federal law enforcement, or a child-welfare agency designated by the Justice Department.

Daniels's report echoes the advice of experts. In "Sexual Abuse and Sport: A Model to Prevent and Prevent and Protect Athletes," professors Sylvie Parent and Guylaine Demers found that sex abuse was a "low priority" for the sports organizations they analyzed—that administrators considered the issue a "burden," felt they lacked the resources and competence to address it, or worried that, if they did address it, it would imply an existing problem and consequently harm the organization's reputation. In addition, parents and athletes do not regularly receive training, documents, or awareness-raising materials about sexual abuse. Most codes of conduct do not define appropriate boundaries between athletes, coaches, trainers, and physicians. Too many organizations do not thoroughly screen applicants, do not require administrators, coaches, officials, physicians, trainers, and volunteers to undergo training, and lack a clear and enforced protocol for allegations or suspicions of abuse. These problems must change to protect the safety of athletes.[42] Finally, the culture of sport also needs to change in ways that empower athletes to maintain autonomy over their bodies, to remove the shame and stigma survivors feel about coming forward, and to believe and support them when they do.

11

MOVING ON

If sport provides so many benefits, why don't all girls and women participate?

As mentioned throughout this book, there are many physical, mental, and social benefits that come from playing sport. In brief, those who play sports suffer fewer health problems, are more confident, learn to work together, learn to deal with setbacks and failure, and cultivate leadership skills. They tend to do better in school, perform better in the labor market, and, as a result, enjoy greater social and economic mobility and success.

It may be tempting, then, to tell girls and women to "get in the game" or, to borrow from Nike, to "just do it." It is not always that simple. A web of social constraints shapes what seems a matter of personal choice. In the United States, sport remains stratified along lines of sex, gender, sexuality, race, ethnicity, impairment, geography, and social class. Those girls and women who start from a place of disadvantage have a more difficult time gaining access, finding the time and the money, and overcoming social stigma en route to sport.

This is true throughout the world, but it is especially striking in developing countries, where female sports participation typically remains low. Girls and women in many such areas must contend with strictly enforced gender roles, cultural and legal restrictions on movement, lack of familial support, the absence of athletic female role models, and financial limitations. Girls and women often internalize proscriptions against their involvement in sport, while those inclined to become athletes may be stymied by a lack of programs, funding, and facilities. For instance, Afghan women encounter nearly insurmountable odds finding safe and accessible spaces to play. As Asad Ziar, CEO of the Afghanistan Rugby Federation explains,

> There are no private grounds and it's impossible for women to train in public. We need secured and proper facilities for the development of women's rugby. When we have those facilities we will start working on the development of women's teams.[1]

For some girls and women, simply appearing in public, especially unaccompanied by a male chaperone or dressed in athletic clothing, incites harassment, potential violence, and even death, as in the case of one girl in Somalia. Militants came to her home. They took her to an empty lot, cut her body and face with shards of glass, shaved her head, and left her to die—all because she dared to play basketball. "It made me really scared for my life," the girl's teammate recalled, "You put your life in danger in this country because of the thing that you love."[2]

Remarkably, however, sport can help. According to a policy brief from the Peterson Institute for International Economics, initiatives such as the Marthare Youth Sports Association in Kenya not only empower participants but also work by "providing a safe space for girls to play and fostering interaction with boys with a view to increasing familiarity between the sexes and deobjectifying women."[3] Sport programs can also help girls deal with social pressures relating to early marriage, pregnancy, abuse, misogyny, and oppressive gender roles. In the Indian state of Jharkhand, for example, girls who attend the Yuwa school play soccer as "a way of cultivating positive peer pressure to keep girls involved when their families and communities pull them in other directions." As one student reflected, through soccer,

> I am learning more things than in the classroom. It also makes me stronger to deal with villagers who do not like that my friends and I wear shorts and play football like boys. Football made me powerful to ignore them because I know what I am doing is right.[4]

Are there any places where it is illegal for women to play sport?

Laws that forbid women's participation in sport and physical activity are slowly disappearing. Even so, lingering ideologies are often just as powerful as legal statutes for keeping women out. There is evidence of this in several Muslim and Muslim-majority countries, particularly those governed by Sharia (Islamic law). As women's rights activist Shaista Gohir explains, "Although there is nothing in the Quran forbidding women and girls from exercising and playing sports, religious scholars are making Islam more restrictive than it should be through misinterpretations."[5]

Under Taliban rule, it was illegal for Afghan girls and women to play sports. The ban, along with the Taliban's formal regime, ended in 2001, but women athletes still face scorn, ridicule, and danger. Sportswomen report that antagonists chastise them as "immodest," "infidels," and "prostitutes." Khalida Popal, the first captain of the Afghan National Football team, recalls the vitriol she and her teammates experienced: "People threw rocks and garbage at us. I received many death threats." As a result, a number of sportswomen—including Popal—have fled the country.[6]

In Somalia, women's basketball flourished under former dictator Siad Barre. When the Islamic Courts Union, a group of militia-backed Sharia courts, assumed control, leaders declared sports to be satanic acts; "girls couldn't go to stadiums to watch basketball, handball, or track and field, let alone compete in them," reported *The New Yorker*. Today, under new rule, sport is no longer illegal in Somalia, but that does not mean it is accepted. Rebels continue to terrorize female athletes. Despite all this, women who dare to compete can affect social change. As one Somali basketball player remarked, "Since we started playing, community perception of us has completely changed. People who used to shame us, now clap for us."[7]

The situation for Saudi female athletes also appears to be improving, albeit incrementally. Whereas observers applauded the Saudi Arabian Olympic Committee for including women in its 2012 delegation, critics called it a "fig leaf" that did little to inspire lasting change.[8] Four years later, Saudi women could still not participate in state-organized sports leagues, national tournaments, or attend men's national team competitions. At that time, there were 150 official sports clubs in the kingdom, none of which were open to women due to strict gender segregation. Women could not exercise in fitness studios, and those who sought to open women-only facilities were denied licenses. Until 2017, girls' public schools did not provide physical education, a mandatory subject for boys. Even with the change, however, few girls' schools have facilities or trained teachers to lead these classes.

Saudi Arabia's high rates of obesity and diabetes were a major impetus behind finally providing physical education for girls, which is a reminder that sport is also about health and well-being. Sport can also be a matter of survival by helping women fend off attackers, as promoted in self-defense and martial arts programs such as the Sure Start Project in Mifumi, Uganda. "Through the practice of karate, girls are encouraged to develop a sense of self-awareness and a sense of ownership over their bodies," according to Women Win, a Dutch advocacy organization.[9] To that end, Women Win partnered with the Women's Sport and Fitness Foundation Malaysia to offer self-defense training to women with physical impairments, who are especially vulnerable to physical and sexual violence. The results are astounding. As one participant reflected,

Most of the time I live isolated in the house of my family, who are ashamed of my circumstances. But this week I have met so many other women in the same circumstances as myself. We could talk about so many things: marrying, the ability to get babies, work, studying, but also how to cope with the prejudices because we are disabled. I feel so powerful and aware of my abilities. Also, the respect that the teachers gave me, and the role model of the teacher who is in a wheelchair too, has taught me that I can do more things with my impairment than I ever thought.[10]

Swimming is another vital skill. The 2004 tsunami that hit southern India killed four times as many women as men. Lacking the abilities to swim or to climb to higher ground, women accounted for up to 80 percent of the casualties in some villages. "Due to the absence of sporting activities for women in many of the affected areas women lack strength and confidence," concluded Women Without Borders, an international research and advocacy organization. Consequently, the organization teamed with the Austrian Swimming Association, the Austrian Youth Red Cross, and the Austrian Life Saving Association to devise a program for Indian girls and women. After just seven days, more than two-thirds of the participants were able to swim the length of a swimming pool—a potentially life-saving competency.[11]

Is sport a human right?

A number of high-profile organizations have recognized sport as a human right. In fact, the eighth Fundamental Principle of Olympism, as specified in the Olympic Charter, reads, "The practice of sport is a human right. Every individual must have the possibility of practicing sport in accordance with his or her needs."

In that spirit, the United Nations Educational, Scientific and Cultural Organization (UNESCO) adopted the International Charter of Physical Education and Sport in 1978, which states,

> One of the essential conditions for the effective exercise of human rights is that everyone should be free to develop and preserve his or her physical, intellection, and moral powers, and that access to physical education and sport should consequently be assured and guaranteed for all human beings.[12]

Delegates amended the charter in 1991 (and again in 2015) to affirm that "the practice of physical education and sport is a fundamental right for all."[13]

The UN has also made sport part of its 2030 Agenda for Sustainable Development, a "plan of action for people, planet and prosperity" that "seeks to strengthen universal peace in larger freedom." In 2015, UN representatives laid out a series of goals designed to eradicate poverty, hunger, ameliorate climate change, and foster peace. Paragraph 37 of the agenda reads,

> Sport is also an important enabler of sustainable development. We recognize the growing contribution of sport to the realization of development and peace in its promotion of tolerance and respect and the contributions it makes to the empowerment of women and of young people, individuals and communities as well as to health, education and social inclusion objectives.[14]

In recognizing the value of sport, the UN and other powerful establishments clearly view it as a human right and a tool for development and peace.

What is Sport for Development and Peace?

Organizers have long employed sport as an instrument of social change, but programs specifically designated as Sport for Development and Peace (SDP) began to take off in the 1990s. SDP refers to an amalgam of programs, instituted by governments, corporations, private donors, and nongovernmental organizations, that use sport as a strategy for social intervention. In 2002, UN Secretary-General Kofi Annan convened the Inter-Agency Task Force on Sport for Development and Peace (the UN has since established an Office of Sport for Development and Peace and recognizes August 6 as the International Day of Sport for Development and Peace). The report from that initial task force, "Sport as a Tool for Development and Peace: Towards Achieving the United Nations Millennium Development Goals," identifies a range of objectives, including the promotion of gender equality and the empowerment of women (Table 11.1). Indeed, there are a number of SDP programs specific to the needs of girls and women, and in recent years, the focus of those programs has shifted from advocating for "gender equity in sport" toward the use of "sport for gender equity and personal development."[15]

In the Kenyan program Moving the Goalposts, for example, soccer is an entry point for providing peer education programs on reproductive health, women's rights, and economic empowerment. In much the same way, India's Naz Foundation Trust implemented its Goal program, which uses netball as "a vehicle for social inclusion . . . aimed at building self-confidence, knowledge and leadership amongst adolescent girls." Each session pairs netball training with the promotion of a variety of life skills. In Afghanistan, Cambodia, and South

Table 11.1 Sport and the Millennium Development Goals

Goal 1: Eradicate extreme poverty and hunger. Providing development opportunities will help fight poverty. The sport industry, as well as the organization of large sporting events, creates opportunities for employment.

Sport provides life skills essential for a productive life in society. The opportunity to acquire such skills is often more limited for women, making their access to sport of critical importance.

Goal 2: Achieve universal primary education. Sport and physical education are an essential element of quality education. They promote positive values and skills that have an immediate and lasting impact on young people. Sport activities and physical education generally make school more attractive and improve attendance.

Goal 3: Promote gender equality and empower women. Increasing access for women and girls to physical education and sport helps build confidence and promotes stronger social integration. Involving girls in sport activities alongside boys can help overcome prejudice that often contributes to social vulnerability of women and girls.

Goals 4 and 5: Reduce child mortality and improve maternal health. Sport can be an effective means to provide women with a healthy lifestyle as well as to convey important messages on a wide range of health issues.

Goal 6: Combat HIV/AIDS, malaria and other diseases. Sport can help engage otherwise difficult-to-reach populations and provide positive role models delivering prevention messages. The most vulnerable populations, including women and girls, are highly responsive to sport-targeted programs. Sport can also effectively assist in overcoming prejudice, stigma and discrimination.

Goal 7: Ensure environmental sustainability. Sport is ideal for raising awareness about the need to preserve the environment. The interdependency between the regular practice of outdoor sports and the protection of the environment is clear.

Goal 8: Develop a global partnership for development. Sport offers diverse opportunities for innovative partnerships for development and can be used as a tool to build and foster partnerships between developed and developing nations to work towards achieving the Millennium Development Goals.

Source: United Nations. "Sport and the Millennium Development Goals." 2005. https://www.un.org/sport2005/a_year/mill_goals.html.

Africa, children benefit from Skateistan. As explained on the organization's website,

> Through the hook of skateboarding we engage children, especially girls and children from low income backgrounds, and provide them with access to safe spaces and education. Our innovative programs teach children valuable life skills that go beyond the skatepark and the classroom.[16]

As SDP programs show, sport has an incredible potential to positively affect the lives of participants.

Are things getting better for girls and women in sport?

In so many ways, things have gotten much better for girls and women. To look back over the history of sport and weigh it against girls' and women's participation rates in the twenty-first century, the progress is nothing short of remarkable. The range of sports available to women, their visibility, the continual smashing of social, medical, and aesthetic rationales against their participation, the growing acceptance of powerful sportswomen, and the moves to include more women in leadership positions all speak volumes about how far things have come. At the same time, however, congratulations should not give way to complacency. Despite all the gains women have made in sport, there are still many areas in need of improvement.

The 1994 *Brighton Declaration of Women and Sport* points out some of those areas. The document resulted from the "Women, Sport, and the Challenge of Change" conference held in Brighton, England. There, emissaries from eighty-two countries, representing every continent, convened to strategize ways to "enable and value the full involvement of women in every aspect of sport." The resulting declaration outlined ten principles relating to facilities, school and junior sport, women's participation, high-performance sport, leadership, education, training and development, sports information and research, resources, and domestic and international cooperation—all of which remain important (Table 11.2).[17]

On the occasion of the twentieth anniversary of the *Brighton Declaration*, delegates reconvened and concluded that "a lot of progress has taken place concerning women and sport," but there remains "much work to be done." In the 2014 report, *From Brighton to Helsinki*, the International Working Group on Women and Sport recommended that advocates prioritize four areas in the coming years:

1. The development of child-care provision for people involved in sport in different roles and at different arenas
2. The development of programs to support the retirement of female elite level athletes
3. The development of preventive measures which ensure that sport and exercise is a safe arena for girls and women, particular in relation to
   a. Prevention of bullying, hazing, homophobia, sexual harassment and/or abuse
   b. Prevention of eating disorders
   c. Prevention of injuries
4. Emphasizing increased female leadership in different sporting roles such as
   a. Refereeing
   b. Coaching
   c. Decision-making[18]

The emphasis goes beyond getting girls and women involved in sports, indicating the progress made in that regard. Although participation remains imperative, social change has brought a host of new considerations.

We are still a long way from equality in sport, but we are moving in that direction. Individuals, organizations, advocacy

Table 11.2 Brighton Declaration on Women and Sport: The Principles

1. Equity and Equality in Society and Sport

Every effort should be made by state and government machineries to ensure that institutions and organisations responsible for sport comply with the equality provisions of the Charter of the United Nations, the Universal Declaration of Human Rights and the UN Convention on the Elimination of all Forms of Discrimination Against Women.

Equal opportunity to participate and be involved in sport whether for the purpose of leisure and recreation, health promotion or high performance, is the right of every woman, regardless of race, colour, language, religion, creed, sexual orientation, age, marital status, disability, political belief or affiliation, national or social origin.

Resources, power and responsibility should be allocated fairly and without discrimination on the basis of sex, but such allocation should redress any inequitable balance in the benefits available to women and men.

2. Facilities

Women's participation in sport is influenced by the extent, variety and accessibility of facilities. The planning, design and management of these should appropriately and equitably meet the particular needs of women in the community, with special attention given to the need for childcare provision and safety.

3. School and Junior Sport

Research demonstrates that girls and boys approach sport from markedly different perspectives. Those responsible for sport, education, recreation and physical education of young people should ensure that an equitable range of opportunities and learning experience, which accommodate the values, attitudes and aspirations of girls, is incorporated in programs to develop physical fitness and basic sport skills of young people.

4. Developing Participation

Women's participation in sport is influenced by the range of activities available. Those responsible for delivering sporting opportunities and programs should provide and promote activities which meet women's needs and aspirations.

5. High Performance Sport

Governments and sports organizations should provide equal opportunities to women to reach their sports performance potential by ensuring that all activities and programs relating to performance improvements take account of the specific needs of female athletes. Those supporting elite and/or professional athletes should ensure that competition opportunities, rewards, incentives, recognition, sponsorship, promotion and other forms of support are provided fairly and equitably to both women and men.

(continued)

Table 11.2 Continued

6. Leadership in Sport

Women are under-represented in the leadership and decision making in all sport and sport-related organizations. Those responsible for these areas should develop policies and programs and design structures which increase the number of women coaches, advisers, decision makers, officials, administrators and sports personnel at all levels with special attention given to recruitment, development and retention.

7. Education, Training and Development

Those responsible for the education, training and development of coaches and other sports personnel should ensure that education processes and experiences address issues relating to gender equity and the needs of female athletes, equitably reflect women's role in sport and take account of women's leadership experiences, values and attitudes.

8. Sports Information and Research

Those responsible for research and providing information on sport should develop policies and programs to increase knowledge and understanding about women and sport and ensure that research norms and standards are based on research on women and men.

9. Resources

Those responsible for the allocation of resources should ensure that support is available for sportswomen, women's programmes and special measures to advance this Declaration of Principles.

10. Domestic and International Cooperation

Government and non-government organizations should incorporate the promotion of issues of gender equity and the sharing of examples of good practice in women and sport policies and programs in their associations with other organizations, within both domestic and international arenas.

Source: WomenSport International. "Brighton Declaration on Women and Sport." 1994. http://www.sportsbiz.bz/womensportinternational/conferences/brighton_declaration.htm.

groups, and progress and policy reports keep propelling us forward, even as obstructionists try to hold us back. The importance of sport runs the gamut—encompassing everything from fun and games to matters of life and death. But when we support, promote, and celebrate girls and women in sport, we all win.

NOTES

Chapter 1
1. PERFORM, Kantar Media, and SportBusiness Group, "Know the Fan: The Global Sports Media Consumption Report, 2014," http://www.knowthefan.com.
2. Plunkett Research, "Sports Industry Statistic and Market Size Overview, Business and Industry Statistics," https://www. plunkettresearch.com/statistics/Industry-Statistics-Sports-Industry-Statistic-and-Market-Size-Overview. All monetary figures in this manuscript are in US dollars, except where noted.
3. Rick Porter, "Summer Olympics Are the Lowest-Rated and Least Watched Since 2000," *TV by the Numbers*, August 23, 2016, http:// tvbythenumbers.zap2it.com/uncategorized/summer-olympics-are-the-lowest-rated-and-least-watched-since-2000.
4. International Olympic Committee, "London 2012 Olympic Games: Global Broadcast Report," 2012, https://www.olympic. org; Fédération Internationale de Football Association, "2014 FIFA World Cup Reached 3.2 Billion Viewers, One Billion Watched," December 16, 2015, http://www.fifa.com/worldcup/ news/y=2015/m=12/news=2014-fifa-world-cuptm-reached-3-2-billion-viewers-one-billion-watched--2745519.html; Fédération Internationale de Football Association, "Record-Breaking FIFA Women's World Cup Tops 750 Million TV Viewers," December 17, 2015, http://www.fifa.com/womensworldcup/ news/y=2015/m=12/news=record-breaking-fifa-women-s-world-cup-tops-750-million-tv-viewers-2745963.html; Joe Flint, "Super Bowl 50 Ranks as Third Most-Watched Title Game," *Wall Street Journal*, February 8, 2016, https://www.wsj.com/

articles/super-bowl-50-ranks-as-third-most-watched-title-game-
1454962962; Barry Jackson, "Sports Media Analysis: Social Media
Brings Instant Updates, but There Are Drawbacks," *Miami
Herald*, July 18, 2015, http://www.miamiherald.com/sports/spt-
columns-blogs/article27687346.html#storylink=cpy.

5. Ellen J. Staurowsky et al., *Her Life Depends on It III: Sport, Physical
Activity and the Health and Well-Being of American Girls and Women*
(East Meadow, NY: Women's Sports Foundation, 2015).

6. Women in Sport and Investec, "Sport for Success: The Socioeconomic Benefits of Women Playing Sport," 2016, https://www.
womeninsport.org/resources/sport-for-success; Ernst & Young,
"Female Executives Say Participation in Sport Helps Accelerate
Leadership and Career Potential," October 14, 2014, https://
www.prnewswire.com/news-releases/female-executives-say-
participation-in-sport-helps-accelerate-leadership-and-career-
potential-278614041.html.

7. EY Women Athletes Business Network and espnW, "Female
Athletes Make Winning Entrepreneurs, According to New EY/
espnW Report," 2017, http://www.ey.com/gl/en/newsroom/
news-releases/news-ey-female-athletes-make-winning-
entrepreneurs-ey-espn2-report.

8. Martha Brady, "Olympics Remind Us That Sports Can
Empower Women in Developing Countries," *Newsday*, August
10, 2012, https://www.newsday.com/opinion/oped/brady-
olympics-remind-us-that-sports-can-empower-women-in-
developing-countries-1.3895855; Right to Play, "Sport and
Gender: Empowering Girls and Women," 2010, http://www.
righttoplay.com/Pages/default.aspx.

9. June Larkin, Sherene Razack, and Fiona Moole, "Gender, Sport,
and Development," in *Literature Reviews on Sport for Development
and Peace*, commissioned by Sport for Development and Peace
International Working Group Secretariat (Toronto: University
of Toronto, 2007), 89–123. United Nations, "Sport as a Means to
Promote Education, Health, Development and Peace," November
3, 2005, https://www.un.org/sport/resources/documents/
secretary-generals-reports-general-assembly; Nilanjana
Bhowmick, "India's Golden Girls: How Sport and the Olympics
Can Uplift Women," *Time*, August 21, 2012, http://olympics.
time.com/2012/08/21/indias-golden-girls-how-sports-and-the-
olympics-can-uplift-women/#ixzz24TMCOcjB.

10. United Nations Women, "UN Women Signs Partnership Agreement with the International Olympic Committee to Advance Gender Equity," August 23, 2012.

11. Nancy Theberge, "Toward a Feminist Alternative to Sport as a Male Preserve," *Quest* 37, no. 2 (1985): 193–202. For a critique, see Niko Bresier, Susan Brownell, and Thomas F. Carter, *The Anthropology of Sport: Bodies, Borders, Biopolitics* (Oakland: University of California Press, 2018), 147–151.

12. Nancy L. Struna, " 'Good Wives' and 'Gardeners,' Spinners and 'Fearless Riders': Middle- and Upper-rank Women in Early American Sporting Culture," in J. A. Mangan and Roberta J. Park, *From "Fair Sex" to Feminism: Sport and the Socialization of Women in the Industrial and Post-Industrial Eras* (London: Routledge, 1987), 244.

13. "Organized Cheering," *The Nation*, January 5, 1911, 5–6.

14. Quoted in Welch Suggs, *A Place on the Team: The Triumph and Tragedy of Title IX* (Princeton, NJ: Princeton University Press, 2005), 73.

15. Frederick O. Mueller, "Cheerleading Injuries and Safety," *Journal of Athletic Training* 44 (2009): 565; Frederick O. Mueller and Robert C. Cantu, "Catastrophic Sports Injury Research: Twenty-Ninth Annual Report, Fall 1982–Spring 2011," http://nccsir.unc.edu.

16. Jaime Schultz, "Cheerleading's Peculiar Path to Potential Olympic Sport," *The Conversation,* February 1, 2018, https://theconversation.com/cheerleadings-peculiar-path-to-potential-olympic-sport-70386.

Chapter 2

1. June Kennard and John Marshall Carter, "In the Beginning: The Ancient and Medieval Worlds," in *Women and Sport: Interdisciplinary Perspectives,* ed. D. Margaret Costa and Sharon R. Guthrie (Champaign, IL: Human Kinetics, 1994), 20.

2. Susan Brownell, *Beiging's Games: What the Olympics Means to China* (Lanham, MD: Rowman and Littlefield, 2008), 20.

3. Allen Guttmann, *Women's Sports: A History* (New York: Columbia University Press, 1991), 26.

4. T. J. Desch Obi, *Fighting for Honor: The History of African Martial Arts Traditions in the Atlantic World* (Columbia: University of South Carolina Press, 2008).

5. Allen Guttmann, *From Ritual to Record: The Nature of Modern Sports* (New York: Columbia University Press, 1978), 16.

6. Quoted in Janice A. Beran, *From Six-on-Six to Full Court Press: A Century of Iowa Girls' Basketball* (Iowa City: University of Iowa Press, 2007), 8.

7. Dahn Shaulis, "Pedestriennes: Newsworthy but Controversial Women in Sporting Entertainment," *Journal of Sport History* 26, no. 1 (1999): 29–51.

8. "A Great Pedestrian Feat: Mme. Anderson Completes Her Task," *New York Times*, January 13, 1879, 5.

9. "The Female Pedestrians: A Sorry Spectacle at Gilmore's Garden—The Walking Record up to Last Evening," *New York Times*, March 28, 1879, 2.

10. Theresa Kay and Ruth Jeanes, "Women, Sport, and Gender Inequity," in *Sport and Society: A Student Introduction*, ed. Barrie Houlihan (Thousand Oaks: Sage, 2008), 131.

11. Quoted in Gertrude Pfister, "The Medical Discourse on Female Physical Culture in the 19th and Early 20th Centuries," *Journal of Sport History* 17, no. 2 (1990): 191.

12. Carmen Rial, "Women's Soccer in Brazil," *Revista*, Spring 2012, https://revista.drclas.harvard.edu/book/womens-soccer-brazil.

13. Collette Dowling, *The Frailty Myth: Women Approaching Physical Equality* (New York: Random House, 2000), 4; 6.

14. E. L. Wolven, "College Sports and Motherhood," *New York Times*, July 3, 1921, 42.

15. Patricia A. Vertinsky, *The Eternally Wounded Woman: Women, Doctors, and Exercise in the Late Nineteenth Century* (Manchester, UK: Manchester University Press, 1990).

16. Stephen K. Westmann, *Sport, Physical Education, and Womanhood* (Baltimore: Williams & Wilkins, 1939), 46; 49. Emphasis in original.

17. Paul Gallico, *A Farewell to Sport* (New York: Knopf, 1938), 233.

18. "Things Seen and Heard," *Sportsman* 20 (October 1936): 18.

19. Coubertin quoted in Mary Henson Leigh, "The Evolution of Women's Participation in the Summer Olympic Games, 1900–1948" (PhD diss., Ohio State University, 1974), 61.

20. Dudley A. Sargent, "Are Athletics Making Girls Masculine? A Practical Answer to a Question Every Girl Asks," *Ladies' Home Journal*, March 1912, 11.

21. Radhika Sanghani, " 'Get More Women Into Sport Through Cheerleading—It's Feminine,' Says Sports Minister Helen Grant," *Telegraph*, February 20, 2014, http://www.telegraph. co.uk/women/womens-politics/10652074/Get-more-women-into-sport-through-cheerleading-its-feminine-says-sports-minister-Helen-Grant.html.

22. Paul Gallico, "The Golden Decade," *Saturday Evening Post*, September 5, 1931, 12–13; 113–116.

23. Lynne Emery, "From Lowell Mills to Halls of Fame: Industrial League Sport for Women," in *Women and Sport: Interdisciplinary Perspectives*, ed. D. Margaret Costa and Sharon R. Guthrie (Champaign, IL: Human Kinetics, 1994), 107; 112.

24. John R. Tunis, "Women and the Sport Business," *Harper's Magazine*, July 1929, 213.

25. Nicole Willms, *When Women Rule the Court: Gender, Race, and Japanese American Basketball* (New Brunswick, NJ: Rutgers University Press, 2017), 8.

26. Linda J. Borish, "Settlement Houses to Olympic Stadiums: Jewish American Women, Sports and Social Change," *International Sports Studies* 21, no. 1 (2001): 10.

27. Willms, *When Women Rule the Court.*

28. Jennifer H. Lansbury, *A Spectacular Leap: Black Women Athletes in Twentieth-Century America* (Fayetteville: University of Arkansas Press, 2014), 18–32.

29. Amira Rose Davis, "No League of Their Own: Baseball, Black Women, and the Politics of Representation," *Radical History Review* 125 (2016): 77.

30. Samuel O. Regalado, "Incarcerated Sport: Nisei Women's Softball and Athletics During Japanese American Internment," *Journal of Sport History* 27 no. 3 (2000): 439.

Chapter 3

1. Quoted in George Vecsey, "Help on the Way for Title IX," *New York Times*, April 22, 1984, S3.

2. Alia Wong, "Where Girls Are Missing Out on High-School Sports," *The Atlantic*, June 26, 2015, https://www.theatlantic. com/education/archive/2015/06/girls-high-school-sports-inequality/396782.

3. The authors defined schools as "heavily minority" as schools in which 10 percent or less of enrolled students are white and "heavily white" if 90 percent or more of enrolled students were white. National Women's Law Center and the Poverty and Race Research Action Council, "Finishing Last: Girls of Color and Schools Sports Opportunities," 2015, https://nwlc.org/wp-content/uploads/2015/08/final_nwlc_girlsfinishinglast_report.pdf.

4. Richard Lapchick et al., "The 2016 Racial & Gender Report Card: College Sport," The Institute for Diversity and Ethics in Sport, April 6, 2017, http://www.tidesport.org/college-sport.html, 6.

5. Don Sabo and Phil Veliz, *Go Out and Play: Youth Sports in America* (East Meadow, NY: Women's Sports Foundation, 2008).

6. Michael L. Williams, "Accommodating Disabled Students Into Athletic Programs," National Federation of State High School Associations, July 27, 2014, https://www.nfhs.org/articles/accommodating-disabled-students-into-athletic-programs.

7. Eastern College Athletic Conference, "ECAC Board of Directors Cast Historic Vote to Add Varsity Sport Opportunities for Students With Disabilities in ECAC Leagues and Championships," January 22, 2015, http://www.ecacsports.com.

8. Kevin Trahan, " 'Nobody's Watching': Are Major College Sports Programs Treating Title IX Like a Suggestion?" *Vice Sports,* June 15, 2016, https://sports.vice.com/en_us/article/8qygwz/nobodys-watching-are-major-college-sports-programs-treating-title-ix-like-a-suggestion.

9. National Coalition for Girls and Women in Education, "Title IX and Athletics," 2017, http://www.ncwge.org/athletics.html.

10. Brian Burnsed, "Athletics Departments That Make More Money Than They Spend Still a Minority," September 18, 2015, http://www.ncaa.org/about/resources/media-center/news/athletics-departments-make-more-they-spend-still-minority.

11. Quoted in Doug Lederman, "North Carolina and Coach Settle Sexual Harassment Suit," *Inside Higher Ed,* January 15, 2008, https://www.insidehighered.com/news/2008/01/15/unc.

12. See Jessica Luther, *Unsportsmanlike Conduct: College Football and the Politics of Rape* (New York: Akashic, 2016).

13. Marc Tracy and Dan Berry, "The Rise, Then Shame, of Baylor Nation," *New York Times,* March 9, 2017, https://www.nytimes.com/2017/03/09/sports/baylor-football-sexual-assault.html.

14. Sofi Sinozich and Lynn Langton, "Rape and Sexual Assault Victimization Among College Females, 1995–2013," Bureau of Justice Statistics (December 2014): 1–19.

15. Quoted in J. B. Smith, "Report Shows Systemic Failure in Sex Crime Response at Baylor," *Waco Tribune-Herald*, May 26, 2016, http://www.wacotrib.com/news/higher_education/report-shows-systemic-failure-in-sex-crime-response-at-baylor/article_432b820a-6e64-5864-92c2-f3081f020384.html.

Chapter 4

1. Eleanor Metheny, "Symbolic Forms of Movement: The Feminine Image in Sports," in *Connotations of Movement in Sport and Dance* (Dubuque, IA: William C. Brown, 1965), 48–52. Emphasis in original.

2. Mary Louise Adams, *Artistic Impressions: Figure Skating, Masculinity, and the Limits of Sport* (Toronto: University of Toronto Press, 2011); Susan K. Cahn, *Coming on Strong: Gender and Sexuality in Women's Sport* (Urbana: University of Illinois Press, 2015).

3. Dvora Meyers, *The End of the Perfect 10: The Making and Breaking of Gymnastics' Top Score* (New York: Touchstone, 2016), 37.

4. USA Gymnastics, "Women's Artistic Gymnastics Event Descriptions," https://usagym.org/pages/gymnastics101/women/events.html.

5. "No Women Athletes for American Team," *New York Times*, March 31, 1914, 9.

6. Shireen Ahmed, "After a Long Fight, FIBA Finally Lifts Ban on Religious Headwear," *VICE*, May 4, 2017, https://sports.vice.com/en_ca/article/nz8bvg/after-a-long-fight-fiba-finally-lifts-its-ban-on-religious-headwear.

7. Jan Felshin, "The Triple Option . . . for Women in Sport," *Quest* 21, no. 1 (1974): 36–40.

8. Pat Griffin, *Strong Women, Deep Closets: Lesbians, Homophobia, and Sport* (Champaign, IL: Human Kinetics, 1998), 68.

9. K. L. Broad, "The Gendered Unapologetic: Queer Resistance in Women's Sport," *Sociology of Sport Journal* 18, no. 2 (2001): 181–204.

10. See Tanya Bunsell, *Strong and Hard Women: An Ethnography of Female Bodybuilding* (London: Routledge, 2013), 31. Emphasis in original.

11. Anne Bolin, "Buff Bodies and the Beast: Emphasized Femininity, Labor, and Power Relations Among Fitness, Figure, and Women Bodybuilding Competitors 1985–2010," in *Critical Readings in Bodybuilding*, ed. Adam Locks and Niall Richardson (London: Routledge, 2013): 29–57.

12. Caroline Praderio, "The First American in 16 Years to Win a Weightlifting Medal Is Championing Body Positivity," *Business Insider*, August 15, 2016, http://www.businessinsider.com/sarah-robles-weightlifting-medal-2016-8.

13. Cahn, *Coming on Strong*, 2.

14. Moya Bailey, "They Aren't Talking About Me . . ." *Crunk Feminist Collective*, March 14, 2010, http://www.crunkfeministcollective.com/2010/03/14/they-arent-talking-about-me.

15. Ben Rothenberg, "Tennis's Top Women Balance Body Image With Ambition," *New York Times*, July 10, 2015, https://www.nytimes.com/2015/07/11/sports/tennis/tenniss-top-women-balance-body-image-with-quest-for-success.html?_r=0&mtrref=undefined&assetType=nyt_now.

Chapter 5

1. Susan K. Cahn, *Coming on Strong: Gender and Sexuality in Twentieth-Century Women's Sport* (Cambridge, MA: Harvard University Press, 2005).

2. Quoted in Geoffrey C. Ward and Ken Burns, *Baseball: An Illustrated History* (New York: Knopf, 1994), 280.

3. Quoted in Cahn, *Coming on Strong*, 133.

4. Barry McDermott, "More Than a Pretty Face," *Sports Illustrated*, January 18, 1982, https://www.si.com/vault/1982/01/18/540914/more-than-a-pretty-face.

5. Chris Isidore, "Sex in Play in Women's Sports," *CNN*, August 23, 2002, http://money.cnn.com/2002/08/23/commentary/column_sportsbiz/women_sex/index.htm.

6. Emily Andrews and Colin Fernandez, "Babe, Set and Match: Why Looks Count for More Than Talent When Wimbledon Decides Which Girls Will Play on Centre Court," *Daily Mail*, June 29, 2009, http://www.dailymail.co.uk/news/article-1196155/Babe-set-match-How-looks-count-talent-Wimbledon-decides-girls-play-Centre-Court.html.

7. "Make-up and Short Shorts Improving Women's Football, Says Brazilian Official," *Guardian*, June 16, 2015,

https://www.theguardian.com/football/2015/jun/16/
make-up-shorts-improving-womens-game-brazil.

8. Mary Jo Kane, "Sex Sells Sex, Not Women's Sports," *The Nation*, July 27, 2010, https://www.thenation.com/article/ sex-sells-sex-not-womens-sports.

9. Saman Shad, "How to Get Men Watching Women's Football? Have Them Play in Lingerie," *Guardian*, June 7, 2012, https:// www.theguardian.com/commentisfree/2012/jun/07/ american-lingerie-football-league-women.

10. Gregory M. Herek, "The Psychology of Sexual Prejudice," *Current Directions in Psychological Science* 9, no. 1 (2000): 19–22.

11. Dennis Altman, "The Term 'LGBTI' Confuses Desire, Behavior and Identity—It's Time for a Rethink," *The Conversation*, January 19, 2018, https://theconversation.com/the-term-lgbti-confuses-desire-behaviour-and-identity-its-time-for-a-rethink-90175.

12. Quoted in Annie Kelly, "Raped and Killed for Being a Lesbian: South Africa Ignores 'Corrective' Attacks," *The Guardian*, March 12, 2009, https://www.theguardian.com/world/2009/ mar/12/eudy-simelane-corrective-rape-south-africa.

13. Pat Griffin, *Strong Women, Deep Closets: Lesbians and Homophobia in Sport* (Champaign, IL: Human Kinetics, 1998).

14. Helen Jefferson Lenskyj, "Reflections on Communication and Sport: On Heteronormativity and Gender Identities," *Communication & Sport* 1, no. 1–2 (2013): 138–150.

15. "Laila Ali Says She's Not Gay," *UPI*, November 11, 2005, http:// www.upi.com/Laila-Ali-says-shes-not-gay/34361131763228.

16. Pat Griffin, "Changing the Game: Homophobia and Lesbians in Sport," *Quest* 44, no. 2 (1992): 251–265.

17. Luke Cyphers and Kate Fagan, "Unhealthy Climate," ESPN, February 7, 2011, http://www.espn.com/ncw/news/story?page =Mag15unhealthyclimate.

18. Quoted in Tim Nash, "Jess Fishlock Reveals Her Struggles With Social Media and How She Handles Anti-Gay Bullying," *excellsports*, June 29, 2017, http://www.excellsports.com/ news/jess-fishlock-social-media-bullying.

19. Quoted in Jesse Jackman, "For Closeted Gay Athletes, Endorsement Fears Persist," *Huffington Post*, February 19, 2016, https://www.huffingtonpost.com/jesse-jackman/for-closeted-gay-athletes_b_9269956.html.

20. Mary G. McDonald, "Rethinking Resistance: The Queer Play of the Women's National Basketball Association, Visibility Politics and Late Capitalism," *Leisure Studies* 27, no. 1 (2008): 77–93.

Chapter 6

1. Eileen McDonagh and Laura Pappano, *Playing With the Boys: Why Separate Is Not Equal* (New York: Oxford University Press, 2007), 34. Emphasis in original.

2. Katie McDonough, "School Won't Let 12-Year-Old Girl Play Football Because of 'Lusting' Male Teammates," *Salon*, June 24, 2013, https://www.salon.com/2013/06/24/school_wont_let_12_year_old_girl_play_football_because_of_lusting_male_teammates; Christina Cauterucci, "An Arizona Boys' Soccer Team Refused to Play a Team With Girls for Religious Reasons," *Slate*, September 26, 2016, http://www.slate.com/blogs/xx_factor/2016/09/26/an_arizona_boys_soccer_team_refused_to_play_a_team_with_girls_for_religious.html; Anna North, "7 Sports in Which Women Have Beaten Men," *BuzzFeed*, August 2, 2012, https://www.buzzfeed.com/annanorth/7-sports-in-which-women-have-beaten-men?utm_term=.oh30mAnyzO#.pv1arQnWVz.

3. Michael A. Messner, *Taking the Field: Women, Men, and Sports* (Minneapolis: University of Minnesota Press, 2002).

4. Quoted in Harry Slavin, "Female Drivers Would 'Not Physically Be Able to Drive an F1 Car Quickly,' Claims Supremo Bernie Ecclestone," *Daily Mail*, April 19, 2016, http://www.dailymail.co.uk/sport/formulaone/article-3548844/Bernie-Ecclestone-Female-drivers-not-physically-able-drive-F1-car-quickly.html.

5. Eric Anderson, "'I Used to Think Women Were Weak': Orthodox Masculinity, Gender Segregation, and Sport," *Sociological Forum* 23, no. 2 (2008): 257–280.

6. McDonagh and Pappano, *Playing With the Boys*, 199.

7. Anne Crittenden Scott, "Closing the Muscle Gap: New Facts About Strength, Endurance—and Gender," *Ms.*, September 1974, 49–52.

8. Valérie Thibault et al., "Women and Men in Sport Performance: The Gender Gap Has Not Evolved Since 1983," *Journal of Sports Science and Medicine* 9, no. 2 (2010): 214–223.

9. Simone de Beauvoir, *The Second Sex*, trans. Constance Borde and Sheila Malovany-Chevallier (New York: Vintage, 2011), 400.

10. International Quidditch Association, "IQA Rulebook, 2016–2018," www.iqaquidditch.org/IQARulebook2016-2018.pdf, 12.

11. Jennifer Ring, *Stolen Bases: Why American Girls Don't Play Baseball* (Urbana: University of Illinois Press, 2009).

12. Gai Ingham Berlage, "Transition of Women's Baseball: An Overview," *NINE: A Journal of Baseball History and Culture* 9, no. 1 (2000): 72–81.

13. Quoted in Barbara Gregorich, *Women at Play: The Story of Women in Baseball* (San Diego, CA: Harcourt Brace, 1993), 69.

14. Katherine M. Jamieson, "Advance at Your Own Risk: Latinas, Families, and Collegiate Softball," in *Mexican Americans and Sport: A Reader on Athletics and Barrio Life*, ed. Jorge Iber and Samuel O. Regalado (College Station: Texas A&M University Press, 2006), 216.

15. Amira Rose Davis, "No League of Their Own: Baseball, Black Women, and the Politics of Representation," *Radical History Review* 125 (May 2016): 77.

16. Quoted in McDonagh and Pappano, *Playing With the Boys*, 209.

17. Joseph B. Treaster, "Little League Baseball Yields to 'Social Climate' and Accepts Girls," *New York Times*, June 13, 1974, 26.

18. Mary Peters with Ian Wooldridge, *Mary P.: Autobiography* (London: Paul, 1974), 55–56.

19. "Preserving la Difference," *Time*, September 16, 1966, 72.

20. Quoted in "Sex Test Disqualifies Athlete," *New York Times*, September 16, 1967, 28.

21. "Records of Polish Girl Sprinter Who Flunked Sex Test Barred," *New York Times*, February 26, 1968, 50.

22. "IAAF Regulations Governing Eligibility of Females With Hyperandrogenism to Compete in Women's Competition," http://www.iaaf.org/medical/policy.

23. Mianne Bagger, e-mail, February 13, 2018.

24. Susan Birrell and C. L. Cole, "Double Fault: Renee Richards and the Construction and Naturalization of Difference," *Sociology of Sport Journal* 7, no. 1 (1990): 1–21.

25. USA Wrestling, "USA Wrestling Transgender Guidelines," 2017, http://content.themat.com/forms/USAWrestling-Transgender-Policy.pdf.

26. Nebraska School Activities Association, "Gender Participation Policy," 2015, http://www.rockcountyschools.org/wp-content/uploads/2014/07/NSAA-Transgender-Policy.pdf.

Chapter 7

1. International Olympic Committee, "The Organisation," https://www.olympic.org/about-ioc-institution.
2. All data in this chapter is related to: Emily J. Houghton, Lindsay Parks Pieper, and Maureen M. Smith, *Women in the 2016 Olympic and Paralympic Games: An Analysis of Participation, Leadership, and Media Coverage* (East Meadow, NY: Women's Sports Foundation, 2017).
3. Ibid.
4. Quoted in Dikaia Chatziefstathiou, "Reading Baron Pierre de Coubertin: Issues of Gender and Race," *Aethlon* 25, no. 2 (2008): 101–102.
5. Quoted in John W. Loy, Fiona McLachlan, and Douglas Booth. "Connotations of Female Movement and Meaning," *Olympika*, XVIII (2009): 12.
6. Quoted in Fr. M. Messerli, "Women's Participation in the Modern Olympic Games," *Bulletin du Comité International Olympique* (May 1952): 25.
7. Mary H. Leigh and Thérèse M. Bonin, "The Pioneering Role of Madame Alice Milliat and the FSFI in Establishing International Track and Field Competition for Women," *Journal of Sport History* 4, no. 1 (1977): 72–83.
8. John R. Tunis, "Women and the Sport Business," *Harper's Magazine* (July 1929): 213; *Chicago Herald-Tribune*, July 17, 1930; Stephanie Daniels and Anita Tedder, *"A Proper Spectacle": Women Olympians 1900–1936* (Bedfordshire, UK: ZeNaNA Press, 2000), 70–75.
9. Wythe Williams, "Americans Beaten in Four Olympic Tests," *New York Times*, August 3, 1928, 3.
10. Quoted in Roseanne Montillo, *Fire on the Track: Betty Robinson and the Triumph of the Early Olympic Women* (New York: Crown, 2017), 85.
11. Jaime Schultz, "Going the Distance: The Road to the 1984 Olympic Women's Marathon," *International Journal of the History of Sport* 32, no. 1 (2015): 72–88.
12. Andrea Rodriguez, "Women Demand Cuba Support 1st Female Boxing Team," *Miami Herald*, February 1, 2017, http://www.miamiherald.com/news/nation-world/world/americas/cuba/article130041039.html.

13. Amanda Ruggeri, "Why It Took 90 Years for Women's Ski Jumping to Make the Olympics," *Deadspin,* February 11, 2014, https://deadspin.com/why-it-took-90-years-for-womens-ski-jumping-to-make-the-1520520342.

14. Quoted in Katie Thomas, "After Long Fight for Inclusion, Women's Ski Jumping Gains Olympic Status," *New York Times,* April 6, 2011, http://www.nytimes.com/2011/04/07/sports/skiing/07skijumping.html?mcubz=1; quoted in Michelle Kaufman, "Women's Ski Jumping Competitions in 2014 Winter Olympics a Giant Leap for Womankind," *Miami Herald,* February 12, 2014, http://www.miamiherald.com/sports/olympics/article1960265.html; quoted in Mireille Silcoff, "Who Said Girls Can't Jump?" *New York Times Magazine,* November 22, 2013, http://www.nytimes.com/2013/11/24/magazine/who-said-girls-cant-jump.html.

15. International Olympic Committee, "Tokyo 2020 Event Programme to See Major Boost for Female Participation, Youth and Urban Appeal," June 9, 2017, https://www.olympic.org/news/tokyo-2020-event-programme-to-see-major-boost-for-female-participation-youth-and-urban-appeal.

16. Helen Jefferson Lenskyj, *Gender Politics and the Olympic Industry* (New York: Palgrave Macmillan, 2013), 43–44.

17. Ibid.

18. Quoted in Jeré Longman, "A Giant Leap for Women, but Hurdles Remain," *New York Times,* July 29, 2012, http://www.nytimes.com/2012/07/30/sports/olympics/despite-gains-for-female-athletes-fight-for-true-equality-remains.html?mcubz=1&mtrref=www.google.com&gwh=36B7A8DA464A5741442B819DA9E248A2&gwt=pay.

19. Jennifer L. Berdahl, Eric Luis Uhlmann, and Feng Bai, "Win–Win: Female and Male Athletes From More Gender Equal Nations Perform Better in International Sports Competitions," *Journal of Experimental Social Psychology* 56 (2015): 1–3.

20. Danyel Reiche, *Success and Failure of Countries at the Olympic Games* (New York: Routledge, 2016).

21. Ian Brittain, *The Paralympic Games Explained* (London: Routledge, 2010).

22. Paralympic Movement, "Classification Introduction," n.d., https://www.paralympic.org/classification.

23. Women on Boards, "Gender Balance in Global Sport," 2016, https://www.womenonboards.net/en-GB/Resources/Voice-for-Women/Gender-Balance-in-Global-Sport.

24. International Olympic Committee, "Sochi 2014," https://www.paralympic.org/sochi-2014.

25. International Paralympic Committee, "IPC Women in Sport Leadership Toolkit," October 2010, https://www.paralympic.org/sites/default/files/document/130130154714620_2010_10_01++IPC+Women+in+Sport+Leadership+Toolkit.pdf.

26. John Affleck, "Why Do the Paralympics Get So Little Media Attention in the United States?" *The Conversation*, September 14, 2016, https://theconversation.com/why-do-the-paralympics-get-so-little-media-attention-in-the-united-states-65205.

27. Kayla Parker, "A Primer to the 2016 Rio Paralympic Games," ESPN.com, September 5, 2016, http://www.espn.com/espnw/sports/article/17101834/a-primer-2016-rio-paralympics-games.

28. "Rio 2016 Paralympics Smash All TV Viewing Records," *Women's Sport Report*, March 16, 2017, http://www.womensportreport.com/rio-2016-paralympics-smash-all/wn/20419.

29. Women's Sports Foundation, "Women in the 2016 Olympic and Paralymic Games: An Analysis of Participation, Leadership, and Media Coverage," November 27, 2017, https://www.womenssportsfoundation.org/research/article-and-report/elite-athletes/women-2016-olympic-paralympic-games.

30. "What Are Your Chances of Becoming a Summer Olympic Athlete?" *Visually*, August 6, 2012, https://visual.ly/community/infographic/olympics/what-are-your-chances-becoming-summer-olympic-athlete.

Chapter 8

1. Emma Sherry, Angela Osborne, and Matthew Nicholson, "Images of Sports Women: A Review," *Sex Roles* 74, no. 7 (2015): 299–309; Toni Bruce, "Assessing the Sociology of Sport: On Media and Representations of Sportswomen," *International Review for the Sociology of Sport* 50, no. 4–5 (2015): 380–384; Roxane Coche, "The Amount of Women's Sports Coverage on International Sports News Websites' Home Pages: Content Analysis of the Top Two Sites From Canada, France, Great Britain, and the United States," *Electronic*

News 9, no. 4 (2015): 223–241; Thomas Horky and Jorge-Uwe Nieland, "Comparing Sports Reporting From Around the World—Numbers and Facts on Sports in Daily Newspapers," *International Sports Press Survey 2011* 5 (2013): 22; Toni Bruce, Jorid Hovden, and Pirkko Markula, eds. *Sportswomen at the Olympics: A Global Content Analysis of Newspaper Coverage* (Rotterdam: Sense Publishers, 2010); Gerd Von der Lippe, "Media Image: Sport, Gender and National Identities in Five European Countries," *International Review for the Sociology of Sport* 37, no. 3–4 (2002): 371–395; Janet Fink, "Female Athletes, Women's Sport, and the Sport Media Commercial Complex: Have We Really 'Come A Long Way, Baby'?" *Sport Management Review* 18 (2015): 331–342.

2. Gaye Tuchman, "The Symbolic Annihilation of Women by the Mass Media," in *Hearth and Home: Images of Women in the Mass Media*, ed. Gaye Tuchman, Arlene Kaplan Daniels, and James Walker Benét (New York: Oxford University Press, 1978).

3. Tucker Center for Research on Girls and Women in Sport, "Media Coverage and Female Athletes," http://www.cehd.umn.edu/ tuckercenter/multimedia/mediacoverage.html.

4. Cheryl Cooky, Michael A. Messner, and Michaela Musto, " 'It's Dude Time!': A Quarter Century of Excluding Women's Sports in Televised News and Highlight Shows," *Communication & Sport* 3, no. 3 (2015): 261–287.

5. Ibid., 278, 275.

6. Kelly Wallace, "How to Keep Girls in the Game After Puberty," CNN.com, June 28, 2016, http://www.cnn.com/2016/06/28/ health/girls-sports-puberty-likeagirl/index.html.

7. Cooky, Messner, and Musto, " 'It's Dude Time!' " 269.

8. Cambridge University Press, "Aesthetics or Athletics?" August 1, 2016, http://www.cambridge.org/about-us/media/press-releases/aesthetics-or-athletics.

9. Reprinted in " 'We Must Continue to Dream Big': An Open Letter From Serena Williams," *The Guardian*, November 29, 2016, https://www.theguardian.com/lifeandstyle/2016/nov/ 29/dream-big-open-letter-serena-williams-porter-magazine-incredible-women-of-2016-issue-women-athletes.

10. "#Cover the Athlete," YouTube video, 1:22, posted by CoverTheAthlete, October 28, 2015, https://www.youtube.com/ watch?v=Ol9VhBDKZs0.

11. Frank Deford, "She Won't Win the French Open, but Who Cares? Anna Kournikova Is Living Proof That Even in This Age of Supposed Enlightenment, a Hot Body Can Count as Much as a Good Backhand," *Sports Illustrated,* June 5, 2000, https://www. si.com/vault/2000/06/05/282062/she-wont-win-the-french-open-but-who-cares-anna-kournikova-is-living-proof-that-even-in-this-age-of-supposed-enlightenment-a-hot-body-can-count-as-much-as-a-good-backhand.

12. See, for example, Sally Jenkins, "Stalking Is Not Just a Sports Issue," *Washington Post,* July 4, 2002, https://www. washingtonpost.com/archive/sports/2002/07/04/stalking-is-not-just-a-sports-issue/a2f1e508-8159-40e3-8e6e-0b16f353e304/ ?utm_term=.ece92c3b4457.

13. Dennis Romero, "Danica Patrick, Racing Warrior, Is a Word That 'Starts With B' Says SoCal Sports Anchor Ross Shimabuku," *LA Weekly,* February 2, 2012, http://www. laweekly.com/news/danica-patrick-racing-warrior-is-a-word-that-starts-with-b-says-socal-sports-anchor-ross-shimabuku-2391709.

14. Katherine M. Jamieson, "Reading Nancy Lopez: Decoding Representations of Race, Class, and Sexuality," *Sociology of Sport Journal* 15, no. 4 (1998): 355.

15. Gilbert Rogin, "Flamin' Mamie's Bouffant Belles," *Sports Illustrated,* April 20, 1964, https://www.si.com/vault/1964/04/ 20/612942/flamin-mamies-bouffant-belles.

16. Linda D. Williams, "Sportswomen in Black and White: Sport History From an Afro-American Perspective," in *Women, Media and Sport: Challenging Gender Values,* ed. Pamela J. Creedon (Thousand Oaks, CA: Sage, 1994), 45–66.

17. Susan Tyler Eastman and Andrew C. Billings, "Biased Voice of Sports: Racial and Gender Stereotyping in College Basketball Announcing," *Howard Journal of Communication* 12, no. 4 (2001): 183–202. See also Marie Hardin, Julie E. Dodd, Jean Chance, and Kristie Walsdorf, "Sporting Images in Black and White: Race in Newspaper Coverage of the 2000 Olympic Games," *Howard Journal of Communications* 15, no. 4 (2004): 211–227.

18. Akilah R. Carter-Francique, " 'Re'Presenting 'Gabby': Examining the Digital Media Coverage of Gabrielle Douglas at the 2012

London Olympic Games," *International Journal of Sport Studies* 4, no. 9 (2014): 1080–1091.

19. Yomee Lee, "A New Voice: Korean American Women in Sports," *International Review for the Sociology of Sport* 40, no. 4 (2005): 481–495.

20. See, for example, Valerie J. Nelson and Nathan Fenno, "Sammy Lee, Diver Who Became First Asian American to Win Olympic Medal, Dies at 96," *LA Times*, December 3, 2016, http://www.latimes.com/local/obituaries/la-me-sammy-lee-snap-20161203-story.html.

21. Devin Israel Cabanilla, "Media Fail to Give REAL First Asian American Olympic Gold Medalist Her Due," *The Seattle Globalist*, December 15, 2016, http://www.seattleglobalist.com/2016/12/15/real-first-asian-american-olympic-gold-medalist-doesnt-get-due/60115.

22. Claire Jean Kim, "The Racial Triangulation of Asian Americans," *Politics & Society* 27, no. 1 (1999): 126–127.

23. Mary Yu Danico and Franklin Ng, *Asian American Issues* (Westport, CT: Greenwood Press, 2004), 39.

24. Jamieson, "Reading Nancy Lopez."

25. Cynthia M. Frisby, "A Content Analysis of Serena Williams and Angelique Kerber's Racial and Sexist Microaggressions," *Open Journal of Social Sciences* 5 (2017): 263–281.

26. Quoted in Michael Rosenberg, "Ibtihaj Muhammad Didn't Need a Medal to Leave Her Mark on U.S., Olympics," *Sports Illustrated*, August 8, 2016, https://www.si.com/olympics/2016/08/08/ibtihaj-muhammad-team-usa-fencing-rio-olympics.

27. Shireen Ahmed, "Breaking: Women in Hijab Play Sports," *Daily Beast*, August 12, 2016, https://www.thedailybeast.com/breaking-women-in-hijab-play-sports.

28. Anthanasios (Sakis) Pappous, Anne Marcellini, and Eric de Leseleuc, "Contested Issues in Research on the Media Coverage of Female Paralympic Athletes," *Sport in Society* 14, no. 9 (2011): 1182–1191; Helen Meekosha and Leanne Dowse, "Distorting Images, Invisible Images: Gender, Disability, and the Media," *Media International Australia* 84 (1997): 91–101; Lea Ann Schell and Stephanie Rodriguez, "Subverting Bodies/Ambivalent Representations; Media Analysis of Paralympian, Hope Lewellen," *Sociology of Sport Journal* 18 (2001): 127–135.

29. Andrew Smith and Nigel Thomas, "The 'Inclusion' of Elite
    Athletes With Disabilities in the 2002 Manchester Commonwealth
    Games: An Exploratory Analysis of British Newspaper
    Coverage," *Sport, Education and Society* 10, no. 1 (2005): 52.
30. Ronald J. Berger, "Disability and the Dedicated Wheelchair
    Athlete: Beyond the 'Supercrip' Critique," *Journal of Contemporary
    Ethnography* 37, no. 6 (2008): 647–678.
31. Jan Grue, "The Problem With Inspiration Porn: A Tentative
    Definition and a Provisional Critique," *Disability & Society* 31,
    no. 6 (2016): 839.
32. David E. J. Purdue and P. David Howe, "Who's in and Who's
    Out? Legitimate Bodies Within the Paralympic Games," *Sociology
    of Sport Journal* 30, no. 1 (2013): 24–40.
33. International Paralympic Committee, "Guide to Reporting
    on Persons With an Impairment," October 2014, https://
    m.paralympic.org/sites/default/files/document/
    141027103527844_2014_10_31+Guide+to+reporting+on+persons
    +with+an+impairment.pdf.
34. Dunja Antunovic and Marie Hardin, "Women and the
    Blogosphere: Exploring Feminist Approaches to Sport,"
    International Review for the Sociology of Sport 50, no. 6
    (2015): 661–677.
35. Sarah Wolter, "A Qualitative Analysis of Photographs and
    Articles on espnW: Positive Progress for Female Athletes,"
    Communication and Sport 3, no. 2 (2015): 454–471.
36. Sarah Wolter, " 'It Just Makes Good Business Sense': A Media
    Political Economy Analysis of espnW," *Journal of Sports Media* 9,
    no. 2 (2014): 73–96.
37. Jennings Brown, "Where Are All the Women Sports Stars
    in Video Games?" *New York Daily News,* September 11,
    2015, http://www.nydailynews.com/sports/soccer/
    women-sports-stars-video-games-article-1.2356913.
38. Pamela Creedon, "Women in Toyland: A Look at Women in
    American Newspaper Sports Journalism," in *Women, Media
    and Sport: Challenging Gender Values* (Thousand Oaks, CA: Sage,
    1994), 99.
39. Women's Media Center, "The Status of Women in U.S. Media,
    2017," March 21, 2017, http://www.womensmediacenter.com/
    reports/the-status-of-women-in-u.s.-media-2017.
40. Cooky, Messner, and Musto, " 'It's Dude Time!' " 278.

41. Marie Hardin and Stacie Shain, "Strength in Numbers? The Experiences and Attitudes of Women in Sport Media," *Journalism and Mass Communication Quarterly* 82, no. 4 (2005): 804–819.

42. Quoted in Julie DiCaro, "Safest Bet in Sports: Men Complaining About a Female Announcer's Voice," *New York Times*, September 18, 2017, https://www.nytimes.com/2017/09/18/sports/nfl-beth-mowins-julie-dicaro.html?mcubz=1.

43. Kavitha A. Davidson, "That Visceral Feeling of Hearing Someone Like Me in the Monday Night Football Booth," espnW, September 13, 2017, http://www.espn.com/espnw/voices/article/20681034/that-visceral-feeling-hearing-the-monday-night-football-booth.

44. Pam Oliver, as told to Jeannine Amber, "Game Change: Pam Oliver Breaks Her Silence on Her Career Shake-up," *Essence*, September 3, 2014, https://www.essence.com/2014/09/04/pam-oliver-game-change.

45. Quoted in Donald McRae, "Chris Gayle: 'You're With Men. You're Good-Looking. What Do You Expect," *The Guardian*, June 14, 2016, https://www.theguardian.com/sport/2016/jun/14/chris-gayle-mel-mclaughlin-sexism-row-west-indies-cricket.

46. Sarah Spain, "Grace Under Fire: Women in Media Shouldn't Have to 'Ignore' Abuse," espnW, April 28, 2016, http://www.espn.com/espnw/voices/article/15412369/women-sports-media-ignore-abuse.

47. Korryn D. Mozisek, "No Girls Allowed! Female Reporters as Threats to the Male Domain of Sports," *Journal of Sports Media* 10, no. 2 (2015): 17–29.

48. See Lisa Disch and Mary Jo Kane, "When a Looker Is Really a Bitch: Lisa Olson, Sport, and the Heterosexual Matrix," *Signs: Journal of Women in Culture and Society* 21, no. 2 (1996): 278–308.

Chapter 9

1. Nevin Caple, Richard Lapchick, and Nicole M. LaVoi, "Gender, Race, and LGBT Inclusion of Head Coaches of Women's Teams: A Special Collaborative Report on Select NCAA Division I Conferences for the 45th Anniversary of Title IX," June 2017, http://www.cehd.umn.edu/tuckercenter/library/docs/research/2017_Title_IX_at_45_Report.pdf.

2. Ellen J. Staurowsky and Michael Proska, "Gender Equity at the High School Level," Women in Coaching (blog), July 15, 2013,

http://stream.goodwin.drexel.edu/womenincoaching/tag/female-high-school-athletic-directors.

3. Aspen Institute's Project Play, "State of Play 2016: Trends and Developments," https://www.aspenprojectplay.org/sites/default/files/StateofPlay_2016_FINAL.pdf.

4. Jacqui L. Kalin and Jennifer J. Waldron, "Preferences Toward Gender of Coach and Perceptions of Roles of Basketball Coaches," *International Journal of Exercise Science* 8, no. 4 (2015): 303–317.

5. Rachel Stark, "Where Are the Women?" *Champion Magazine,* Winter 2017, http://www.ncaa.org/static/champion/where-are-the-women/index.html; Don Sabo, Philip Veliz, and Ellen J. Staurowsky, *Beyond X's and O's: Gender Bias and Coaches of Women's College Sports* (East Meadow, NY: Women's Sports Foundation, 2016).

6. C. Bonnie Everhart and Packianathan Chelladurai, "Gender Differences in Preferences for Coaching as an Occupation: The Role of Self-Efficacy, Valence, and Perceived Barriers," *Research Quarterly for Exercise and Sport,* 69, no. 2 (1998): 188–200.

7. Quoted in Linda Flanagan, "The Field Where Men Still Call the Shots," *The Atlantic,* July 28, 2017, https://www.theatlantic.com/education/archive/2017/07/the-field-where-men-still-call-the-shots/535167.

8. Amada Hess, "Male Basketball Coach Says a Female Coach Could Never 'Mold Boys Into Successful Men,'" *Slate,* August 6, 2016, http://www.slate.com/blogs/xx_factor/2014/08/06/female_basketball_coaches_will_a_woman_ever_coach_a_men_s_college_basketball.html.

9. David Berri, "Why the NBA Should Give Female Coaches Like Becky Hammon a Shot," *Vice,* July 22, 2015, https://sports.vice.com/en_us/article/bmeq34/why-the-nba-should-give-female-coaches-like-becky-hammon-a-shot.

10. Quoted in Jim Buzinski, "San Francisco 49ers Assistant Katie Sowers Is First Out LGBT Coach in NFL," *Outsports,* August 22, 2017, https://www.outsports.com/2017/8/22/16175286/katie-sowers-san-francisco-49ers-coach-gay-coming-out.

11. Quoted in Charlie Eccleshare, "'Next You'll Be Saying You're Going to Work With a Dog'—Andy Murray Reveals Player's Response to Hiring a Female Coach," *Telegraph,* August 23, 2017, http://www.telegraph.co.uk/tennis/2017/08/23/

next-saying-going-work-dog-andy-murray-reveals-players-response.

12. Women on Boards, "Gender Balance of Global Sport Report," 2016, https://www.womenonboards.net/en-GB/Resources/Voice-for-Women/Gender-Balance-in-Global-Sport.

13. Staurowsky and Proska, "Gender Equity at the High School Level."

14. Amy Wilson, *45 Years of Title IX: The Status of Women in Intercollegiate Athletics* (NCAA, 2017), http://www.ncaa.org/sites/default/files/TitleIX45-295-FINAL_WEB.pdf.

15. Bob Cook, "Women Are Largely Untapped Resource in Alleviating Youth Sports Referee Shortage," *Forbes,* June 16, 2017, https://www.forbes.com/sites/bobcook/2017/06/16/women-are-largely-untapped-resource-in-alleviating-youth-sports-referee-shortage/#4626be5a4cbc.

16. Michael Popke, "More Women Coaching High School Boys Teams," *Athletic Business,* November 2008, https://www.athleticbusiness.com/high-school/more-women-coaching-high-school-boys-teams.html.

17. Quoted in Taylor Link, "LaVar Ball Bullied Female Referee at Las Vegas Tournament, Had Her Replaced With Male Ref," *Salon,* July 30, 2017, http://www.salon.com/2017/07/30/lavar-ball-bullied-female-referee-at-las-vegas-tournament-had-her-replaced-with-male-ref.

18. Eduardo Gonzalez, "Referee Company Cuts Ties With Adidas After LaVar Ball Has Female Official Removed From Game," *Los Angeles Times,* July 31, 2017, http://www.latimes.com/sports/highschool/la-sp-company-cut-ties-with-adidas-lavar-ball-female-referee-20170731-story.html.

19. Angelina Chapin, "Four Decades after the Battle of the Sexes, the Fight for Equality Goes On," *Guardian,* March 11, 2017, https://www.theguardian.com/sport/2017/mar/11/billie-jean-king-battle-of-the-sexes-tennis.

20. Venus Williams, "Wimbledon Has Sent Me a Message: I'm Only a Second-Class Champion," *Times,* June 26, 2006, https://www.thetimes.co.uk/article/wimbledon-has-sent-me-a-message-im-only-a-second-class-champion-f056h05hmzq.

21. Ben Rothenberg, "Roger Federer, $731,000; Serena Williams, $495,000: The Pay Gap in Tennis," *New York Times,* April 12, 2016, https://www.nytimes.com/2016/04/13/sports/tennis/

equal-pay-gender-gap-grand-slam-majors-wta-atp.html?ref=tenn
is&module=ArrowsNav&contentCollection=Tennis&action=key
press&region=FixedLeft&pgtype=article.

22. "Prize Money in Sport—BBC Sport Study," June 19, 2017, http://
www.bbc.com/sport/40300519.

23. "The World's Highest Paid Athletes," *Forbes*, 2017, https://www.
forbes.com/athletes/list.

24. Max Saffer, "Dollars but No Sense: Golf's Long History
of Shortchanging Women," espnW, April 8, 2016, http://
www.espn.com/espnw/sports/article/15160220/
big-gap-earnings-men-women-professional-golfers.

25. Tim Wigmore, "Sports Gender Pay Gap: Why Are Women
Still Paid Less Than Men?" *New Statesman*, August 5, 2016,
https://www.newstatesman.com/politics/sport/2016/08/
sport-s-gender-pay-gap-why-are-women-still-paid-less-men.

26. Gwendolyn Oxenham, " 'Pele With a Skirt': The Unequal
Fortunes of Brazil's Soccer Stars," *The Atlantic*, June 4, 2015,
https://www.theatlantic.com/entertainment/archive/2015/06/
neymar-marta-world-cup-brazil/394856.

27. Louisa Thomas, "Equal Pay for Equal Play: The Case for
the Women's Soccer Team," *New Yorker*, May 27, 2016,
https://www.newyorker.com/culture/cultural-comment/
the-case-for-equal-pay-in-womens-sports.

28. Seth Berkman, "Pay Cuts Jolt Women's Pro League and Leave Its
Future Uncertain," *New York Times*, November 22, 2016, https://
www.nytimes.com/2016/11/22/sports/hockey/nwhl-pay-cut-
salary.html?mcubz=1.

29. Jonathan Tannenwald, "Glenside Native Maddy Evans'
Retirement From Playing Soccer an Example of Ugly Truth About
NWSL Salaries," *Philadelphia Inquirer*, August 16, 2017, http://
www.philly.com/philly/sports/soccer/national-women-soccer-
league-salaries-maddy-edwards-retirement-orlando-pride-marta-
alex-morgan-20170816.html.

30. Meg Linehan, "NWSL Minimum Salary to Double for Fifth
Season," *excellesports*, January 26, 2017, http://www.excellesports.
com/news/nwsl-minimum-salary-double-fifth-season; Christian
Simmons, "Orlando Pride Midfielder Maddy Evans Says Low
Salary Was Factor in Retirement," *Orlando Sentinel*, September 11,
2017, http://www.orlandosentinel.com/sports/orlando-pride-
soccer/os-sp-orlando-pride-news-0814-story.html.

31. National Collegiate Athletic Association, "Estimated Probability of Competing in Professional Athletics," March 10, 2017, http://www.ncaa.org/about/resources/research/estimated-probability-competing-professional-athletics.

32. Carl Stoffers, "Equal Pay for Equal Play? As Women's Sports Become More Popular, Female Athletes Are Demanding to Be Paid Like Their Male Counterparts," *Junior Scholastic/Current Events*, January 9, 2017.

33. David George Surdam, *The Rise of the National Basketball Association* (Urbana: University of Illinois Press, 2012).

34. Quoted in "Football Club Become First to Give Equal Pay to Both Men's and Women's Teams," *The Independent*, July 12, 2017, http://www.independent.co.uk/sport/football/news-and-comment/lewes-fc-equal-pay-club-statement-equality-fc-a7836601.html.

35. Jeanette Howard, "Sad Ending, but Deserved," *Chicago Tribune*, September 17, 2003, http://articles.chicagotribune.com/2003-09-17/sports/0309170215_1_wusa-women-s-sports-pax.

Chapter 10

1. Women's Sports Foundation, "Factors Influencing Girls' Participation in Sport," September 9, 2016, https://www.womenssportsfoundation.org/support-us/do-you-know-the-factors-influencing-girls-participation-in-sports.

2. "Half of Girls Quit Sports by the End of Puberty," *Business Wire*, June 28, 2016, https://www.businesswire.com/news/home/20160628005793/en/Girls-Quit-Sports-Puberty*-New-Always%C2%AE-LikeAGirl.

3. Aspen Institute's Project Play, "Facts: Sports Activity and Children," https://www.aspenprojectplay.org/the-facts.

4. Sally Jenkins, "There's a Legal Remedy to the Doping Issue," *Washington Post*, October 12, 2007, http://www.washingtonpost.com/wp-dyn/content/article/2007/10/11/AR2007101102285.html.

5. Andrew Wolanin, Eugene Hong, Donald Marks, Kelly Panchoo, and Michael Gross, "Prevalence of Clinically Elevated Depressive Symptoms in College Athletes and Differences by Gender and Sport," *British Journal of Sports Medicine* 50, no. 3 (2016): 167–171.

6. Thomas Hammond, Christie Gialloreto, Hanna Kubas, and Henry Hap Davis IV, "The Prevalence of Failure-Based

Depression Among Elite Athletes," *Clinical Journal of Sport Medicine* 23, no. 4 (2013): 273–277.

7. Neeru Jayanthi, "Sports Specialized Risks for Reinjury in Young Athletes: A 2+ Year Clinical Prospective Evaluation," *British Journal of Sports Medicine* 51, no. 4 (2017): 334.

8. American Medical Society for Sports Medicine, "Effectiveness of Early Sport Specialization Limited in Most Sports, Sport Diversification May Be Better Approach at Young Ages," 2013, https://www.amssm.org/News-Release-Article.php?NewsID=69.

9. Martin Rogers, "U.S. Women Were Multi-Sport Athletes Before Focusing on Soccer," *USA Today*, July 3, 2015, https://www.usatoday.com/story/sports/soccer/2015/07/03/abby-wambach-morgan-brian-lauren-holiday/29665797.

10. Joel S. Brenner, "Sports Specialization and Intensive Training in Young Athletes," *Pediatrics* 138, no. 3 (2016): e20162148.

11. Natalie Voskanian, "ACL Injury Prevention in Female Athletes: Review of the Literature and Practical Considerations in Implementing an ACL Prevention Program," *Current Reviews in Musculoskeletal Medicine* 6, no. 2 (2013): 158–163.

12. Jennifer M. Hootman, Randall Dick, and Julie Agel, "Epidemiology of Collegiate Injuries for 15 Sports: Summary and Recommendations for Injury Prevention Initiatives," *Journal of Athletic Training* 42, no. 2 (2007): 311–319; Andrew E. Lincoln, Shane V. Caswell, and Jon L. Almquist, "Trends in Concussion Incidence in High School Sports: A Prospective 11-Year Study," *American Journal of Sports Medicine* 39, no. 5 (2011): 958–963.

13. Tyler Maland, "My Legacy: Brandi Chastain Pledges Brain," *Concussion Legacy Foundation*, March 3, 2016, https://concussionfoundation.org/story/my-legacy-brandi-chastain.

14. Quoted in Malaka Gharib, "A Swimmer's 'Period' Comment Breaks Taboos in Sports—And in China," NPR.org, August 17, 2016, https://www.npr.org/sections/goatsandsoda/2016/08/17/490121285/a-swimmers-period-comment-breaks-taboos-in-sports-and-in-china.

15. Mary Jane De Souza et al., "2014 Female Athlete Triad Coalition Consensus Statement on Treatment and Return to Play of the Female Athlete Triad," *British Journal of Sports Medicine* 48, no. 4 (2014): 289.

16. D'Arcy Maine, "The Pressure of Pulling Your Own Weight," espnW, n.d., http://www.espn.com/espn/feature/story/_/id/19232937/espnw-body-image-confidential#!pressure.
17. Quoted in Philip Hersh, "Are Ski Jumpers Too Thin?" *Chicago Tribune,* January 16, 2002, http://articles.chicagotribune.com/2002-01-16/sports/0201160397_1_top-jumpers-alan-alborn-sven-hannawald.
18. American College of Obstetrics and Gynecology, *Technical Bulletin: Exercise During Pregnancy and the Postnatal Period* (Washington, DC: American College of Obstetrics and Gynecology, 1985).
19. Roger L. Hammer, Jan Perkins, and Richard Parr, "Exercise During the Childbearing Year," *Journal of Perinatal Education* 9, no. 1 (2000): 1–14.
20. Uğur Erdener and Richard Budgett, "Exercise and Pregnancy: Focus on Advice for the Competitive and Elite Athlete," *British Journal of Sports Medicine* 50, no. 10 (2016): 567–567.
21. Quoted in Marissa Payne, "With a Boost From Wonder Woman, Pregnant Alysia Montaño Returns to the Track," *Washington Post,* June 23, 2017, https://www.washingtonpost.com/news/early-lead/wp/2017/06/23/with-a-boost-from-wonder-woman-pregnant-alysia-montano-returns-to-the-track/?utm_term=.c6aecadad1d8.
22. Elisabeth Braw, "East Germany's Steroid Shame," *Newsweek,* June 8, 2014, http://www.newsweek.com/2014/06/13/east-germanys-steroid-shame-253840.html.
23. World Anti-Doping Agency, "Prohibited List Q&A," n.d., https://www.wada-ama.org/en/questions-answers/prohibited-list-qa#item-391.
24. World Anti-Doping Agency, "Prohibited List, 2018," https://www.wada-ama.org/sites/default/files/prohibited_list_2018_en.pdf.
25. World Health Organization, "Sexual Violence," n.d., http://www.who.int/reproductivehealth/topics/violence/sexual_violence/en.
26. National Sexual Violence Resource Center, "What Is Sexual Violence? Fact Sheet," January 2016, https://www.nsvrc.org/publications/fact-sheets.
27. Quoted in Alyssa Roenigk, "In Wake of Sexual Abuse Scandal, What's Next for USA Gymnastics?" espnW, August 17, 2017,

http://www.espn.com/espnw/sports/article/20370014/
in-wake-sexual-abuse-scandal-usa-gymnastics.

28. Celia Brackenridge and Kari Fasting, "The Grooming Process in Sport: Narratives of Sexual Harassment and Abuse," *Auto/Biography* 13, no. 1 (2005): 35.

29. Katherine Starr, "Breaking Down Sexual Abuse in Sports," *Huffington Post*, March 20, 2013, http://www.huffingtonpost.com/katherine-starr/breaking-down-sexual-abus_b_2500956.html. See also Helen Owton, *Sexual Abuse in Sport: A Qualitative Case Study* (New York: Springer, 2016).

30. Kristy L. McCray, "Intercollegiate Athletes and Sexual Violence: Review of Literature and Recommendations for Future Study," *Trauma Violence Abuse* 16, no. 4 (2015): 438–443.

31. Scot B. Boeringer, "Associations of Rape-Supportive Attitudes With Fraternal and Athletic Participation," *Violence Against Women* 5, no. 1 (1999): 82; Robin G. Sawyer, Estina E. Thompson, and Anne Marie Chicorelli, "Rape Myth Acceptance Among Intercollegiate Student Athletes: A Preliminary Examination," *American Journal of Health Studies* 18, no. 1 (2002): 19–25.

32. Belinda-Rose Young, Sarah L. Desmarais, Julie A. Baldwin, and Rasheeta Chandler, "Sexual Coercion Practices Among Undergraduate Male Recreational Athletes, Intercollegiate Athletes, and Non-Athletes," *Violence Against Women* 23, no. 7 (2016): 795–812.

33. Sofi Sinozich and Lynn Langton, "Rape and Sexual Assault Victimization Among College Females, 1995–2013," *Bureau of Justice Statistics* (December 2014): 1–19.

34. Celia Brackenridge, "Sexual Harassment and Sexual Abuse in Sport," in *Researching Women and Sport*, ed. Gill Clarke and Barbara Humberstone (London: Macmillan, 1997), 127.

35. Mark Alesia, Marisa Kwiatkowski, and Tim Evans, "Sexual Predators Left Off List of Banned USA Gymnastic Coaches," *Indianapolis Star*, August 7, 2016, https://www.indystar.com/story/news/2016/08/07/holes-child-abuse-safety-net/88118404.

36. Mark Alesia, Marisa Kwiatkowski, and Tim Evans, "Rachael Denhollander's Courage Led Army of Larry Nassar Accusers," *USA Today*, January 26, 2018, https://www.usatoday.com/story/news/nation-now/2018/01/25/rachael-denhollander-larry-nassar-public-accuser/1065313001/.

37. David Eggert, "Abuse Victims Say They Were Required to See Disgraced Doctor," *Merced Sun-Star,* January 31, 2018, http://www.mercedsunstar.com/news/article197540424.html.
38. Matt Mencarini, "Larry Nassar: 2014 Police Report Sheds Light on How He Avoided Criminal Charges," *USA Today,* January 26, 2018, https://www.usatoday.com/story/news/nation-now/2018/01/26/larry-nassar-michigan-state-university-investigation/1069151001/.
39. Alice Park, "Aly Raisman Opens Up About Sexual Abuse by USA Gymnastics Doctor Larry Nassar," *Time,* November 13, 2017, http://time.com/5020885/aly-raisman-sexual-abuse-usa-gymnastics-doctor-larry-nassar/.
40. Eggert, "Abuse Victims"; "Accuser Tells Larry Nassar: 'The Bad Guy Never Wins,'" *Washington Post,* January 31, 2018, https://www.washingtonpost.com/sports/victim-to-nassar-what-you-did-to-me-was-twisted/2018/01/31/2a8d84a0-06c4-11e8-aa61-f3391373867e_story.html?utm_term=.44db47f96c2f.
41. Deborah J. Daniels, "Report to USA Gymnastics on Proposed Policy and Procedural Changes for the Protection of Young Athletes," June 26, 2017, https://assets.documentcloud.org/documents/3879574/USA-Gymnastics-Sexual-Abuse-Report-Independent.txt.
42. Sylvie Parent and Guylaine Demers, "Sexual Abuse and Sport: A Model to Prevent and Prevent and Protect Athletes," *Child Abuse Review* 20 (2011): 120-133.

Chapter 11
1. Quoted in Barbara Kotschwar, "Women, Sports, and Development: Does It Pay to Let Girls Play?," Policy Brief 14-8, Peterson Institute for International Economics, March 2014, 3, https://piie.com/publications/policy-briefs/women-sports-and-development-does-it-pay-let-girls-play.
2. Quoted in Alexis Okeowo, "The Fight Over Women's Basketball in Somalia," *The New Yorker,* September 11, 2017, https://www.newyorker.com/magazine/2017/09/11/the-fight-over-womens-basketball-in-somalia.
3. Kotschwar, "Women, Sports, and Development," 12.
4. Quoted in Serena de Sanctis, "Yuwa Is Hope," espnW, March 27, 2017, http://www.espn.com/espn/feature/story/_/id/18732237/espnw-yuwa-gives-girls-rural-india-rare-opportunity.

5. Quoted in "Why Muslim Countries Fail to Shine in the Olympic Games," *Inquirer,* August 12, 2016, http://sports.inquirer. net/219177/why-muslim-countries-fail-to-shine-at-olympic-games#ixzz4qUUfZO7m.

6. Quoted in Rachel Moss, "Former Football Captain Khalida Popal on the Dangers Facing Afghan Women in Sport," *Huffington Post,* July 29, 2016, http://www.huffingtonpost.co.uk/entry/ khalida-popal-afghanistan-womens-football-team_uk_ 579b2de2e4b07cb01dcf72b1.

7. Quoted in Karla Christensen, "Girls' Basketball Bounces Back in Somalia," *Frontlines,* September/October, 2016, https://www. usaid.gov/news-information/frontlines/september-october-2016/girls-basketball-bounces-back-somalia.

8. Julia Case-Levine, "Saudi Arabia Lets Women Compete in Olympics, but Bans Them From Playing Sports Back Home," *Quartz,* August 8, 2016, https://qz.com/752289/even-as-saudi-female-olympians-compete-women-face-discrimination-back-home.

9. Saripah bintin A. Hamad, quoted in Sarvenaz Fasshih, *Empowering Girls and Women Through Sport and Physical Activity* (Amsterdam: Women Win, 2009),15.

10. Ibid., 10.

11. Women Without Borders, "India—Women Swimming Into the Future," 2010, http://www.women-without-borders.org/ projects/underway/21.

12. United Nations Educational, Scientific and Cultural Organization, "The International Charter of Physical Education and Sport," 1978, https:// www.sportanddev.org/en/article/publication/ international-charter-physical-education-and-sport.

13. United Nations Educational, Scientific and Cultural Organization, "The International Charter of Physical Education and Sport," 2015, http://www.unesco.org/new/en/social-and-human-sciences/themes/physical-education-and-sport/ sport-charter.

14. United Nations, "Transforming Our World: The 2030 Agenda," 2015, https://sustainabledevelopment.un.org/post2015/ transformingourworld.

15. "The Role of Sport in Addressing Gender Issues," https://www.sportanddev.org/en/learn-more/gender/ role-sport-addressing-gender-issues-0.
16. "Skateistan," https://www.skateistan.org.
17. WomenSport International, "Brighton Declaration on Women and Sport," 1994, http://www.sportsbiz.bz/ womensportinternational/conferences/brighton_declaration. htm.
18. Kari Fasting, Trond Svela Sand, Elizabeth Pike, and Jordan Matthews, *From Brighton to Helsinki: Women and Sport Progress Report 1994–2014* (Valo: Finnish Sports Confederation, 2014), 94.

BIBLIOGRAPHY

"Accuser Tells Larry Nassar: 'The Bad Guy Never Wins.'" *Washington Post*, January 31, 2018. https://www.washingtonpost.com/sports/victim-to-nassar-what-you-did-to-me-was-twisted/2018/01/31/2a8d84a0-06c4-11e8-aa61-f3391373867e_story.html?utm_term=.44db47f96c2f.

Adams, Mary Louise. *Artistic Impressions: Figure Skating, Masculinity, and the Limits of Sport.* Toronto: University of Toronto Press, 2011.

Affleck, John. "Why Do the Paralympics Get So Little Media Attention in the United States?" *The Conversation,* September 14, 2016. https://theconversation.com/why-do-the-paralympics-get-so-little-media-attention-in-the-united-states-65205.

Ahmed, Shireen. "Breaking: Women in Hijab Play Sports." *Daily Beast,* August 12, 2016. https://www.thedailybeast.com/breaking-women-in-hijab-play-sports.

Ahmed, Shireen. "After a Long Fight, FIBA Finally Lifts Ban on Religious Headwear." *VICE,* May 4, 2017. https://sports.vice.com/en_ca/article/nz8bvg/after-a-long-fight-fiba-finally-lifts-its-ban-on-religious-headwear.

Alesia, Mark, Marisa Kwiatkowski, and Tim Evans. "Sexual Predators Left Off List of Banned USA Gymnastics Coaches." *Indianapolis Star,* August 7, 2016. https://www.indystar.com/story/news/2016/08/07/holes-child-abuse-safety-net/88118404.

Altman, Dennis. "The Term 'LGBTI' Confuses Desire, Behavior and Identity—It's Time for a Rethink." *The Conversation,* January 19, 2018. https://theconversation.com/the-term-lgbti-confuses-desire-behaviour-and-identity-its-time-for-a-rethink-90175.

American College of Obstetrics and Gynecology. *Technical Bulletin: Exercise During Pregnancy and the Postnatal Period*. Washington, DC: American College of Obstetrics and Gynecology, 1985.

American Medical Society for Sports Medicine. "Effectiveness of Early Sport Specialization Limited in Most Sports, Sport Diversification May Be Better Approach at Young Ages." News release, 2013. https://www.amssm.org/News-Release-Article.php?NewsID=69.

Anderson, Eric. "'I Used to Think Women Were Weak': Orthodox Masculinity, Gender Segregation, and Sport." *Sociological Forum* 23, no. 2 (2008): 257–280.

Andrews, Emily, and Colin Fernandez. "Babe, Set and Match: Why Looks Count for More Than Talent When Wimbledon Decides Which Girls Will Play on Centre Court." *Daily Mail*, June 29, 2009. http://www.dailymail.co.uk/news/article-1196155/Babe-set-match-How-looks-count-talent-Wimbledon-decides-girls-play-Centre-Court.html.

Antunovic, Dunja, and Marie Hardin. "Women and the Blogosphere: Exploring Feminist Approaches to Sport." *International Review for the Sociology of Sport* 50, no. 6 (2015): 661–677.

Aspen Institute's Project Play. "Facts: Sports Activity and Children." https://www.aspenprojectplay.org/the-facts.

Aspen Institute's Project Play. "State of Play 2016: Trends and Developments." https://www.aspenprojectplay.org/sites/default/files/StateofPlay_2016_FINAL.pdf.

Bailey, Moya. "They Aren't Talking About Me . . ." *Crunk Feminist Collective*, March 14, 2010. http://www.crunkfeministcollective.com/2010/03/14/they-arent-talking-about-me.

Beran, Janice A. *From Six-on-Six to Full Court Press: A Century of Iowa Girls' Basketball*. Iowa City: University of Iowa Press, 2007.

Berdahl, Jennifer L., Eric Luis Uhlmann, and Feng Bai. "Win–Win: Female and Male Athletes from More Gender Equal Nations Perform Better in International Sports Competitions." *Journal of Experimental Social Psychology* 56 (2015): 1–3.

Berger, Ronald J. "Disability and the Dedicated Wheelchair Athlete: Beyond the 'Supercrip' Critique." *Journal of Contemporary Ethnography* 37, no. 6 (2008): 647–678.

Berkman, Seth. "Pay Cuts Jolt Women's Pro League and Leave Its Future Uncertain." *New York Times*, November 22, 2016. https://www.nytimes.com/2016/11/22/sports/hockey/nwhl-pay-cut-salary.html?mcubz=1.

Berlage, Gai Ingham. "Transition of Women's Baseball: An Overview." *NINE: A Journal of Baseball History and Culture* 9, no. 1 (2000): 72–81.

Berri, David. "Why the NBA Should Give Female Coaches Like Becky Hammon a Shot." *Vice*, July 22, 2015. https://sports.vice.com/en_us/article/bmeq34/why-the-nba-should-give-female-coaches-like-becky-hammon-a-shot.

Bhowmick, Nilanjana. "India's Golden Girls: How Sport and the Olympics Can Uplift Women." *Time*, August 21, 2012. http://olympics.time.com/2012/08/21/indias-golden-girls-how-sports-and-the-olympics-can-uplift-women/#ixzz24TMCOcjB.

Birrell, Susan, and C. L. Cole. "Double Fault: Renee Richards and the Construction and Naturalization of Difference." *Sociology of Sport Journal* 7, no. 1 (1990): 1–21.

Blackmun, Scott. "Open Letters to Team USA Athletes Regarding Nassar Case." January 24, 2018. https://www.teamusa.org/News/2018/January/24/Open-Letters-To-Team-USA-Athletes-Regarding-Nassar-Case.

Boeringer, Scot B. "Associations of Rape-Supportive Attitudes With Fraternal and Athletic Participation." *Violence Against Women* 5, no. 1 (1999): 81–90.

Bolin, Anne. "Buff Bodies and the Beast: Emphasized Femininity, Labor, and Power Relations Among Fitness, Figure, and Women Bodybuilding Competitors 1985–2010." In *Critical Readings in Bodybuilding*, edited by Adam Locks and Niall Richardson, 29–57. London: Routledge, 2013.

Borish, Linda J. "Settlement Houses to Olympic Stadiums: Jewish American Women, Sports and Social Change." *International Sports Studies* 21, no. 1 (2001): 5–24.

Borish, Linda J., David K. Wiggins, and Gerald R. Gems, eds. *The Routledge History of American Sport*. London: Routledge, 2016.

Brackenridge, Celia. "Sexual Harassment and Sexual Abuse in Sport." In *Researching Women and Sport*, edited by Gill Clarke and Barbara Humberstone, 126–141. London: Macmillan, 1997.

Brackenridge, Celia, and Kari Fasting. "The Grooming Process in Sport: Narratives of Sexual Harassment and Abuse." *Auto/Biography* 13, no. 1 (2005): 33–52.

Brady, Martha. "Olympics Remind Us That Sports Can Empower Women in Developing Countries." *Newsday*, August 10, 2012. https://www.newsday.com/opinion/oped/brady-olympics-remind-us-that-sports-can-empower-women-in-developing-countries-1.3895855.

Braw, Elisabeth. "East Germany's Steroid Shame." *Newsweek,* June 8, 2014. http://www.newsweek.com/2014/06/13/east-germanys-steroid-shame-253840.html.

Brenner, Joel S. "Sports Specialization and Intensive Training in Young Athletes." *Pediatrics* 138, no. 3 (2016): e20162148.

Bresier, Niko, Susan Brownell, and Thomas F. Carter. *The Anthropology of Sport: Bodies, Borders, Biopolitics.* Oakland: University of California Press, 2018.

Brittain, Ian. *The Paralympic Games Explained.* London: Routledge, 2010.

Broad, K. L. "The Gendered Unapologetic: Queer Resistance in Women's Sport." *Sociology of Sport Journal* 18, no. 2 (2001): 181–204.

Brown, Jennings. "Where Are All the Women Sports Stars in Video Games?" *New York Daily News,* September 11, 2015. http://www.nydailynews.com/sports/soccer/women-sports-stars-video-games-article-1.2356913.

Brownell, Susan. *Beiging's Games: What the Olympics Means to China.* Rowman and Littlefield, 2008.

Bruce, Toni. "Assessing the Sociology of Sport: On Media and Representations of Sportswomen." *International Review for the Sociology of Sport* 50, no. 4–5 (2015): 380–384.

Bruce, Toni, Jorid Hovden, and Pirkko Markula, eds. *Sportswomen at the Olympics: A Global Content Analysis of Newspaper Coverage.* Rotterdam: Sense Publishers, 2010.

Bunsell, Tanya. *Strong and Hard Women: An Ethnography of Female Bodybuilding.* London: Routledge, 2013.

Burnsed, Brian. "Athletics Departments That Make More Money Than They Spend Still a Minority." September 18, 2015. http://www.ncaa.org/about/resources/media-center/news/athletics-departments-make-more-they-spend-still-minority.

Buzinski, Jim. "San Francisco 49ers Assistant Katie Sowers Is First Out LGBT Coach in NFL." *Outsports,* August 22, 2017. https://www.outsports.com/2017/8/22/16175286/katie-sowers-san-francisco-49ers-coach-gay-coming-out.

Cahn, Susan K. *Coming on Strong: Gender and Sexuality in Twentieth-Century Women's Sport.* Cambridge, MA: Harvard University Press, 2005.

Cahn, Susan K. *Coming on Strong: Gender and Sexuality in Women's Sport.* Urbana: University of Illinois Press, 2015.

Cambridge University Press, "Aesthetics or Athletics?" August 1, 2016. http://www.cambridge.org/about-us/media/press-releases/aesthetics-or-athletics.

Caple, Nevin, Richard Lapchick, and Nicole M. LaVoi. "Gender, Race, and LGBT Inclusion of Head Coaches of Women's Teams: A Special Collaborative Report on Select NCAA Division I Conferences for the 45th Anniversary of Title IX." June 2017. http://www.cehd. umn.edu/tuckercenter/library/docs/research/2017_Title_IX_at_ 45_Report.pdf.

Carter-Francique, Akilah R. "'Re'Presenting 'Gabby': Examining the Digital Media Coverage of Gabrielle Douglas at the 2012 London Olympic Games." *International Journal of Sport Studies* 4, no. 9 (2014): 1080–1091.

Case-Levine, Julia. "Saudi Arabia Lets Women Compete in Olympics, but Bans Them From Playing Sports Back Home." *Quartz*, August 8, 2016. https://qz.com/752289/even-as-saudi-female-olympians-compete-women-face-discrimination-back-home.

Cauterucci, Christina. "An Arizona Boys' Soccer Team Refused to Play a Team With Girls for Religious Reasons." *Slate*, September 26, 2016. http://www.slate.com/blogs/xx_factor/2016/09/26/an_ arizona_boys_soccer_team_refused_to_play_a_team_with_girls_ for_religious.html.

Chapin, Angelina. "Four Decades after the Battle of the Sexes, the Fight for Equality Goes On." *Guardian*, March 11, 2017. https://www.theguardian.com/sport/2017/mar/11/ billie-jean-king-battle-of-the-sexes-tennis.

Chatziefstathiou, Dikaia. "Reading Baron Pierre de Coubertin: Issues of Gender and Race." *Aethlon* 25, no. 2 (2008): 95–115.

Christensen, Karla. "Girls' Basketball Bounces Back in Somalia." *Frontlines*, September/October, 2016. https://www.usaid. gov/news-information/frontlines/september-october-2016/ girls-basketball-bounces-back-somalia.

Coche, Roxane. "The Amount of Women's Sports Coverage on International Sports News Websites' Home Pages: Content Analysis of the Top Two Sites From Canada, France, Great Britain, and the United States." *Electronic News* 9, no. 4 (2015): 223–241.

Cook, Bob. "Women Are Largely Untapped Resource in Alleviating Youth Sports Referee Shortage." *Forbes*, June 16, 2017. https:// www.forbes.com/sites/bobcook/2017/06/16/women-are-largely-untapped-resource-in-alleviating-youth-sports-referee-shortage/ #4626be5a4cbc.

Cooky, Cheryl, Michael A. Messner, and Michaela Musto. "'It's Dude Time!': A Quarter Century of Excluding Women's Sports in

Televised News and Highlight Shows." *Communication & Sport* 3, no. 3 (2015): 261–287.

Costa, D. Margaret, and Sharon R. Guthrie, eds. *Women and Sport: Interdisciplinary Perspectives.* Champaign, IL: Human Kinetics, 1994.

"#Cover the Athlete." YouTube video, 1:22. Posted by CoverTheAthlete, October 28, 2015. https://www.youtube.com/watch?v=Ol9VhBDKZs0.

Creedon, Pamela. "Women in Toyland: A Look at Women in American Newspaper Sports Journalism." In *Women, Media and Sport: Challenging Gender Values,* 67–107. Thousand Oaks, CA: Sage, 1994.

Cyphers, Luke, and Kate Fagan. "Unhealthy Climate." ESPN, February 7, 2011. http://www.espn.com/ncw/news/story?page=Mag15unh ealthyclimate.

Danico, Mary Yu, and Franklin Ng. *Asian American Issues.* Westport, CT: Greenwood Press, 2004.

Daniels, Deborah J. "Report to USA Gymnastics on Proposed Policy and Procedural Changes for the Protection of Young Athletes." June 26, 2017. https://assets.documentcloud.org/documents/3879574/USA-Gymnastics-Sexual-Abuse-Report-Independent.txt.

Daniels, Stephanie, and Anita Tedder. *"A Proper Spectacle": Women Olympians 1900–1936.* Bedfordshire, UK: ZeNaNA Press, 2000.

Davidson, Kavitha A. "That Visceral Feeling of Hearing Someone Like Me in the Monday Night Football Booth." espnW, September 13, 2017. http://www.espn.com/espnw/voices/article/20681034/that-visceral-feeling-hearing-the-monday-night-football-booth.

Davis, Amira Rose. "No League of Their Own: Baseball, Black Women, and the Politics of Representation." *Radical History Review* 125 (2016): 74–96.

de Beauvoir, Simone. *The Second Sex.* Translated by Constance Borde and Sheila Malovany-Chevallier. New York: Vintage, 2011.

de Sanctis, Serena. "Yuwa Is Hope." espnW, March 27, 2017. http://www.espn.com/espn/feature/story/_/id/18732237/espnw-yuwa-gives-girls-rural-india-rare-opportunity.

De Souza, Mary Jane, Aurelia Nattiv, Elizabeth Joy, Madhusmita Misra, Nancy I. Williams, Rebecca J. Mallinson, Jenna C. Gibbs, Marion Olmsted, Marci Goolsby, and Gordon Matheson. "2014 Female Athlete Triad Coalition Consensus Statement on Treatment and

Return to Play of the Female Athlete Triad." *British Journal of Sports Medicine* 48, no. 4 (2014): 289.

Deford, Frank. "She Won't Win the French Open, but Who Cares? Anna Kournikova Is Living Proof That Even in This Age of Supposed Enlightenment, a Hot Body Can Count as Much as a Good Backhand." *Sports Illustrated,* June 5, 2000. https://www.si.com/vault/2000/06/05/282062/she-wont-win-the-french-open-but-who-cares-anna-kournikova-is-living-proof-that-even-in-this-age-of-supposed-enlightenment-a-hot-body-can-count-as-much-as-a-good-backhand.

DiCaro, Julie. "Safest Bet in Sports: Men Complaining About a Female Announcer's Voice." *New York Times,* September 18, 2017. https://www.nytimes.com/2017/09/18/sports/nfl-beth-mowins-julie-dicaro.html?mcubz=1.

Disch, Lisa, and Mary Jo Kane. "When a Looker Is Really a Bitch: Lisa Olson, Sport, and the Heterosexual Matrix." *Signs: Journal of Women in Culture and Society* 21, no. 2 (1996): 278–308.

Dowling, Collette. *The Frailty Myth: Women Approaching Physical Equality.* New York: Random House, 2000.

Eastern College Athletic Conference. "ECAC Board of Directors Cast Historic Vote to Add Varsity Sport Opportunities for Students With Disabilities in ECAC Leagues and Championships." January 22, 2015. http://www.ecacsports.com.

Eastman, Susan Tyler, and Andrew C. Billings. "Biased Voice of Sports: Racial and Gender Stereotyping in College Basketball Announcing." *Howard Journal of Communication* 12, no. 4 (2001): 183–202.

Eccleshare, Charlie. " 'Next You'll Be Saying You're Going to Work With a Dog'—Andy Murray Reveals Player's Response to Hiring a Female Coach." *Telegraph,* August 23, 2017. http://www.telegraph.co.uk/tennis/2017/08/23/next-saying-going-work-dog-andy-murray-reveals-players-response.

Eggert, David. "Abuse Victims Say They Were Required to See Disgraced Doctor." *Merced Sun-Star,* January 31, 2018. http://www.mercedsunstar.com/news/article197540424.html.

Emery, Lynne. "From Lowell Mills to Halls of Fame: Industrial League Sport for Women." In *Women and Sport: Interdisciplinary Perspectives,* edited by D. Margaret Costa and Sharon R. Guthrie, 107–121. Champaign, IL: Human Kinetics, 1994.

Erdener, Uğur, and Richard Budgett. "Exercise and Pregnancy: Focus on Advice for the Competitive and Elite Athlete." *British Journal of Sports Medicine* 50, no. 10 (2016): 567–567.

Ernst & Young. "Female Executives Say Participation in Sport Helps Accelerate Leadership and Career Potential." October 14, 2014. https://www.prnewswire.com/news-releases/female-executives-say-participation-in-sport-helps-accelerate-leadership-and-career-potential-278614041.html.

Everhart, C. Bonnie, and Packianathan Chelladurai. "Gender Differences in Preferences for Coaching as an Occupation: The Role of Self-Efficacy, Valence, and Perceived Barriers." *Research Quarterly for Exercise and Sport* 69, no. 2 (1998): 188–200.

EY Women Athletes Business Network and espnW. "Female Athletes Make Winning Entrepreneurs, According to New EY/espnW Report." 2017. http://www.ey.com/gl/en/newsroom/news-releases/news-ey-female-athletes-make-winning-entrepreneurs-ey-espn2-report.

Fasshih, Sarvenaz. *Empowering Girls and Women Through Sport and Physical Activity.* Amsterdam: Women Win, 2009.

Fasting, Kari, Trond Svela Sand, Elizabeth Pike, and Jordan Matthews. *From Brighton to Helsinki: Women and Sport Progress Report 1994–2014.* Helsinki, Finland: Valo, Finnish Sports Confederation, 2014.

Fédération Internationale de Football Association. "2014 FIFA World Cup Reached 3.2 Billion Viewers, One Billion Watched." December 16, 2015. http://www.fifa.com/worldcup/news/y=2015/m=12/news=2014-fifa-world-cuptm-reached-3-2-billion-viewers-one-billion-watched--2745519.html

Fédération Internationale de Football Association. "Record-Breaking FIFA Women's World Cup Tops 750 Million TV Viewers." December 17, 2015. http://www.fifa.com/womensworldcup/news/y=2015/m=12/news=record-breaking-fifa-women-s-world-cup-tops-750-million-tv-viewers-2745963.html.

Felshin, Jan. "The Triple Option . . . for Women in Sport." *Quest* 21, no. 1 (1974): 36–40.

Fink, Janet. "Female Athletes, Women's Sport, and the Sport Media Commercial Complex: Have We Really 'Come a Long Way, Baby'?" *Sport Management Review* 18 (2015): 331–342.

Flanagan, Linda. "The Field Where Men Still Call the Shots." *The Atlantic*, July 28, 2017. https://www.theatlantic.com/education/archive/2017/07/the-field-where-men-still-call-the-shots/535167.

Flint, Joe. "Super Bowl 50 Ranks as Third Most-Watched Title Game." *Wall Street Journal*, February 8, 2016. https://www.wsj.com/articles/super-bowl-50-ranks-as-third-most-watched-title-game-1454962962.

"Football Club Become First to Give Equal Pay to Both Men's and Women's Teams." *The Independent*, July 12, 2017. http://www.independent.co.uk/sport/football/news-and-comment/lewes-fc-equal-pay-club-statement-equality-fc-a7836601.html.

Frisby, Cynthia M. "A Content Analysis of Serena Williams and Angelique Kerber's Racial and Sexist Microaggressions." *Open Journal of Social Sciences* 5 (2017): 263–281.

Gallico, Paul. *A Farewell to Sport*. New York: Knopf, 1938.

Gallico, Paul. "The Golden Decade." *Saturday Evening Post*, September 5, 1931, 12–13, 113–116.

Gharib, Malaka. "A Swimmer's 'Period' Comment Breaks Taboos in Sports—And in China." NPR.org, August 17, 2016. https://www.npr.org/sections/goatsandsoda/2016/08/17/490121285/a-swimmers-period-comment-breaks-taboos-in-sports-and-in-china.

Gonzalez, Eduardo. "Referee Company Cuts Ties With Adidas After Lavar Ball Has Female Official Removed From Game." *Los Angeles Times*, July 31, 2017. http://www.latimes.com/sports/highschool/la-sp-company-cut-ties-with-adidas-lavar-ball-female-referee-20170731-story.html.

Gregorich, Barbara. *Women at Play: The Story of Women in Baseball*. San Diego, CA: Harcourt Brace, 1993.

Griffin, Pat. "Changing the Game: Homophobia and Lesbians in Sport." *Quest* 44, no. 2 (1992): 251–265.

Griffin, Pat. *Strong Women, Deep Closets: Lesbians, Homophobia, and Sport*. Champaign, IL: Human Kinetics, 1998.

Grue, Jan. "The Problem With Inspiration Porn: A Tentative Definition and a Provisional Critique." *Disability & Society* 31, no. 6 (2016): 838–849.

Guttmann, Allen. *From Ritual to Record: The Nature of Modern Sports*. New York: Columbia University Press, 1978.

Guttmann, Allen. *Women's Sports: A History*. New York: Columbia University Press, 1991.

Haegele, Justin Anthony, and Samuel Hodge. "Disability Discourse: Overview and Critiques of the Medical and Social Models." *Quest* 68, no. 2 (2016): 193–206.

"Half of Girls Quit Sports by the End of Puberty." *Business Wire*, June 28, 2016. https://www. businesswire.com/news/home/20160628005793/en/ Girls-Quit-Sports-Puberty*-New-Always%C2%AE-LikeAGirl.

Hammer, Roger L., Jan Perkins, and Richard Parr. "Exercise During the Childbearing Year." *Journal of Perinatal Education* 9, no. 1 (2000): 1–14.

Hammond, Thomas, Christie Gialloreto, Hanna Kubas, and Henry Hap Davis IV. "The Prevalence of Failure-Based Depression Among Elite Athletes." *Clinical Journal of Sport Medicine* 23, no. 4 (2013): 273–277.

Hardin, Marie, Julie E. Dodd, Jean Chance, and Kristie Walsdorf. "Sporting Images in Black and White: Race in Newspaper Coverage of the 2000 Olympic Games." *Howard Journal of Communications* 15, no. 4 (2004): 211–227.

Hardin, Marie, and Stacie Shain. "Strength in Numbers? The Experiences and Attitudes of Women in Sport Media." *Journalism and Mass Communication Quarterly* 82, no. 4 (2005): 804–819.

Herek, Gregory M. "The Psychology of Sexual Prejudice." *Current Directions in Psychological Science* 9, no. 1 (2000): 19–22.

Hersh, Philip. "Are Ski Jumpers Too Thin?" *Chicago Tribune*, January 16, 2002. http://articles.chicagotribune.com/2002-01-16/sports/0201160397_1_top-jumpers-alan-alborn-sven-hannawald.

Hess, Amada. "Male Basketball Coach Says a Female Coach Could Never 'Mold Boys Into Successful Men.'" *Slate*, August 6, 2016. http://www.slate.com/blogs/xx_factor/2014/08/06/female_basketball_coaches_will_a_woman_ever_coach_a_men_s_college_basketball.html.

Hootman, Jennifer M., Randall Dick, and Julie Agel. "Epidemiology of Collegiate Injuries for 15 Sports: Summary and Recommendations for Injury Prevention Initiatives." *Journal of Athletic Training* 42, no. 2 (2007): 311–319.

Horky, Thomas, and Jorge-Uwe Nieland. "Comparing Sports Reporting From Around the World—Numbers and Facts on Sports in Daily Newspapers." *International Sports Press Survey 2011* 5 (2013): 22.

Houlihan, Barrie, ed. *Sport and Society: A Student Introduction*. Thousand Oaks, CA: Sage, 2008.

Howard, Jeanette. "Sad Ending, but Deserved." *Chicago Tribune*, September 17, 2003. http://articles.chicagotribune.com/2003-09-17/sports/0309170215_1_wusa-women-s-sports-pax.

"IAAF Regulations Governing Eligibility of Females With Hyperandrogenism to Compete in Women's Competition." https://www.iaaf.org/download/download?filename=58438613-aaa7-4bcd-b730-70296abab70c.pdf&urlslug=IAAF%20Regulations%20Governing%20Eligibility%20of%20Females%20with%20Hyperandrogenism%20to%20Compete%20in%20Women%E2%80%99s%20Competition%20-%20In%20force%20as%20from%201st%20May%202011.

International Olympic Committee. "Factsheet: Women in the Olympic Movement." January 2016. https://stillmed.olympic.org/Documents/Reference_documents_Factsheets/Women_in_Olympic_Movement.pdf.

International Olympic Committee. "London 2012 Olympic Games: Global Broadcast Report." 2012. https://www.olympic.org.

International Olympic Committee. "Olympic Charters." August 2, 2016. https://www.olympic.org/olympic-studies-centre/collections/official-publications/olympic-charters.

International Olympic Committee. "The Organisation." https://www.olympic.org/about-ioc-institution.

International Olympic Committee. "Sochi 2014." https://www.paralympic.org/sochi-2014.

International Olympic Committee. "Tokyo 2020 Event Programme to See Major Boost for Female Participation, Youth and Urban Appeal." June 9, 2017. https://www.olympic.org/news/tokyo-2020-event-programme-to-see-major-boost-for-female-participation-youth-and-urban-appeal.

International Paralympic Committee. "Guide to Reporting on Persons With an Impairment." October 2014. https://m.paralympic.org/sites/default/files/document/141027103527844_2014_10_31+Guide+to+reporting+on+persons+with+an+impairment.pdf.

International Paralympic Committee. "IPC Women in Sport Leadership Toolkit." October 2010. https://www.paralympic.org/sites/default/files/document/130130154714620_2010_10_01++IPC+Women+in+Sport+Leadership+Toolkit.pdf.

International Quidditch Association. "IQA Rulebook, 2016–2018." www.iqaquidditch.org/IQARulebook2016-2018.pdf.

Isidore, Chris. "Sex in Play in Women's Sports." *CNN*, August 23, 2002. http://money.cnn.com/2002/08/23/commentary/column_sportsbiz/women_sex/index.htm.

Israel Cabanilla, Devin. "Media Fail to Give REAL First Asian American Olympic Gold Medalist Her Due." *The Seattle Globalist,* December 15, 2016. http://www.seattleglobalist.com/2016/12/15/real-first-asian-american-olympic-gold-medalist-doesnt-get-due/60115.

Jackman, Jesse. "For Closeted Gay Athletes, Endorsement Fears Persist." *Huffington Post,* February 19, 2016. https://www.huffingtonpost.com/jesse-jackman/for-closeted-gay-athletes_b_9269956.html.

Jackson, Barry. "Sports Media Analysis: Social Media Brings Instant Updates, but There Are Drawbacks." *Miami Herald,* July 18, 2015. http://www.miamiherald.com/sports/spt-columns-blogs/article27687346.html#storylink=cpy.

Jamieson, Katherine M. "Reading Nancy Lopez: Decoding Representations of Race, Class, and Sexuality." *Sociology of Sport Journal* 15, no. 4 (1998): 343–358.

Jamieson, Katherine M. "Advance at Your Own Risk: Latinas, Families, and Collegiate Softball." In *Mexican Americans and Sport: A Reader on Athletics and Barrio Life,* edited by Jorge Iber and Samuel O. Regalado, 213–232. College Station: Texas A&M University Press, 2006.

Jayanthi, Neeru. "Sports Specialized Risks for Reinjury in Young Athletes: A 2+ Year Clinical Prospective Evaluation." *British Journal of Sports Medicine* 51, no. 4 (2017): 334.

Jenkins, Sally. "Stalking Is Not Just a Sports Issue." *Washington Post,* July 4, 2002. https://www.washingtonpost.com/archive/sports/2002/07/04/stalking-is-not-just-a-sports-issue/a2f1e508-8159-40e3-8e6e-0b16f353e304/?utm_term=.ece92c3b4457.

Jenkins, Sally. "There's a Legal Remedy to the Doping Issue." *Washington Post,* October 12, 2007. http://www.washingtonpost.com/wp-dyn/content/article/2007/10/11/AR2007101102285.html.

Kalin, Jacqui L., and Jennifer J. Waldron. "Preferences Toward Gender of Coach and Perceptions of Roles of Basketball Coaches." *International Journal of Exercise Science* 8, no. 4 (2015): 303–317.

Kane, Mary Jo. "Sex Sells Sex, Not Women's Sports." *The Nation,* July 27, 2010. https://www.thenation.com/article/sex-sells-sex-not-womens-sports.

Kaufman, Michelle. "Women's Ski Jumping Competitions in 2014 Winter Olympics a Giant Leap for Womankind." *Miami Herald,* February 12, 2014. http://www.miamiherald.com/sports/olympics/article1960265.html.

Kay, Theresa, and Ruth Jeanes. *Women, Sport, and Gender Inequity*. In
Sport and Society: A Student Introduction, edited by Barrie Houlihan,
130–154. Thousand Oaks, CA: Sage, 2008.

Kelly, Annie. "Raped and Killed for Being a Lesbian: South Africa
Ignores 'Corrective' Attacks." *The Guardian*, March 12, 2009.
https://www.theguardian.com/world/2009/mar/12/
eudy-simelane-corrective-rape-south-africa.

Kennard, June, and John Marshall Carter. "In the Beginning: The
Ancient and Medieval Worlds." In *Women and Sport: Interdisciplinary
Perspectives*, edited by D. Margaret Costa and Sharon R. Guthrie,
15–26. Champaign, IL: Human Kinetics, 1994.

Kim, Claire Jean. "The Racial Triangulation of Asian Americans."
Politics & Society 27, no. 1 (1999): 105–138.

Kotschwar, Barbara. "Women, Sports, and Development: Does
It Pay to Let Girls Play?" Policy Brief 14-8, Peterson
Institute for International Economics. March 2014.
https://piie.com/publications/policy-briefs/
women-sports-and-development-does-it-pay-let-girls-play.

"Laila Ali Says She's Not Gay." *UPI*, November 11, 2005. http://www.
upi.com/Laila-Ali-says-shes-not-gay/34361131763228.

Lansbury, Jennifer H. *A Spectacular Leap: Black Women Athletes in
Twentieth-Century America*. Fayetteville: University of Arkansas
Press, 2014.

Lapchick, Richard, Saahil Marfatia, Austin Bloom, and Stanley
Sylverain. "The 2016 Racial & Gender Report Card: College Sport."
The Institute for Diversity and Ethics in Sport. April 6, 2017. http://
www.tidesport.org/college-sport.html.

Larkin, June, Sherene Razack, and Fiona Moole. "Gender, Sport, and
Development." In *Literature Reviews on Sport for Development
and Peace*, commissioned by Sport for Development and
Peace International Working Group Secretariat, 89–123.
Toronto: University of Toronto, 2007.

Lederman, Doug. "North Carolina and Coach Settle Sexual
Harassment Suit." *Inside Higher Ed*, January 15, 2008. https://www.
insidehighered.com/news/2008/01/15/unc.

Lee, Yomee. "A New Voice: Korean American Women in Sports."
International Review for the Sociology of Sport 40, no. 4 (2005): 481–495.

Leigh, Mary H., and Thérèse M. Bonin. "The Pioneering Role of
Madame Alice Milliat and the FSFI in Establishing International
Track and Field Competition for Women." *Journal of Sport History* 4,
no. 1 (1977): 72–83.

Leigh, Mary Henson. "The Evolution of Women's Participation in the Summer Olympic Games, 1900–1948." PhD diss., Ohio State University, 1974.

Lenskyj, Helen Jefferson. "Reflections on Communication and Sport: On Heteronormativity and Gender Identities." *Communication & Sport* 1, no. 1–2 (2013): 138–150.

Lincoln, Andrew E., Shane V. Caswell, and Jon L. Almquist. "Trends in Concussion Incidence in High School Sports: A Prospective 11-Year Study." *American Journal of Sports Medicine* 39, no. 5 (2011): 958–963.

Linehan, Meg. "NWSL Minimum Salary to Double for Fifth Season." *excellesports*, January 26, 2017. http://www.excellesports.com/news/nwsl-minimum-salary-double-fifth-season.

Link, Taylor. "LaVar Ball Bullied Female Referee at Las Vegas Tournament, Had Her Replaced With Male Ref." *Salon*, July 30, 2017. http://www.salon.com/2017/07/30/lavar-ball-bullied-female-referee-at-las-vegas-tournament-had-her-replaced-with-male-ref.

Locks, Adam, and Niall Richardson, eds. *Critical Readings in Bodybuilding*. London: Routledge, 2013.

Longman, Jeré. "A Giant Leap for Women, but Hurdles Remain." *New York Times*, July 29, 2012. http://www.nytimes.com/2012/07/30/sports/olympics/despite-gains-for-female-athletes-fight-for-true-equality-remains.html?mcubz=1&mtrref=www.google.com&gwh=36B7A8DA464A5741442B819DA9E248A2&gwt=pay.

Loy, John W., Fiona McLachlan, and Douglas Booth. "Connotations of Female Movement and Meaning." *Olympika*, XVIII (2009): 1–23.

Luther, Jessica. *Unsportsmanlike Conduct: College Football and the Politics of Rape*. New York: Akashic, 2016.

Maine, D'Arcy. "The Pressure of Pulling Your Own Weight." espnW, n.d. http://www.espn.com/espn/feature/story/_/id/19232937/espnw-body-image-confidential#!pressure.

"Make-up and Short Shorts Improving Women's Football, Says Brazilian Official." *Guardian,* June 16, 2015. https://www.theguardian.com/football/2015/jun/16/make-up-shorts-improving-womens-game-brazil.

Maland, Tyler. "My Legacy: Brandi Chastain Pledges Brain." Concussion Legacy Foundation, March 3, 2016. https://concussionfoundation.org/story/my-legacy-brandi-chastain.

Mangan, J.A. and Roberta J. Park. *From "Fair Sex" to Feminism: Sport and the Socialization of Women in the Industrial and Post-Industrial Eras*. London: Routledge, 1987.

Mather, Victor. "Olympic Gymnast McKayla Maroney Says She Too Was Molested by Team Doctor." *New York Times*, October 18, 2017. https://www.nytimes.com/2017/10/18/sports/olympics/gymnast-mckayla-maroney-team-doctor-sexual-abuse.html.

McCray, Kristy L. "Intercollegiate Athletes and Sexual Violence: Review of Literature and Recommendations for Future Study." *Trauma Violence Abuse* 16, no. 4 (2015): 438–443.

McDermott, Barry. "More Than a Pretty Face." *Sports Illustrated*, January 18, 1982. https://www.si.com/vault/1982/01/18/540914/more-than-a-pretty-face.

McDonagh, Eileen, and Laura Pappano. *Playing With the Boys: Why Separate Is Not Equal.* New York: Oxford University Press, 2007.

McDonald, Mary G. "Rethinking Resistance: The Queer Play of the Women's National Basketball Association, Visibility Politics and Late Capitalism." *Leisure Studies* 27, no. 1 (2008): 77–93.

McDonough, Katie. "School Won't Let 12-Year-Old Girl Play Football Because of 'Lusting' Male Teammates." *Salon*, June 24, 2013. https://www.salon.com/2013/06/24/school_wont_let_12_year_old_girl_play_football_because_of_lusting_male_teammates.

McRae, Donald. "Chris Gayle: 'You're With Men. You're Good-Looking. What Do You Expect.'" *The Guardian*, June 14, 2016. https://www.theguardian.com/sport/2016/jun/14/chris-gayle-mel-mclaughlin-sexism-row-west-indies-cricket.

Meekosha, Helen, and Leanne Dowse. "Distorting Images, Invisible Images: Gender, Disability, and the Media." *Media International Australia* 84 (1997): 91–101.

Mencarini, Matt. "Larry Nassar: 2014 Police Report Sheds Light on How He Avoided Criminal Charges." *USA Today*, January 26, 2018. https://www.usatoday.com/story/news/nation-now/2018/01/26/larry-nassar-michigan-state-university-investigation/1069151001/.

Messerli, Fr. M. "Women's Participation in the Modern Olympic Games." *Bulletin du Comité International Olympique* (May 1952): 25.

Messner, Michael A. *Taking the Field: Women, Men, and Sports.* Minneapolis: University of Minnesota Press, 2002.

Metheny, Eleanor. *Connotations of Movement in Sport and Dance.* Dubuque, IA: William C. Brown, 1965.

Meyers, Dvora. *The End of the Perfect 10: The Making and Breaking of Gymnastics' Top Score.* New York: Touchstone, 2016.

Montillo, Roseanne. *Fire on the Track: Betty Robinson and the Triumph of the Early Olympic Women.* New York: Crown, 2017.

Moss, Rachel. "Former Football Captain Khalida Popal on the Dangers Facing Afghan Women in Sport." *Huffington Post,* July 29, 2016. http://www.huffingtonpost.co.uk/entry/khalida-popal-afghanistan-womens-football-team_uk_579b2de2e4b07cb01dcf72b1.

Mozisek, Korryn D. "No Girls Allowed! Female Reporters as Threats to the Male Domain of Sports." *Journal of Sports Media* 10, no. 2 (2015): 17–29.

Mueller, Frederick O. "Cheerleading Injuries and Safety." *Journal of Athletic Training* 44 (2009): 565–566.

Mueller, Frederick O., and Robert C. Cantu. "Catastrophic Sports Injury Research: Twenty-Ninth Annual Report, Fall 1982–Spring 2011." http://nccsir.unc.edu.

Nash, Tim. "Jess Fishlock Reveals Her Struggles With Social Media and How She Handles Anti-Gay Bullying." *Excelleports,* June 29, 2017. http://www.excellesports.com/news/jess-fishlock-social-media-bullying.

National Coalition for Girls and Women in Education. "Title IX and Athletics." 2017. http://www.ncwge.org/athletics.html.

National Collegiate Athletic Association. "Estimated Probability of Competing in Professional Athletics." March 10, 2017. http://www.ncaa.org/about/resources/research/estimated-probability-competing-professional-athletics.

National Sexual Violence Resource Center. "What Is Sexual Violence? Fact Sheet." January 2016. https://www.nsvrc.org/publications/fact-sheets.

National Women's Law Center and the Poverty and Race Research Action Council. "Finishing Last: Girls of Color and Schools Sports Opportunities." 2015. https://nwlc.org/wp-content/uploads/2015/08/final_nwlc_girlsfinishinglast_report.pdf.

Nebraska School Activities Association. "Gender Participation Policy." 2015. http://www.rockcountyschools.org/wp-content/uploads/2014/07/NSAA-Transgender-Policy.pdf.

Nelson, Valerie J., and Nathan Fenno. "Sammy Lee, Diver Who Became First Asian American to Win Olympic Medal, Dies at 96." *LA Times,* December 3, 2016. http://www.latimes.com/local/obituaries/la-me-sammy-lee-snap-20161203-story.html.

"No Women Athletes for American Team." *New York Times,* March 31, 1914, 9.

North, Anna. "7 Sports in Which Women Have Beaten Men." *BuzzFeed,* August 2, 2012. https://www.buzzfeed.com/annanorth/

7-sports-in-which-women-have-beaten-men?utm_term=.
oh30mAnyzO#.pv1arQnWVz.

Obi, T. J. Desch. *Fighting for Honor: The History of African Martial Arts Traditions in the Atlantic World.* Columbia: University of South Carolina Press, 2008.

Okeowo, Alexis. "The Fight Over Women's Basketball in Somalia." *The New Yorker,* September 11, 2017. https://www.newyorker.com/magazine/2017/09/11/the-fight-over-womens-basketball-in-somalia.

Oliver, Pam, as told to Jeannine Amber. "Game Change: Pam Oliver Breaks Her Silence on Her Career Shake-up." *Essence,* September 3, 2014. https://www.essence.com/2014/09/04/pam-oliver-game-change.

"Organized Cheering." *The Nation,* January 5, 1911, 5–6.

Owton, Helen. *Sexual Abuse in Sport: A Qualitative Case Study.* New York: Springer, 2016.

Oxenham, Gwendolyn. " 'Pele With a Skirt': The Unequal Fortunes of Brazil's Soccer Stars." *The Atlantic,* June 4, 2015. https://www.theatlantic.com/entertainment/archive/2015/06/neymar-marta-world-cup-brazil/394856.

Pappous, Anthanasios (Sakis), Anne Marcellini, and Eric de Leseleuc. "Contested Issues in Research on the Media Coverage of Female Paralympic Athletes." *Sport in Society* 14, no. 9 (2011): 1182–1191.

Paralympic Movement. "Classification Introduction." n.d. https://www.paralympic.org/classification.

Parent, Sylvie and Guylaine Demers. "Sexual Abuse and Sport: A Model to Prevent and Prevent and Protect Athletes." *Child Abuse Review* 20 (2011): 120–133.

Park, Alice. "Aly Raisman Opens Up About Sexual Abuse by USA Gymnastics Doctor Larry Nassar." *Time,* November 13, 2017. http://time.com/5020885/aly-raisman-sexual-abuse-usa-gymnastics-doctor-larry-nassar/.

Parker, Kayla. "A Primer to the 2016 Rio Paralympic Games." ESPN.com, September 5, 2016. http://www.espn.com/espnw/sports/article/17101834/a-primer-2016-rio-paralympics-games.

Payne, Marissa. "With a Boost From Wonder Woman, Pregnant Alysia Montaño Returns to the Track." *Washington Post,* June 23, 2017. https://www.washingtonpost.com/news/early-lead/wp/2017/06/23/with-a-boost-from-wonder-woman-pregnant-alysia-montano-returns-to-the-track/?utm_term=.c6aecadad1d8.

PERFORM, Kantar Media, and SportBusiness Group. "Know the Fan: The Global Sports Media Consumption Report, 2014." http://www.knowthefan.com.

Peters, Mary, with Ian Wooldridge. *Mary P.: Autobiography*. London: Paul, 1974.

Pfister, Gertrude. "The Medical Discourse on Female Physical Culture in the 19th and Early 20th Centuries." *Journal of Sport History* 17, no. 2 (1990): 183–198.

Plunkett Research. "Sports Industry Statistic and Market Size Overview, Business and Industry Statistics." n.d. https://www.plunkettresearch.com/statistics/Industry-Statistics-Sports-Industry-Statistic-and-Market-Size-Overview.

Popke, Michael. "More Women Coaching High School Boys Teams." *Athletic Business*, November 2008. https://www.athleticbusiness.com/high-school/more-women-coaching-high-school-boys-teams.html.

Porter, Rick. "Summer Olympics Are the Lowest-Rated and Least Watched Since 2000." *TV by the Numbers*, August 23, 2016. http://tvbythenumbers.zap2it.com/uncategorized/summer-olympics-are-the-lowest-rated-and-least-watched-since-2000.

Praderio, Caroline. "The First American in 16 Years to Win a Weightlifting Medal Is Championing Body Positivity." *Business Insider*, August 15, 2016. http://www.businessinsider.com/sarah-robles-weightlifting-medal-2016-8.

"Preserving la Difference." *Time*, September 16, 1966, 72.

"Prize Money in Sport—BBC Sport Study." June 19, 2017. http://www.bbc.com/sport/40300519.

Purdue, David E. J., and P. David Howe. "Who's in and Who's Out? Legitimate Bodies Within the Paralympic Games." *Sociology of Sport Journal* 30, no. 1 (2013): 24–40.

"Records of Polish Girl Sprinter Who Flunked Sex Test Barred." *New York Times*, February 26, 1968, 50.

Regalado, Samuel O. "Incarcerated Sport: Nisei Women's Softball and Athletics During Japanese American Internment." *Journal of Sport History* 27 no. 3 (2000): 431–444.

Reiche, Danyel. *Success and Failure of Countries at the Olympic Games*. New York: Routledge, 2016.

Rial, Carmen. "Women's Soccer in Brazil." *Revista*, Spring 2012. https://revista.drclas.harvard.edu/book/womens-soccer-brazil.

Right to Play. "Sport and Gender: Empowering Girls and Women." 2010. http://www.righttoplay.com/Pages/default.aspx.

Ring, Jennifer. *Stolen Bases: Why American Girls Don't Play Baseball.* Urbana: University of Illinois Press, 2009.

"Rio 2016 Paralympics Smash All TV Viewing Records." *Women's Sport Report,* March 16, 2017. http://www.womensportreport.com/rio-2016-paralympics-smash-all/wn/20419.

Rodriguez, Andrea. "Women Demand Cuba Support 1st Female Boxing Team." *Miami Herald,* February 1, 2017. http://www.miamiherald.com/news/nation-world/world/americas/cuba/article130041039.html.

Roenigk, Alyssa. "In Wake of Sexual Abuse Scandal, What's Next for USA Gymnastics?" espnW, August 17, 2017. http://www.espn.com/espnw/sports/article/20370014/in-wake-sexual-abuse-scandal-usa-gymnastics.

Rogers, Martin. "U.S. Women Were Multi-Sport Athletes Before Focusing on Soccer." *USA Today,* July 3, 2015. https://www.usatoday.com/story/sports/soccer/2015/07/03/abby-wambach-morgan-brian-lauren-holiday/29665797.

Rogin, Gilbert. "Flamin' Mamie's Bouffant Belles." *Sports Illustrated,* April 20, 1964. https://www.si.com/vault/1964/04/20/612942/flamin-mamies-bouffant-belles.

Romero, Dennis. "Danica Patrick, Racing Warrior, Is a Word That 'Starts With B' Says SoCal Sports Anchor Ross Shimabuku." *LA Weekly,* February 2, 2012. http://www.laweekly.com/news/danica-patrick-racing-warrior-is-a-word-that-starts-with-b-says-socal-sports-anchor-ross-shimabuku-2391709.

Rosenberg, Michael. "Ibtihaj Muhammad Didn't Need a Medal to Leave Her Mark on U.S., Olympics." *Sports Illustrated,* August 8, 2016. https://www.si.com/olympics/2016/08/08/ibtihaj-muhammad-team-usa-fencing-rio-olympics.

Rothenberg, Ben. "Tennis's Top Women Balance Body Image With Ambition." *New York Times,* July 10, 2015. https://www.nytimes.com/2015/07/11/sports/tennis/tenniss-top-women-balance-body-image-with-quest-for-success.html?_r=0&mtrref=undefined&assetType=nyt_now.

Rothenberg, Ben. "Roger Federer, $731,000; Serena Williams, $495,000: The Pay Gap in Tennis." *New York Times,* April 12, 2016. https://www.nytimes.com/2016/04/13/sports/tennis/equal-pay-gender-gap-grand-slam-majors-wta-atp.html?ref=tennis&module=ArrowsNav&contentCollection=Tennis&action=keypress&region=FixedLeft&pgtype=article.

Ruggeri, Amanda. "Why It Took 90 Years for Women's Ski Jumping to Make the Olympics." *Deadspin*, February 11, 2014. https://deadspin.com/why-it-took-90-years-for-womens-ski-jumping-to-make-the-1520520342.

Sabo, Don, and Phil Veliz. *Go Out and Play: Youth Sports in America*. East Meadow, NY: Women's Sports Foundation, 2008.

Sabo, Don, Philip Veliz, and Ellen J. Staurowsky. *Beyond X's and O's: Gender Bias and Coaches of Women's College Sports*. East Meadow, NY: Women's Sports Foundation, 2016.

Saffer, Max. "Dollars but No Sense: Golf's Long History of Shortchanging Women." espnW, April 8, 2016. http://www.espn.com/espnw/sports/article/15160220/big-gap-earnings-men-women-professional-golfers.

Sanghani, Radhika. " 'Get More Women Into Sport Through Cheerleading—It's Feminine,' Says Sports Minister Helen Grant." *Telegraph*, February 20, 2014, http://www.telegraph.co.uk/women/womens-politics/10652074/Get-more-women-into-sport-through-cheerleading-its-feminine-says-sports-minister-Helen-Grant.html.

Sargent, Dudley A. "Are Athletics Making Girls Masculine? A Practical Answer to a Question Every Girl Asks." *Ladies' Home Journal*, March 1912.

Sawyer, Robin G., Estina E. Thompson, and Anne Marie Chicorelli. "Rape Myth Acceptance Among Intercollegiate Student Athletes: A Preliminary Examination." *American Journal of Health Studies* 18, no. 1 (2002): 19–25.

Schell, Lea Ann, and Stephanie Rodriguez. "Subverting Bodies/Ambivalent Representations: Media Analysis of Paralympian, Hope Lewellen." *Sociology of Sport Journal* 18 (2001): 127–135.

Schultz, Jaime. *Qualifying Times: Points of Change in US Women's Sport*. Champaign: University of Illinois Press, 2014.

Schultz, Jaime. "Going the Distance: The Road to the 1984 Olympic Women's Marathon." *International Journal of the History of Sport* 32, no. 1 (2015): 72–88.

Schultz, Jaime. "Cheerleading's Peculiar Path to Potential Olympic Sport." *The Conversation*, February 1, 2018. https://theconversation.com/cheerleadings-peculiar-path-to-potential-olympic-sport-70386.

Scott, Anne Crittenden. "Closing the Muscle Gap: New Facts About Strength, Endurance—and Gender." *Ms.*, September 1974, 49–52.

"Sex Test Disqualifies Athlete." *New York Times*, September 16, 1967, 28.

Shad, Saman. "How to Get Men Watching Women's Football? Have Them Play in Lingerie." *Guardian*, June 7, 2012. https://www.theguardian.com/commentisfree/2012/jun/07/american-lingerie-football-league-women.

Shaulis, Dahn. "Pedestriennes: Newsworthy but Controversial Women in Sporting Entertainment." *Journal of Sport History* 26, no. 1 (1999): 29–51.

Sherry, Emma, Angela Osborne, and Matthew Nicholson. "Images of Sports Women: A Review." *Sex Roles* 74, no. 7 (2015): 299–309.

Silcoff, Mireille. "Who Said Girls Can't Jump?" *New York Times Magazine*, November 22, 2013. http://www.nytimes.com/2013/11/24/magazine/who-said-girls-cant-jump.html.

Simmons, Christian. "Orlando Pride Midfielder Maddy Evans Says Low Salary Was Factor in Retirement." *Orlando Sentinel*, September 11, 2017. http://www.orlandosentinel.com/sports/orlando-pride-soccer/os-sp-orlando-pride-news-0814-story.html.

Sinozich, Sofi, and Lynn Langton. "Rape and Sexual Assault Victimization Among College Females, 1995–2013." Bureau of Justice Statistics, December 2014, 1–19.

Skateistan. https://www.skateistan.org.

Slavin, Harry. "Female Drivers Would 'Not Physically Be Able to Drive an F1 Car Quickly,' Claims Supremo Bernie Ecclestone." *Daily Mail*, April 19, 2016. http://www.dailymail.co.uk/sport/formulaone/article-3548844/Bernie-Ecclestone-Female-drivers-not-physically-able-drive-F1-car-quickly.html.

Smith, Andrew, and Nigel Thomas. "The 'Inclusion' of Elite Athletes With Disabilities in the 2002 Manchester Commonwealth Games: An Exploratory Analysis of British Newspaper Coverage." *Sport, Education and Society* 10, no. 1 (2005): 49–67.

Smith, J.B. "Report Shows Systemic Failure in Sex Crime Response at Baylor." *Waco Tribune-Herald*, May 26, 2016. http://www.wacotrib.com/news/higher_education/report-shows-systemic-failure-in-sex-crime-response-at-baylor/article_432b820a-6e64-5864-92c2-f3081f020384.html.

Spain, Sarah. "Grace Under Fire: Women in Media Shouldn't Have to 'Ignore' Abuse." espnW, April 28, 2016. http://www.espn.com/espnw/voices/article/15412369/women-sports-media-ignore-abuse.

Stapleton, AnneClaire, and Eric Levenson. "McKayla Maroney Alleges USA Gymnastics Doctor Abused Her at 13." CNN.com, October 19, 2017. http://www.cnn.com/2017/10/18/us/mckayla-maroney-me-too-abuse/index.html.

Stark, Rachel "Where Are the Women?" *Champion Magazine*, Winter 2017. http://www.ncaa.org/static/champion/where-are-the-women/index.html.

Starr, Katherine. "Breaking Down Sexual Abuse in Sports." *Huffington Post*, March 20, 2013. http://www.huffingtonpost.com/katherine-starr/breaking-down-sexual-abus_b_2500956.html.

Staurowsky, Ellen J., Mary Jane De Souza, Kathleen E. Miller, Don Sabo, Sohaila Shakib, Nancy Theberge, Phil Veliz, A. Weaver, and Nancy I. Williams. *Her Life Depends on It III: Sport, Physical Activity and the Health and Well-Being of American Girls and Women*. East Meadow, NY: Women's Sports Foundation, 2015.

Staurowsky, Ellen J., and Michael Proska. "Gender Equity at the High School Level." Women in Coaching (blog), July 15, 2013.

Stoffers, Carl. "Equal Pay for Equal Play? As Women's Sports Become More Popular, Female Athletes Are Demanding to Be Paid Like Their Male Counterparts." *Junior Scholastic/Current Events*, January 9, 2017.

Struna, Nancy L. " 'Good Wives' and 'Gardeners,' Spinners and 'Fearless Riders': Middle- and Upper-rank Women in Early American Sporting Culture." In *From "Fair Sex" to Feminism: Sport and the Socialization of Women in the Industrial and Post-Industrial Eras*, edited by J.A. Mangan and Roberta J. Park, 235–255. London: Routledge, 1987.

Suggs, Welch. *A Place on the Team: The Triumph and Tragedy of Title IX*. Princeton, NJ: Princeton University Press, 2005.

Surdam, David George. *The Rise of the National Basketball Association*. Urbana: University of Illinois Press, 2012.

Tannenwald, Jonathan. "Glenside Native Maddy Evans' Retirement From Playing Soccer an Example of Ugly Truth About NWSL Salaries." *Philadelphia Inquirer*, August 16, 2017. http://www.philly.com/philly/sports/soccer/national-women-soccer-league-salaries-maddy-edwards-retirement-orlando-pride-marta-alex-morgan-20170816.html.

"The Female Pedestrians: A Sorry Spectacle at Gilmore's Garden—The Walking Record Up to Last Evening." *New York Times*, March 28, 1879, 2.

"The Role of Sport in Addressing Gender Issues." sportanddev. org. https://www.sportanddev.org/en/learn-more/gender/ role-sport-addressing-gender-issues-0.

"The World's Highest Paid Athletes." *Forbes,* 2017. https://www.forbes. com/athletes/list.

Theberge, Nancy. "Toward a Feminist Alternative to Sport as a Male Preserve." *Quest* 37, no. 2 (1985): 193–202.

Thibault, Valérie, Marion Guillaume, Geoffroy Berthelot, Nour El Helou, Karine Schaal, Laurent Quinquis, Hala Nassif, et al. "Women and Men in Sport Performance: The Gender Gap Has Not Evolved Since 1983." *Journal of Sports Science and Medicine* 9, no. 2 (2010): 214–223.

"Things Seen and Heard." *Sportsman* 20 (October 1936): 18.

Thomas, Katie. "After Long Fight for Inclusion, Women's Ski Jumping Gains Olympic Status." *New York Times,* April 6, 2011. http:// www.nytimes.com/2011/04/07/sports/skiing/07skijumping. html?mcubz=1.

Thomas, Louisa. "Equal Pay for Equal Play: The Case for the Women's Soccer Team." *New Yorker,* May 27, 2016. http:// www.newyorker.com/culture/cultural-comment/ the-case-for-equal-pay-in-womens-sports.

Tracy, Marc, and Dan Berry. "The Rise, Then Shame, of Baylor Nation." *New York Times,* March 9, 2017. https://www.nytimes.com/2017/ 03/09/sports/baylor-football-sexual-assault.html.

Trahan, Kevin. " 'Nobody's Watching': Are Major College Sports Programs Treating Title IX Like a Suggestion?" *Vice Sports,* June 15, 2016. https://sports.vice.com/en_us/article/8qygwz/nobodys- watching-are-major-college-sports-programs-treating-title-ix-like-a- suggestion.

Treaster, Joseph B. "Little League Baseball Yields to 'Social Climate' and Accepts Girls." *New York Times,* June 13, 1974, 26.

Tuchman, Gaye. "The Symbolic Annihilation of Women by the Mass Media." In *Hearth and Home: Images of Women in the Mass Media,* edited by Gaye Tuchman, Arlene Kaplan Daniels, and James Walker Benét. New York: Oxford University Press, 1978.

Tucker Center for Research on Girls and Women in Sport. "Media Coverage and Female Athletes." 2017. http://www.cehd.umn.edu/ tuckercenter/multimedia/mediacoverage.html.

Tunis, John R. "Women and the Sport Business." *Harper's Magazine,* July 1929: 213.

United Nations. "Sport and the Millennium Development Goals." 2005.
    https://www.un.org/sport2005/a_year/mill_goals.html.

United Nations. "Sport as a Means to Promote Education,
    Health, Development and Peace." November 3, 2005.
    https://www.un.org/sport/resources/documents/
    secretary-generals-reports-general-assembly.

United Nations. "Transforming Our World: The 2030 Agenda."
    2015. https://sustainabledevelopment.un.org/post2015/
    transformingourworld.

United Nations Educational, Scientific and Cultural Organization.
    "The International Charter of Physical Education and Sport."
    1978. https://www.sportanddev.org/en/article/publication/
    international-charter-physical-education-and-sport.

United Nations Educational, Scientific and Cultural Organization.
    "The International Charter of Physical Education and Sport." 2015.
    http://www.unesco.org/new/en/social-and-human-sciences/
    themes/physical-education-and-sport/sport-charter.

United Nations Women. "UN Women Signs Partnership Agreement
    With the International Olympic Committee to Advance Gender
    Equity." August 23, 2012.

USA Gymnastics. "Women's Artistic Gymnastics Event Descriptions."
    n.d. https://usagym.org/pages/gymnastics101/women/events.
    html.

USA Wrestling. "USA Wrestling Transgender Guidelines." 2017. http://
    content.themat.com/forms/USAWrestling-Transgender-Policy.pdf.

Vecsey, George. "Help on the Way for Title IX." *New York Times*, April
    22, 1984, S3.

Vertinsky, Patricia A. *The Eternally Wounded Woman: Women, Doctors, and
    Exercise in the Late Nineteenth Century*. Manchester, UK: Manchester
    University Press, 1990.

Von der Lippe, Gerd. "Media Image: Sport, Gender and National
    Identities in Five European Countries." *International Review for the
    Sociology of Sport* 37, no. 3–4 (2002): 371–395.

Voskanian, Natalie. "ACL Injury Prevention in Female Athletes: Review
    of the Literature and Practical Considerations in Implementing
    an ACL Prevention Program." *Current Reviews in Musculoskeletal
    Medicine* 6, no. 2 (2013): 158–163.

Wallace, Kelly. "How to Keep Girls in the Game After Puberty." CNN.
    com, June 28, 2016. http://www.cnn.com/2016/06/28/health/
    girls-sports-puberty-likeagirl/index.html.

Ward, Geoffrey C., and Ken Burns. *Baseball: An Illustrated History.* New York: Knopf, 1994.

" 'We Must Continue to Dream Big': An Open Letter From Serena Williams." *The Guardian,* November 29, 2016. https://www. theguardian.com/lifeandstyle/2016/nov/29/dream-big-open-letter-serena-williams-porter-magazine-incredible-women-of-2016-issue-women-athletes.

Westmann, Stephen K. *Sport, Physical Education, and Womanhood.* Baltimore: Williams & Wilkins, 1939.

"What Are Your Chances of Becoming a Summer Olympic Athlete?" *Visually,* August 6, 2012. https://visual.ly/community/infographic/olympics/what-are-your-chances-becoming-summer-olympic-athlete.

"Why Muslim Countries Fail to Shine in the Olympic Games." *Inquirer,* August 12, 2016. http://sports.inquirer.net/219177/why-muslim-countries-fail-to-shine-at-olympic-games#ixzz4qUUfZO7m.

Wigmore, Tim. "Sports Gender Pay Gap: Why Are Women Still Paid Less Than Men?" *New Statesman,* August 5, 2016. https://www.newstatesman.com/politics/sport/2016/08/sport-s-gender-pay-gap-why-are-women-still-paid-less-men.

Williams, Linda D. "Sportswomen in Black and White: Sport History From an Afro-American Perspective." In *Women, Media and Sport: Challenging Gender Values,* edited by Pamela J. Creedon, 45–66. Thousand Oaks, CA: Sage, 1994.

Williams, Michael L. "Accommodating Disabled Students Into Athletic Programs." National Federation of State High School Associations, July 27, 2014. https://www.nfhs.org/articles/accommodating-disabled-students-into-athletic-programs.

Williams, Venus. "Wimbledon Has Sent Me a Message: I'm Only a Second-Class Champion." *Times,* June 26, 2006. https://www.thetimes.co.uk/article/wimbledon-has-sent-me-a-message-im-only-a-second-class-champion-f056h05hmzq.

Williams, Wythe. "Americans Beaten in Four Olympic Tests." *New York Times,* August 3, 1928, 3.

Willms, Nicole. *When Women Rule the Court: Gender, Race, and Japanese American Basketball.* New Brunswick, NJ: Rutgers University Press, 2017.

Wilson, Amy. *45 Years of Title IX: The Status of Women in Intercollegiate Athletics.* NCAA, 2017. http://www.ncaa.org/sites/default/files/TitleIX45-295-FINAL_WEB.pdf.

Wolanin, Andrew, Eugene Hong, Donald Marks, Kelly Panchoo, and Michael Gross. "Prevalence of Clinically Elevated Depressive Symptoms in College Athletes and Differences by Gender and Sport." *British Journal of Sports Medicine* 50, no. 3 (2016): 167–171.

Wolter, Sarah. " 'It Just Makes Good Business Sense': A Media Political Economy Analysis of espnW." *Journal of Sports Media* 9, no. 2 (2014): 73–96.

Wolter, Sarah. "A Qualitative Analysis of Photographs and Articles on espnW: Positive Progress for Female Athletes." *Communication and Sport* 3, no. 2 (2015): 454–471.

Wolven, E. L. "College Sports and Motherhood." *New York Times*, July 3, 1921, 42.

Women in Sport and Investec. "Sport for Success: The Socioeconomic Benefits of Women Playing Sport." 2016. https://www.womeninsport.org/resources/sport-for-success.

Women on Boards. "Gender Balance in Global Sport." 2016. https://www.womenonboards.net/en-GB/Resources/Voice-for-Women/Gender-Balance-in-Global-Sport.

Women Without Borders. "India—Women Swimming Into the Future." 2010. http://www.women-without-borders.org/projects/underway/21.

Women's Media Center. "The Status of Women in U.S. Media, 2017." March 21, 2017. http://www.womensmediacenter.com/reports/the-status-of-women-in-u.s.-media-2017.

Women's Sports Foundation. "Factors Influencing Girls' Participation in Sport." September 9, 2016. https://www.womenssportsfoundation.org/support-us/do-you-know-the-factors-influencing-girls-participation-in-sports.

Women's Sports Foundation. "Women in the 2016 Olympic and Paralymic Games: An Analysis of Participation, Leadership, and Media Coverage." November 27, 2017. https://www.womenssportsfoundation.org/research/article-and-report/elite-athletes/women-2016-olympic-paralympic-games.

WomenSport International. "Brighton Declaration on Women and Sport." 1994. http://www.sportsbiz.bz/womensportinternational/conferences/brighton_declaration.htm.

Wong, Alia. "Where Girls Are Missing Out on High-School Sports." *The Atlantic*, June 26, 2015. https://www.theatlantic.com/education/archive/2015/06/girls-high-school-sports-inequality/396782.

World Anti-Doping Agency. "Prohibited List Q&A." n.d. https://www.
    wada-ama.org/en/questions-answers/prohibited-list-qa#item-391.
World Anti-Doping Agency. "Prohibited List, 2018." https://www.
    wada-ama.org/sites/default/files/prohibited_list_2018_en.pdf.
World Health Organization. "Sexual Violence." n.d. http://www.who.
    int/reproductivehealth/topics/violence/sexual_violence/en.
Young, Belinda-Rose, Sarah L. Desmarais, Julie A. Baldwin,
    and Rasheeta Chandler. "Sexual Coercion Practices Among
    Undergraduate Male Recreational Athletes, Intercollegiate
    Athletes, and Non-Athletes." *Violence Against Women* 23, no. 7
    (2016): 795–812.

INDEX

Adigun, Seun, 101
Ahmed, Shireen, 118
Al-Attar, Sarah, 100
Ali, Laila, 61
All-American Red Heads
    (basketball team), 44
American Tennis Association
    (ATA), 24–5, 26, 116
ancient Greece, 10–11
ancient Rome, 11–12
Anderson, Ada, 15
Anthony, Susan B., 16
apologetic in women's sports,
    48–9, 54, 61
Association of Intercollegiate
    Athletics for Women
    (AIAW), 28
athletics (track and field), 91
Azzi, Jennifer, 61

Bagger, Mianne, 84
Ballard, Lula, 24
baseball, women and girls in
    All-American Girls
        Professional Baseball League
        (AAGBPL), 54, 74
    Bloomer girls, 16, 73
    Cuban Estrellas (baseball), 74

Little League Baseball (LLB), 74
    women's teams and leagues, 73
basketball, 14–15, 22, 116
    men's, 36
    six-player game, 44
Bauer, Sybil, 21
Baugh, Laura, 55
beach volleyball, 47, 135, 137
Beggs, Mack, 84–5
Berenson, Senda, 14, 44
bicycle, 16, 19, 24
Biles, Simone, 159
Blankers-Koen, Fanny, 153
bloomers, 16
bodybuilding, 49–50
Bonaly, Surya, 51, 116
Braid, Dawn, 131

Cambel, Halet, 100
Chand, Dutee, 82
Channels, Isador, 24
cheerleading, 6–9, 20, 43, 47
coaching, women in, 129–32
Colonial America, 6, 12–13
"coming out straight," 61

Davenport, Lindsay, 51
Davis, Mo'ne, 76

de Beauvoir, Simone, 71
de Coubertin, Baron Pierre,
    19–20, 87
Defrantz, Anita, 87
Delhollander, Rachel, 166
disability sport, *see* parasport
doping, 89, 155–60. *See also*
    performance-enhancing drugs
Draves, Victoria Manalo, 23, 116–17

Ederle, Gertrude, 21, 70

Fédération Internationale de Football
    Association/International
    Federation of Association
    Football (FIFA) 48, 56, 85–6,
    122, 138, 163
    Women's World Cup, 2, 139
Fédération Sportive Féminine
    Internationale, 93–4
femininity, 4, 20–1, 41–3, 44–5,
    48–9, 53, 54–6, 61, 90, 112
field hockey, 43, 35–6
figure skating, 43, 46, 50–1, 71, 88,
    117, 148
Firth, Sharon and Shirley, 117
football (American)
    women in, 57, 67, 76, 110,
        124, 130
    Lingerie Football League (LFL)
        (Legends Football League),
        57, 114
    men in, 14, 29, 38–40, 42, 67, 76,
        109, 150
Fort Shaw Indian Boarding
    School, 26
frailty myth, 18

Gay Games, 63–4
gender-appropriate sport, 42
gender marking, 111–12, 135
Gera, Bernice, 134
Gibson, Althea, 25–6, 115
Grant, Helen, 20
Griffin, Pat, 48–9, 60

Griner, Brittney, 61, 64
gymnastics, 14, 20, 42, 45–6, 148,
    152, 159

Haggman, Pirjo, 87
Hammon, Becky, 131
health concerns
    anterior cruciate
        ligament, 148–9
    concussions, 148–50
    disordered eating, 151–3
    female athlete triad, 151
    pregnancy and sport, 153–4
Henie, Sonja, 46
Herean Games, 11
hijab in sport, 48
hockey, women's, 45, 57, 63, 76,
    139, 149
Holm, Eleanor, 113
Holtkamp, Lauren, 134
homophobia, 53–5, 60–3, 65, 129
    terminology, 58–60
    homophobic violence, 59–60
hyperandrogenism, 81–3

inspiration porn, 120
International Association of Athletics
    Federations (IAAF)
    and doping, 155
    and hyperandrogenism, 81–3
    and sex testing, 78–81
International Olympic Committee
    (IOC), 4, 5, 8, 59, 63, 71, 72,
        78–81, 82, 86, 87–103
    and hyperandrogenism, 81–3
    and sex testing, 78–81
International Paralympic
    Committee (IPC), 103–4, 106,
        108, 120
Isava-Fonseca, Flor, 87

Japanese Internment, 27
Johnson, Kathryn and "Tubby's
    Rule," 74
Jones, Rosie, 64

Joyner, Florence Griffith, 116
Joyner-Kersee, Jackie, 115

Kanter, Dee, 134
King, Billie Jean, 55, 60–1
Klobukowska, Ewa, 80
Kournikova, Anna, 113
Kwan, Michelle, 117

"lady," use of in women's
    sport, 46
Ladies Professional Golf
    Association (LPGA), 55–6,
    62, 137–8
Lenglen, Suzanne, 21
Lenskyj, Helen Jefferson, 61, 98
Lingerie Football League (LFL)
    (Legends Football League),
    57, 114
Lopez, Nancy, 62, 118
Lopiano, Donna, 30, 34

Marble, Alice, 26
Major League Baseball (MLB),
    124, 126, 134, 144, 148
Marshall, Mary, 15
Martínez Patiño, María José, 80
masculinity, 6, 14, 19, 20, 41–4, 46,
    48–9, 53, 67, 75, 78–9, 91, 162
Mauresmo, Amélie, 51, 64
media
    Muslim women in, 118
    parasport and para athletes in,
        106–8, 119–20
    social media, 2, 62–3, 121–2
    women of color in, 114–8
    women journalists in, 122–8
    women's sport in, 109–14
Mendoza, Jessica, 124–5
menstruation, 18–19, 150–1
Miller, Shannon, 63
Milliat, Alice, 91–3
misogynoir, 51
Mitchell, Jackie, 73
modernization of sport, 13

Moran, Gussy, 113
Mowins, Beth, 124
Muhammad, Ibtihaj, 118
Mulkey, Kim, 61
Murray, Andy, 131–2
muscularity, 20, 49–52

Nassar, Larry, 164–6
National Basketball Association
    (NBA), 45, 67, 128, 131, 134,
    140–2, 145
National Collegiate Acrobatics
    and Tumbling Association
    (NCATA), 8
National Collegiate Athletic
    Association (NCAA), 8
    Gender Equity Taskforce, 36–7
National Football League (NFL),
    57, 110, 113, 122, 124, 125, 131,
    134, 144, 147–8
National Hockey League (NHL),
    126, 131, 134, 139, 148
Native American boarding
    schools, 26
Navratilova, Martina, 51, 55, 64
netball, 44–5

officials, umpires, and
    referees, 133–5
Olson, Lisa, 127
Omeoga, Akuoma, 101
Onwumere, Ngozi, 101
"othering," 84, 111–12, 119, 128

Palmer, Violet, 134
parasport, 32–3, 101–8,
    119–20, 160
Patrick, Danica, 114
pedestrianism (competitive
    walking), 15
Pepe, Maria, 74
performance-enhancing drugs, 89,
    155–60. See also doping
Peters, Roumaina and
    Margaret, 25

physical education, 27–8
play days, 21
theory of moderation in, 21
Portland, Rene, 62

Quidditch, 71–2

racial and ethnic segregation,
23–7, 43, 74, 115–16
Radcliffe, Paula, 151
Raisman, Aly, 165
Rapinoe, Megan, 64
Reed-Francois, Desiree, 133
religion, 24, 67–8, 118
Renaissance period, 12
Richards, Renée, 84
Rudolph, Wilma, 25, 115
rule differences, men's and
women's sport, 44–5

Saelua, Jaiyah, 85
salaries, 137–41
Sargent, Dudley Singer, 20
Semenya, Caster, 81–2
settlement homes, 24
sex appeal in women's sport, 54–5
and uniforms, 47
sex differences in sport
physical differences, 70
rule differences for men and
women, 44–5
sex-integrated sport, 71
benefits of, 68–9
previously-integrated sports, 72
sexual harassment, 37–40
sexual violence, 13, 160–8
"corrective rape," 60
and male athletes, 38–40, 162–3
and Title IX, 37–40
and USA Gymnastics, 164–6
sex testing, 78–81
Shahrkhani, Wojdan Ali Seraj
Abdulrahim, 100

Sharapova, Maria, 52
Simelane, Eudy, 60
Smith, Kathryn, 131
soccer (football), 17, 43
professional women's soccer
leagues, 145
salary disputes in, 138–40
women banned from, 17–18
Sowers, Katie, 131
spinning competitions, 6
sport clothes
and gender, 46–9
and religion, 48
and sexuality, 47, 152
skirts, 16, 19, 46–7
Stephenson, Jan, 55
"supercrip" stereotype, 119
swimming, 67, 70, 88, 95, 97, 113,
156, 173

Temple, Ed, 54
Tennessee State Agricultural
and Industrial State College
(Tennessee State University), 25
Tennis, 24, 44, 51–2
Virginia Slims Tennis
Circuit, 135–6
Thomas, Debi, 46
Thomas, Sarah, 134
Title IX, (Patsy T. Mink Equal
Opportunity in Education
Act), 7, 8, 28, 30, 29–40, 76–8,
129, 144, 165
and cheerleading, 8
contact sports exemption, 76–7
Equity in Athletics Disclosure
Act, 33
Grove City v. Bell, 34–5
limitations of, 31–3
and men's programs, 35–6
and sex segregation, 76–8
three-prong test for
compliance, 33–4

transgender athletes
    terminology, 83–4
    sport policies for, 83–6
Tunis, John, 22, 95
Tuskegee Institute (Tuskegee
    University), 25

Ultimate Fighting
    Championship, 50
Uniforms, *see* Sport Clothing
USA Gymnastics, 8
    sex abuse scandal, 164–6

Vanderveer, Tara, 130
Victorian era, 14
Vital Energy Theory, 18
Von Hillern, Bertha, 15

Wambach, Abby, 64
Washington, Ora, 24–5

Welter, Jen, 110, 131
Williams, Serena, 70–1
Williams, Venus, 136
Wills, Helen, 21
Witt, Katarina, 46
Women's National Basketball
    Association (WNBA), 45, 64–
    5, 66, 128, 131, 140–2, 145
    and "kiss-in" protest, 64–5
    Lesbian fans and, 64–5
World Anti-Doping Agency
    (WADA), 155, 157,
    158, 159–60
Worley, Kristin, 83

Yamaguchi, Kristi, 117
Yuanhui, Fu, 151

Zaharias, Mildred "Babe"
    Didrikson, 22–3